The College Hook

The College Hook

Packaging Yourself

to Win the College Admissions Game

by

Pam Proctor

CENTER
STREET®

New York Boston Nashville

Center Street
Hachette Book Group USA
237 Park Avenue
New York, NY 10017
Visit our website at www.centerstreet.com

The Center Street name and logo are registered trademarks of the Hachette Book Group USA.
Printed in the United States of America

First edition: July 2007

10 9 8 7 6 5 4 3 2 1

Library of Congress Cataloging-in-Publication Data

Proctor, Pam
  The College hook : packaging yourself to win the college admissions game / Pam Proctor.
    p. cm.
  Includes index.
  ISBN-13: 978-1-931722-81-0
  ISBN-10: 1-931722-81-1
  1. College applications. 2. Universities and colleges—Admission. I. Title.

LB2351.5.P76 2007
378.1'616—dc22

2006034837

To my students,
who have found not only a Hook,
but also a vision for the future.

Acknowledgments

Without my students, who have put their faith in me as their guide through the college process, this book would never have come to fruition. Their enthusiasm for the project, and their willingness to share the intimate details of their college application experiences, energized me through every stage of the manuscript.

I also owe a debt of gratitude to the staff of Sebastian River High School, where I have served for many years as a consultant to the International Baccalaureate (IB) program. In particular, the support of IB coordinators Donna Olson and Cathie Ziegler, Vice-Principal Judy Kloski, Director of IB Guidance Enrique Valencia, Athletic Director Michael Stutzke, and Principal Dr. Peggy Jones gave me a platform to develop the ideas in this book and the confidence to assert them boldly.

But it was only through the vision of my agent, Carol Mann, my editor, Christina Boys, and my publisher, Rolf Zettersten, that *The College Hook* is now poised to reach a larger audience. They were quick to embrace the concept of the "Hook" and put their full energies behind its development as a book for Center Street. Thanks are also due assistant editor Meredith Pharaoh for her never-ending efficiency and thoroughness.

Finally, I wish to thank my husband, Bill, who has sustained me as my partner, professional colleague, and biggest cheerleader. I suppose it's no accident that we first met in college, when I was a student at Mount Holyoke College, and he was at Harvard Law School. One could argue that the seeds of *The College Hook* were sown back then; it just took a few years to blossom.

Pam Proctor, President
College Application Consultants, Inc.
Vero Beach, Florida

CONTENTS

Acknowledgments   vii
Introduction: The Powerful College Hook Strategy   xi

PART I: Discovering Your Hook   1
    Chapter One: The Power of the Hook   3
    Chapter Two: Hooks That Worked   11
    Chapter Three: Cooking Up a Hook   15

PART II: The Top Ten College Hooks   27
    Chapter Four: The Athletic Hook   29
    Chapter Five: The International Hook   35
    Chapter Six: The Music Hook   41
    Chapter Seven: The Political Hook   47
    Chapter Eight: The Technology Hook   53
    Chapter Nine: The Humanitarian Hook   59
    Chapter Ten: The Science Hook   65
    Chapter Eleven: The Writing Hook   73
    Chapter Twelve: The Drama Hook   81
    Chapter Thirteen: The Multicultural Hook   87

PART III: Packaging Your Hook   91
    Chapter Fourteen: Your College Application
        Marketing Plan   93
    Chapter Fifteen: Bolstering Your Hook   103
    Chapter Sixteen: The Résumé Power Play   109
    Chapter Seventeen: Hooking Your Essay   121
    Chapter Eighteen: Scoring Bigger with Test Scores   137

Chapter Nineteen: Making the Grade 145

Chapter Twenty: Pulling Your Package Together 151

PART IV: Selling Your Hook 159

Chapter Twenty-One: Pitching Your Package to Colleges 161

Chapter Twenty-Two: Acing the Interview 169

Chapter Twenty-Three: Romancing Admissions 175

Chapter Twenty-Four: Courting Coaches 183

Chapter Twenty-Five: Working the Wait List 189

Conclusion: From College to Self-Confidence 199

Appendix A: Sample Essays 201

Appendix B: Sample Supplements and Letters 225

Selected References 241

Endnotes 243

Index 247

Introduction: The Powerful College Hook Strategy

This book is your guide to the powerful packaging weapon known as the Hook—a special talent, achievement, or personal quality that will leap off the page of a college application and catch the eye of admissions officers. At a time when competition for entry to the nation's top colleges is at an all-time high—and intensifying every year—the "packaging" secrets you'll find in this book will help you maximize the odds of admission to the college of your choice.

Harvard and other elite universities are flooded with perfect or near-perfect SATs and straight As. Typical of the trend is Princeton, which in 2006 "took only 17% of the 1,886 valedictorians that applied," according to the *Wall Street Journal*.[1] The university itself boasted on its Web site that more than 7,000 of its "record" 17,563 applicants in 2006 "had average high school grades of A to A–, combined with scores of 700 or higher on each of the three sections of the SAT."[2]

At UCLA, Chancellor Albert Carnesale deemed the scope of applicants' academic achievement "extraordinary." According to the school's office of media relations, nearly 21,000 students—a whopping 44 percent of the 47,258 applicants for the Class of 2010—earned GPAs of 4.0 or above (4.0 is an "A"), while the 12,094 students UCLA admitted clocked in with overall GPAs of 4.27.[3]

Under such circumstances, even if you have the right stuff academically, you must have that "something extra"—a Hook—if you hope to gain admission to your dream school.

In the following chapters you'll find real-life anecdotes and examples from winning applications. Most of these examples cite the student by name. In a few of them, the names and identifying details are masked. But in every case you'll be reading true accounts of students who found a Hook and used it to advantage.

What's more, a step-by-step program will enable you to develop your own unique Hook and then package and market yourself at every stage of the admissions process. Without such a plan, you will be much more likely to become a victim of what has been described by several guidance counselors as the current "college admissions bloodbath."

The Admissions Bloodbath

Because of demographic pressures, enhanced SAT coaching opportunities, and related factors, competition for coveted college slots has heated to the boiling point. Students whose credentials would have made them shoo-ins for the Ivies and Little Ivies* just a few years ago have discovered, to their chagrin, that they just didn't cut it. "If only I had found a vaccine for avian flu or figured out how to solve the Arab-Israeli conflict, then I *might* have had a shot at Yale," lamented one rejected applicant.

The result has also created a high-pressure trickle-down effect, as schools at the middle and lower end of the *U.S. News & World Report* rankings have found applications soaring. As a result, many schools have been forced to raise the bar on standardized test scores and to defer or wait-list stellar academic students whose scores didn't pass muster. Baylor responded to the application deluge by creating its first-ever wait list in February 2006. For the 2006–2007 admissions cycle, the school also dropped its rolling admission policy in favor of set deadlines, including two rounds of Early Action.

The Demographic Details

At the root of the increased competition are demographics and the ever-widening web of accessible information. As the children of baby boomers have reached college age, there are simply more students in the applicant pool—a trend that is expected to continue. What's more, the Internet has enabled students to discover schools far beyond their home states and has provided the on-line capability to fire off as many applications as they can muster. According to *USA Today,* online applications submitted through the Common Application, a form used by more than 300 public and private colleges, "skyrocketed" over a four-year period, "from just under 41,000 in 2000–01 to a predicted 700,000" for the 2005–2006 application cycle.[4] What's more, as the *New York Times* has reported, it's not uncommon for students these days to apply to a dozen or more schools—sometimes even as many as thirty—to cover their bases.[5]

Adding to the admissions crunch is the increased trend toward grade inflation in high schools, which translates into applications rife with grade point

---

* The "Ivies," or Ivy League schools, include Brown, Columbia, Cornell, Dartmouth, Harvard, Princeton, University of Pennsylvania, and Yale. The "Little Ivies" include Amherst, Wesleyan, and Williams.

averages well over 4.0 or even 5.0. The student population's increased awareness of the advantages of prepping for standardized tests has fueled the competition even further. Stellar academic achievement has become commonplace.

"This really is a remarkable generation of college students," says Dr. Jerome Lucido, vice provost for enrollment policy and management at the University of Southern California. "When we are choosing among them, the fact that a student can be academically successful doesn't carry the day, because almost everyone in our applicant pool will be academically successful."

As a result, he says, "we must ask ourselves a different set of questions. We need to ask what characteristics, talents, and attitudes of mind a student brings that can improve the campus. Sometimes it might be leadership. Sometimes it might be athletic accomplishment or the potential to be a great researcher. Or it might be a deep understanding of various cultures that enables us to achieve our goals.

"That's why we read applications—to understand the student," explains Lucido. Admissions decisions, he says, often revolve around a fundamental question: "What is the essence of you?"

In such a climate, when admissions committees are desperate for ways to differentiate candidates, the message for students is clear: *You've got to set yourself apart. You've got to have a Hook.*

From the start of my work as an independent college counselor and IB consultant nearly a decade ago, I recognized the Hook as an essential tool in a successful application. That's why every time I conduct a student workshop, speak at a parent night, or work with a student one on one, I hammer away at one theme: Find your Hook! Over the past few years, hundreds of my students have heard and heeded that message. They have worked hard to find a Hook and package it through every page of their application in order to get a leg up in admissions.

The College Hook will provide you with that same edge and give you the packaging tools to increase your odds of admission to the colleges at the top of your list. These packaging secrets aren't really so secret in some quarters: the savviest of high school guidance counselors and independent consultants have been sharing them with students for years. But even if you don't have access to such guidance face to face, you are now holding in your hands the packaging secrets to level the playing field and give you an equal shot at success in admissions.

As you read, keep in mind that *The College Hook* is designed to talk directly to *you*, the prospective college student, as though we were sitting face to face in a series of one-on-one counseling sessions. Furthermore, parents, grandparents, mentors, and school professionals can and should enter into the dialogue by posing questions, giving suggestions, and evaluating options presented in this book. In effect, one or both parents should use *The College Hook* as a tool to step into the role of independent college admissions counselor for their child.

Finally, as you'll discover, learning to package your Hook is more than a mere ploy to win over college admissions committees. Rather, it can become a confidence-building, inspirational vehicle for self-discovery.

So now, turn the page and begin to experience the power of the Hook, a power that can put you in the driver's seat on the road to college admissions—and beyond.

PART I

Discovering Your Hook

CHAPTER ONE

The Power of the Hook

Every high school student actually *has* a College Hook—that one special interest that will cause admissions officials to salivate over an application and significantly increase the odds of getting into a favorite college.

Sometimes students have an obvious Hook, such as the highly ranked basketball player from Florida or the budding cholesterol researcher from Georgia. One student transformed herself into a "foreign correspondent," and still another became involved in a heart-rending search for a Chinese birth mother.

Other times, I encounter students whose Hook has been as seemingly frivolous or mundane as watching soap operas every afternoon, or reading science fiction, or working during summer vacations at Sears.

In the end, the secret to finding and exploiting a College Hook is to pinpoint a dominant interest, activity, or set of experiences that reflects one of your deepest passions in life—a passion that will set you apart from other students for purposes of college admissions.

"But absolutely nothing about me sticks out!" many of my students protest in initial interviews. "I'm involved in lots of activities, but nothing about me is special."

If that's your attitude too, you're wrong. Somewhere, deep in your background, experience, or interests, lies a talent or passion that you can mine, massage, and market to increase dramatically your chances for admission to the college of your dreams.

This book has been designed to show you how to find and use a special Hook that will cause your true, dynamic identity to leap off the pages of your college application and into the hearts of admissions committees. To get started, take a lesson from Josh, whose Hook took him further than he could ever have imagined.

HOW JOSH DISCOVERED HIS HOOK

Josh's mother was worried.

"He's never going to get into a good college," she lamented at our first independent counseling session.

It was September of Josh's senior year, and based on his numbers, his prospects didn't look too promising. Certainly, his credentials seemed far out of reach for the schools that most piqued his interest: Bard, Hampshire, and Oberlin.

He had struggled in school ever since returning from a year abroad in Israel in ninth grade, exhibiting a kind of culture shock that he found hard to shake. But, finally, he found his niche at a small private school on Manhattan's Upper East Side.

"We have confidence in you, Josh," the admissions director had told him. "We're willing to take a chance because we believe you have what it takes to succeed here."

Josh did, indeed, succeed. By the time senior year rolled around, he had been elected president of the student council and captain of the basketball team. His electrifying personality and precocious verbal ability had made him one of the most popular students among the faculty and his peers.

But it was clear that when it came to schoolwork, Josh lacked confidence. Although his grades were on the upswing, with more Bs on his junior-year transcript, he seemed afraid to face the college application process. As his senior year began, the specter of his rejections during sophomore year hung over him like a cloud, and I could sense his motivation flagging.

"You're a winner," I told him. "Now it's your job to let the colleges know it."

For starters, I gave him his marching orders: "Ace your grades senior year, and prep for the SAT." I knew that by coming on strong the first semester senior year, Josh could appear to colleges as a "late bloomer" who was finally starting to hit his stride.

Next, I helped him zero in on his Hook. Despite his obvious leadership skills, it was clear to me that Josh needed something spectacular to turn the heads of admissions committees.

"You've Got to Have Something More"

"There are thousands of student council presidents," I told Josh bluntly, "and there are even more captains of athletic teams. You've got to have something more."

"Something more" turned out to be photography. After pressing Josh for an hour and a half to describe his activities and passions, I discovered that he had been quietly working away at photography ever since a summer college course prior to sophomore year. With this expertise, he had photographed children on travels abroad with his family in South America and Asia. He had even spent the summer before his senior year working for a nationally famous portrait photographer, assisting him on shoots and around his studio. Inspired by that experience, Josh had set up a darkroom in his own basement.

Clearly, the young man had a passion and a growing array of credentials. The main thing missing was a portfolio.

"Between now and December," I advised him, "create a portfolio to submit with your applications that will knock the socks off the admissions people."

Now, some students might have heard this advice and dismissed it out of hand. Others might have been intrigued by the prospect of doing a portfolio, but when it came down to actually putting one together, they would have shelved the idea until they had "more time." Still others might have begun the project, but then, when the difficulties of the task confronted them, they would have abandoned the effort altogether. Josh's strength—the secret to his ultimate success—was that he jumped right in, started working, and never gave up.

On the advice of his mentor, the professional photographer for whom he had worked the previous summer, he decided to keep the project simple. He came up with a plan to do a series of black-and-white portraits of the members of his class.

Using a camera borrowed from his mentor, Josh set up shop in his living room and rigged up lights and reflective backdrops. Then, every Saturday for the next three months, he scheduled individual portrait sittings for members of his class. Although there were only a small number of students in his graduating class, the project required extensive coordination, as Josh had to juggle schedules for classmates who lived all over New York City. Inevitably, when their Saturday appointment rolled around, kids would call to cancel, and some wouldn't show up at all.

But Josh didn't give up. He kept calling, nudging, and browbeating his friends until they found their way to his doorstep. Working slowly and methodically, he carefully posed each student and gave directions on the facial expression he felt would best set off the student's personality. Some laughed. Some were serious. Some just hinted at a smile. Next Josh positioned the lights, making subtle adjustments to create just the right chiaroscuro effect.

One by one, the portraits started coming together. Stepping into his darkroom to develop the first few shots, Josh watched amazed as portrait after portrait emerged from the chemicals with images so powerful they needed no further explanation. There was Lucy, the bookish Hispanic, looking like she was ready to give a lecture; Phil, the class clown, whose eyes twinkled with some inner joke; Tom, the basketball star, whose lanky frame extended the entire length of the photo.

Josh had caught the personality of each student just as he had intended, and even *he* was bowled over by his accomplishment. "I knew my photos were good," he said. "I just didn't know *how* good."

Week by week, as the photography project progressed, Josh's academic life started to come together as well. He started turning in his homework on time. He edited his English and history papers instead of merely handing in a first draft. And he set aside ample time to study for exams. By the end of October, when first-quarter grades were posted, Josh couldn't believe the results: For the first time in his high school career, he had made the honor roll!

The next two months were a whirlwind as Josh completed his photo shoots, kept studying for the SAT, and worked on his applications, taking care to communicate his Hook clearly every chance he could.

Take the essays, for example. Josh made sure that one of the essays for the Common Application focused on his passion for photography. What made this essay a winner wasn't just his personal anecdote about photographing children in China, which brought to life Josh's incredible eye for detail. Also compelling was Josh's intellectual bent, as he wove into the essay esoteric references to photographic icons such as Irving Penn and *Vogue*'s Alexander Liberman. He used his essay adroitly to demonstrate his profound understanding of the history and art of photography.

Josh's message in his essay was clear: "I'm not just out there taking pictures," he seemed to be saying. "I'm an artist from a great tradition of artists."

Next, Josh attacked his activities list, a standard eight-line grid required by the Common Application and most other applications, which offers space for an abbreviated rundown of school and outside activities. Because the application directs students to list their activities *in order of importance* to them, Josh decided to position his photography Hook first to make it stand out. He realized that although his school leadership positions and community service work were impressive, they weren't unusual enough to deserve top billing. On his application, the first few lines of the list appeared as follows:

Freelance Photographer	Grades 10–12	Portfolio: Portrait of a Class
Photography Workshop	Grade 10	3-wk summer course
Student Council	Grades 11–12	President, Grade 12
Varsity Basketball	Grades 9–12	Captain, Grade 12

Although Josh's list included other activities, ranging from Multicultural Club to volunteer custodial work at a synagogue to efforts to organize friends at a homeless shelter, his work as a photographer was the centerpiece. The guiding principle in devising such an activities list is that the list must not look like a "laundry list," but, rather, must highlight the Hook in some fresh way.

Josh used the same approach in listing his "work experience," another standard category on applications. In order to reiterate his Hook, he listed his photography job first:

Photography Intern *(Name of Famous New York Photographer), Summer, Grade 11*
Day Camp Counselor, *Camp Sho-sho-nee, Summer, Grade 10*

Running with a Résumé

Next came another vital part of Josh's application: the résumé. Often overlooked by students as a selling tool, the résumé gave Josh a way to highlight his photography and explain his achievements in more depth than he could on a short list of activities.

But this was no ordinary résumé. Unlike one he might have written for a job search, this résumé showcased his Hook and other talents. To this end, Josh arranged his activities in categories that communicated his strengths—beginning with photography. The categories had clear subheads that an admissions reader could scan in a few seconds and understand instantly:

Photographer
School Leader
Community Volunteer

Under each category, Josh included specific accomplishments, such as "Photography Intern," "Freelance Photographer," "Photography Course," and "Personal Darkroom," which he described in detail to flesh out his expertise.

But Josh's efforts to market his Hook didn't stop with his application and résumé. To reinforce his photographic expertise, he asked his mentor to write a recommendation.

The photographer not only wrote a letter, but he also went a step further: He invited Josh to help him in the studio the day he was shooting a portrait of a leading photography professor at one of the schools to which Josh was applying. On a visit to the school, Josh met with the professor, thereby cementing his relationship. Finally, on his application, he referred to the professor by name in answer to the question, "Why are you applying?"

A "Genius" at Photography

The pièce de résistance of Josh's application was his portfolio. By the end of December, he had completed more than two dozen photographs, and, by all accounts, they were magnificent.

"Brilliant," said his mentor.

"Amazing," said his headmaster.

As it turned out, Josh was a budding genius at photography. His starkly lit portraits had such a professional quality that everyone who saw them wanted one. The headmaster of Josh's school was so enthralled that he immediately commissioned Josh to shoot a portrait of his family. Next, he hired him to do individual portraits of each member of the faculty, which he promptly displayed in the school's foyer. One commission followed another, and before long, Josh had a backlog of clients waiting for *professional* photo shoots.

Josh's parents were dumbfounded. "Have you seen Josh's work?" they told friends. "He's remarkable. Maybe he has a shot at one of his favorite colleges after all."

For his college application portfolio, Josh selected twelve photos of his classmates and had them reproduced by laser printer for each school. As Christmas break approached, he assembled his applications, essays, résumé, and portfolio, and dropped them in the mail. Then he waited.

The good news started coming in even before April 1. In early March, he received a letter from one liberal arts college in Vermont offering him a $5,000-a-year *merit* scholarship—solely on the strength of his photographs and essays.

A month later, Josh came home from school to discover that he had been accepted at his first choice, Bard, which was ranked that year among the top thirty liberal arts colleges in the country by *U.S. News & World Report.* He was put on the waiting list at another of his top schools, Hampshire College, which eventually accepted him after reviewing his senior grades.

But the good news for Josh went far beyond college admissions. At his high school graduation, he was awarded the Writing Prize for his work in English. And as president of the student body, he was one of the featured speakers.

Recounting the ups and downs of his high school career, Josh thanked the school administration for giving him a chance—a chance to discover who he was and who he could be. As he stood on the podium, speaking before a crowd that included leading New Yorkers whose children were in his class, he oozed confidence—the confidence of someone who was ready to take on the world.

And he has. Josh earned straight As his freshman year in college, and he continued on that track for the next three years. Majoring in creative writing with a minor in photography, he pursued freelance photography on the side, publishing a series of photographs of hip-hop artists in a national magazine. By his senior year, he had plunged into the world of professional photography as an assistant to a top international photographer, whom he accompanied on photo shoots to Brazil, Spain, and Rome.

But Josh didn't stop there. Within two years of graduating from Bard, he was being hailed by the New York art world as an emerging artist for his use of still and video imagery. His first coup was at a group show at a prominent gallery in Manhattan, where his work garnered praise from *New York Times* art critic Holland Cotter. Next came a monthlong solo exhibition at Sarah Lawrence College's new Heimbold Visual Arts Center, where he was invited to give the inaugural lecture to students and professors.

The accolades kept coming. Two museum directors snapped up his work at the Miami Art Fair, a prominent dealer took him on as her client, and *ARTnews* featured him in an interview and photo as one of the leading young artists in the country.

Josh had arrived—by the time he was twenty-four.

And it had all started with his Hook.

"Pulling my portfolio together for my college applications and forcing myself to think and write about my work was the first time I started taking photography seriously," said Josh.

What's more, he said, the wave of enthusiastic feedback he received from his photographs gave a huge boost to his confidence.

"That's when I had a sense of what being an artist was really like. Part of the privilege of being able to make art is that you do have an audience. I want people to see my work. That's why I'm making pictures. Having such an early and positive experience showed me what was possible."

These days, Josh's sights are set on developing a body of work that can carry him into the future. But wherever his career takes him, one thing is certain: He is well on his way to success in life, all because he discovered the right Hook for his college applications—and ran with it all the way through the ivy gates.

FROM COLLEGE TO SELF-CONFIDENCE

As Josh's story illustrates, the college application process doesn't end in April when the final acceptances and rejections roll in. For one thing, many students must next launch a strategy for "working the wait list," a process that involves further fine-tuning and selling of the special Hook (explained in Chapter Twenty-Five).

Perhaps even more important, the design and implementation of a college application strategy almost always starts a typically timid, unsure high school student on the road to new self-confidence and self-esteem. The discovery of a personal College Hook almost always leads to greater self-assurance and performance in college. Many times, the discovery of a Hook will give students such enhanced life focus that they will find themselves on the path to an eventual career.

The Hook may begin as a sophisticated college admissions marketing plan, but it often ends on a much broader field of personal self-fulfillment and significant occupational achievement.

A QUICK GUIDE TO THE COLLEGE HOOK PROGRAM

As you move through the pages of *The College Hook,* you'll discover how to employ a proven strategy for maximizing your odds in the college application process. Specifically, you'll learn the basics of:

Discovering Your Hook: In the remaining chapters of Part I, you'll begin to identify your Hook and jump-start your application efforts by learning how to "cook up a Hook." By probing deeply into your passions and interests with proven preliminary questions that have made my clients successful, you will cut through a potentially confusing and unfocused jumble of facts and activities—and begin to zero in on the one thing that will make you a standout. This section will feature a brief rundown on real Hooks that worked.

The Top Ten College Hooks: Although there are as many Hooks as there are students, those special abilities tend to fall into categories, such as music, science, or athletics, which colleges typically draw on to fill a class. In Part II, you'll get an inside look at the real-life experiences of ten students whose Hooks represent some of the most popular categories. Their Hooks helped shape their applications and paved their way to a wide range of schools that fit their interests.

Packaging Your Hook: Once you've determined your Hook, in Part III you'll pull your application together into a communications vehicle with a single, powerful message as you weave your Hook into your essays, résumé, activities lists, and supplemental submissions. Packaging secrets from professional PR and national journalism, which I've learned from my extensive background in both those fields, will be translated into successful applications.

Among other things, *The College Hook* will guide you step-by-step through the process of developing a smashing lead on your essays and creating eye-catching subheads on your résumé. Every detail of your college admissions package will be designed to communicate your special persona powerfully to admissions personnel. This section will include sample essays, résumés, and activities lists to give you hands-on instruction.

As part of your packaging strategy, you'll also learn how to bolster your Hook by taking your special talents to a sophisticated, or even semi-professional or professional, level. Many students have transformed non-paying avocations or interests into significant summer jobs or special activities involving strong connections with leading professionals in the community.

Practical examples and brainstorming suggestions will help you think outside the box and discover how you can strengthen your strengths with internships, special projects you can pursue at school, and portfolios.

Selling Your Hook: In Part IV, you'll learn the fine points of approaching colleges by using cover letters, e-mail, interviews, and contacts to your advantage—not only during the main application phase, but also in the deferral and wait-list process. A crucial chapter, "Working the Wait List," will empower you to take charge of your destiny until the very end in these high-pressure times.

Now let's immerse ourselves in some creative Hooks that have helped scores of students reach for and gain admission to their dream colleges.

Chapter Two

Hooks That Worked

Whether you're a philosopher, a point guard, a sculptor, a tuba player, or a bookworm, your College Hook could be the deciding factor that catapults you to success in college admissions.

The trouble is, most high school students are so busy doing every activity that comes down the pike—from playing an instrument to community service to athletics—that they don't stop to ask themselves, "What is the *one thing* that sets me apart?"

Without that "one thing," says Amanda, a 2003 graduate of Dartmouth, "top-level college admission is a roll of the dice.

"If you're editor of the newspaper, play three sports, and took lots of AP courses, you don't have a prayer—because everyone else is doing all of these things too," she says.

"Highly selective colleges want superstars," says Amanda. "They want people who twenty years from now will make an impact, and it all starts with who you are right now."

If you're feeling somewhat cowed by Amanda's bluntness, take heart: Dozens of students, including Amanda,* have started out thinking they didn't have a Hook, even though it was right in front of them.

Consider the Hooks of students accepted to New York City's Barnard College in 2006, a year when the admission rate of 22 percent for regular decision set "a new competitive benchmark," according to the school's Web site.[6] Barnard's pool of admitted students boasted "two Junior Olympic Tae Kwon Do medalists (twin sisters); a New York State champion golfer who has played on PGA Junior Tour Tournaments; a state champion fencer; a top-level high school figure skater from China; a winner of the 'Leaders of Tomorrow' Scholarship sponsored by the New York State Lottery; a winner of the New York City Shakespeare Oratory Competition; a world finalist in the Odyssey of the Mind competition; a Massachusetts State speech finalist two years in a row; a semi-finalist in the National Biology Olympiad; and two trapeze circus performers."

---

* See Amanda's story, page 95.

To top it off, the admitted class also included "three professional actresses . . . a world champion Irish dancer . . . an accomplished bag-pipe player . . . a student who helps birth lambs on her family's farm . . . and the winner of an outstanding dairy goat exhibition."[7]

Birthing lambs? Dancing an Irish jig? Performing in a circus?

Yet these are just some of the Hooks that worked at Barnard, a sister school to Columbia. Take a quick look at the Web site of your favorite college and you're likely to find a similar rundown. Whether you've set your sights on Haverford or Harvard, Baylor or Berkeley, Appalachian State or Amherst, Dartmouth or DePaul, you need to have a skill, talent, or interest that stands out clearly on your application and sets you apart.

By now you may be starting to get the picture. But if you need further inspiration, here's a sampling of some Hooks that propelled students to success at a wide range of schools:

- **Peter, an artist with a nose for novelty:** His art portfolio and special art projects, including a painting tutorial with one of Florida's famed African-American Highwaymen, helped him overcome low SATs to get the Early Decision nod from the University of Miami.
- **Laurie, a creative writer with a published poetry "chapbook":** Although she was a C+ student, her poetry "chapbook" (a small book of poetry) was sold on consignment at City Lights Bookstore in San Francisco and helped earn her an unsolicited merit scholarship at a large midwestern university.
- **Asma, a Muslim-American science whiz with an independent streak:** This International Baccalaureate student won a berth at an accelerated medical program with essays that revealed her iconoclastic side: One essay focused on her decision to wear an *hijab,* or head-covering; the other revealed her secret life as a "Trekkie."
- **Jenna, a "best buddy" to a disabled student:** After being *rejected* Early Decision at a top-notch liberal arts college in the South, Jenna resubmitted her application with a focus on her friendship with a severely disabled student and was admitted in the same college's regular admissions pool.
- **Warren, a foreign language ace with a flair for writing Spanish poetry:** His facility with languages, including a stint translating for Spanish-speaking clients in his mother's Lamaze class, opened the door to Amherst Early Decision. His most difficult challenge, he confessed, was translating the word "vagina" to pregnant moms without blushing.
- **Susie, a student with only a 2.0 average but strong leadership skills:** With nearly 600 in each section of the SAT, Susie's strong track record as a leader and mentor was her ace in the hole at Baylor, which awarded her a Provost's Merit Scholarship of $6,000 a year.
- **Chris, a math whiz who ran cribbage tournaments on-line for players around the world:** This offbeat pastime proved unbeatable at the Univer-

sity of California at San Diego, where he majored in economics. He later turned his talents to Texas Hold'em to help pay his way through school.

- **Myra, a singer/songwriter from Appalachia:** A series of professional gigs, along with her homemade videotape performing ballads and bluegrass songs from her repertoire, tipped the scales at NYU's Tisch School of the Arts.
- **David, a successful eBay entrepreneur:** He showcased his business talent in a breezy essay that chronicled his Internet adventures beginning at age eleven, selling everything from Beanie Babies to baseball cards. He made a quick "sale" of his talent to Washington and Lee, which admitted him Early Decision. (See David's essay, page 127.)
- **Robert, a caregiver to his autistic brother:** The summers he spent tossing a football around with his younger brother in rural Michigan offset his lack of extracurricular activities and helped him score with the communications department of a leading college in the South. Majoring in broadcasting, he hopes to become a sports anchor.
- **Stacy, a math team captain with a black belt in jiu-jitsu:** This valedictorian combined her skills in math and martial arts in an essay on the physics of jiu-jitsu that swept Duke's admissions office off their feet.
- **Kira, a South African snake fancier with dreams of using venom to cure cancer:** This immigrant's passion for herpetology gave her research goals an unusual twist that helped charm the admissions committee at Northwestern. (See complete profile of Kira in "The Multicultural Hook," in Chapter Thirteen.)
- **Stan, an auto aficionado who redesigned cars on the Internet:** The hours he spent retooling cars on Web sites for Mercedes and Maserati fueled a career interest in engineering that earned him admission to a top technology school.
- **Charlie, a science guy who became the focus of his own experiment:** His decision to transform himself from an overweight, underachieving teenager to a fitness buff on the fast track for academic success helped him gain entrance to Georgia Tech.

Each of these students had "one thing" that popped off the pages of their applications to make admissions committees take notice. But none of these students started with such a clear focus. Most of them began the application process staring hopelessly at their college applications. Flipping through page after page on the computer screen, they wondered who they were and how they could cut through their endless lists of activities to communicate something meaningful about themselves.

Maybe you feel something like these students: confused and overwhelmed. When you survey your accomplishments, they seem small compared to those of your friends. After all, you're not president of the class, or a starter on the basketball team, or an Eagle Scout. The way you see it, you have nothing particularly outstanding or interesting to offer a college.

I'm just an ordinary high school student, you think to yourself.

But are you?

Chances are, you are sitting on a mother lode—a vein of riches hidden just beneath the surface of your consciousness that can provide the raw material for a fabulous College Hook. To find it, you need to dig deep within yourself to reflect on your true interests and pastimes. Even more important, you need to adopt a Hook mind-set: an expansive vision of yourself that breaks you free of the narrow confines of high school and ushers you into a world of limitless potential—*your* potential.

In the end, you'll find your College Hook in that place where your passion and confidence collide to create "one thing" that will make you stand out in your applications. Furthermore, that one thing may even set you on a successful course for the rest of your life.

Now let's get practical. To find your Hook, we'll start with a simple analysis of what you've done over the past few years and what you care about most. Then we'll develop a recipe that will help you "cook up a Hook," step-by-step.

CHAPTER THREE

Cooking Up a Hook

D iscovering your Hook is like pulling together a meal for dinner," says Erika Pagano, Georgetown Class of 2008. "You look around the kitchen to see what you have—pasta, sauce, vegetables—and then you whip up your own dish.

"In my case, I figured out what that dish was: I had experience as an exchange student, as a writer, as a Model UN leader, and as a publicist through a fan Web site I created for Cirque du Soleil. I put them all together and came up with 'International Communicator.' That was my Hook. It pulled together all my assets with one clear focus."

Like Erika, you may already have at your fingertips all the ingredients you need to create an incredibly appealing Hook. But first you have to look around your "kitchen" to see what you've got. That's Step 1 in a four-part "Recipe for a Hook" that will help you find your own unique interest to whet the appetites of admissions committees.

RECIPE FOR A HOOK: STEP 1

To get started, list the "ingredients" you have on hand—the accomplishments, interests, activities, and passions that have consumed your life in Grades 9 to 12. Write them down on a separate sheet of paper using the categories listed on page 16.

As you're making your list, keep in mind that there are only two guidelines in this exercise: Don't be modest, and be specific. This is not the time accidentally to leave off the fact that you are a National Merit Semifinalist or that you won the top chemistry award in Grade 10. It's also not the time to conveniently ignore the Bucknell Book Award you were given in Grade 11, or the Citizen-of-the-Month Award you received from the Rotary Club last March.

When it comes to activities and interests, be sure to include such accomplishments as leadership positions (e.g., *captain* of the lacrosse team, *president* of

---

RECIPE FOR A HOOK: STEP 1
ACTIVITIES QUESTIONNAIRE

Make a list of all your activities, pastimes, or accomplishments in the following categories:

Honors and Awards

Leadership

Sports

Literature and the Arts

Scientific Achievements

Jobs and Entrepreneurial Ventures

Service

Spiritual Activities

Languages Spoken

Multicultural Connections and Travel

Other Interests and Hobbies

Secret Pastimes and Passions

---

the student government, *founder* of a computer business), positions played, and languages spoken. Also include any publications your work has appeared in, both within school and outside of school. The more details you can include on this initial list, the easier it will be for you to get a clear snapshot of your strengths.

But also don't forget to include those aspects of your life that you don't think of as accomplishments at all. Do you go snowboarding every chance you get? Write it down. How about the time you spend reading Tom Clancy novels? Write it down. What about the video games you play every day, or the T-shirts you design and sell at rock concerts, or the nights you spend playing bingo with your grandmother?

Also, be sure to note your secret life as an on-line trader that has netted you enough money to pay for the first year of college. Then again, think about the months you spent rewiring your entire boarding-school dorm for Linux, the vacations you've enjoyed visiting Civil War battlefields, the vintage Chevy you've been remodeling in your garage, the funky handbags you design and make for your friends, and the graffiti that you inscribe on the sides of abandoned cars in the wee hours of the night. (By the way, *all* of these Hooks have actually been used to great effect by my students.)

Write down *everything* that occupies your time and consumes your passions. Then put the list aside. A few days later, go back over your list and add to it. You'll be surprised at the things you forgot the first time around. Perhaps you forgot the camp musical you wrote and produced when no one else volunteered. That fits under "Literature and the Arts." Maybe you forgot your paid gig playing the saxophone in a local production of *Gypsy*. Put that under "Jobs." Did you include the salsa dancing you do on weekends with your extended Cuban-American family? That goes under "Multicultural Connections."

How about your hobby fixing surfboards for your friends? Write that down under "Other Interests and Hobbies." Or maybe you failed to include the lunches you've had with your father and grandfather every Saturday for the past five years at Stan's Restaurant—lunches where political opinions are flying and your debating skills are regularly put to the test. Put that under "Secret Pastimes."

When you're trying to find your Hook, nothing is too insignificant or frivolous to be considered. What may seem marginal to you—or way too much fun—may actually be the start of the most unusual Hook of all.

When you're satisfied that you've finished your list, ask one or both your parents to review it. You'll be surprised at how much more they may have to add.

RECIPE FOR A HOOK: STEP 2

Next, ask your parents to answer a series of questions that may elicit some very intimate anecdotes and observations about your personality and character.

After your parents have filled in the questionnaire on page 18, take a close look at what they have written, because the answers to these questions could help you see yourself in an entirely new dimension. Here are some actual responses to the questionnaire:

- "Susie's grandmother, who has Alzheimer's, has lived with us for the past five years," wrote one mom. "As a result, Susie has developed a level of patience and compassion beyond her years."
- "Jason has had to work to help pay household expenses," said another mother. "I'll never forget his reaction the day I told him that I needed his Taco Bell money to pay the electric bill. Without saying a word, he went to his dresser, pulled out $200, and handed it over to me."
- "Candace is the most organized person I know. She could take a room full of chimpanzees and put them in order."
- "Kimberly spends every afternoon caring for her sister, Louise, who has Down's syndrome. There are times when Louise behaves inappropriately in public or in the presence of Kimberly's friends. But Kimberly has

RECIPE FOR A HOOK: STEP 2
PARENT QUESTIONNAIRE

Ask your parents to answer the following questions as thoroughly as possible:

1. What do you consider your child's greatest gifts or talents? (Consider especially those that might not be readily apparent in a standard shopping list of "activities.")

2. What are his or her most attractive personal qualities? (For example, sense of humor, diligence, people orientation, trustworthiness, charisma.) Explain.

3. What's your child's biggest passion?

4. What makes your child distinctive? Which of his or her activities, hobbies, or interests might make the biggest selling point to colleges?

5. When you're among friends, family, or acquaintances, what is it about your child that you love to brag about?

6. What do you think your child has to offer a college or university?

7. When you envision America twenty years from now, what is it about your child that will make him or her capable of succeeding?

8. What is the most significant challenge your child has faced, and how has that shaped the person he or she is today? (Health problems, family circumstances, frequent moves, etc.)

9. If you could think of one anecdote that sums up your child's character, what would it be? (This could be something from childhood, or more recently, depending on what comes to mind.)

10. What role has your family's ethnicity or cultural background played in your child's life?

12. Is there anything else important about your child that you'd like to add?

learned to handle these situations with maturity. Observers know immediately that Kimberly loves and protects her little sister."

- "Victoria has an ability to resolve any crisis quickly and efficiently. When she was in elementary school, she and her brother got separated from her father and me in a department store. We went looking for them, only to find that Victoria had gone to the information center and asked them to make an announcement."
- "Because of my husband's work, George has lived in five states and attended seven schools since he was in kindergarten. As a result, he has learned to adapt to new environments and make friends quickly and easily."
- "In ninth grade, Nathaniel chose to switch from a small Christian day school to a large multicultural high school. Through this decision, he gained a wide circle of friends from many different ethnic and religious groups. He is respected by his peers and teachers alike for his ability to care for and communicate with everyone."
- "Tina knows how to think on her feet. That's why she's been so successful arguing cases in the Debate Club."
- "Paul has a very spiritual gift. He is very tuned in to his own feelings and those of others. He has a very special talent to get people on his side and like him."
- "When we crossed into the U.S. from Mexico, Catalina was only nine months old," one parent wrote in Spanish. "We pushed her across the Rio Grande in a spare tire. For many years, we worked as migrant workers all over the United States, and now we both have permanent jobs. Catalina and I became naturalized citizens two years ago."
- "Philip is very logical and a deep thinker. He comes across as very serious, but he has a wonderfully satiric sense of humor. People look up to him because of his height, but also because they can trust him to be honest and do what he says he will. He is not afraid of anything—except maybe insects!"
- "When Robert was in the third grade, the first week of school the teacher had him fill out a questionnaire that asked, 'What do you want people to know about you?' Robert's reply: 'I want to be first.' He's never changed."
- "The one obstacle that stands out is the fact that Sylvia doesn't have a father. When she was six years old, another child asked her where her father was and she pointed to me. She just deals with it."
- "Ever since she was in elementary school, Helen's teachers have said she never hesitates to speak her mind."
- "Jeffrey always seems to know how to take care of himself. When he was too young to be toilet trained and still in diapers, I secretly watched him get a diaper, lie down on the floor, and change his diaper."
- "Rebecca's greatest attribute is that she is not a quitter."

Responses like these can give you a clue to the kind of information you can use when you're searching for your Hook. Although you may blush to read your dad's proud boast that you are "not a quitter" or your mom's fond memory of how you changed your own diaper, you may soon discover that such qualities or anecdotes can become raw material for a Hook. Even personal qualities that seem elusive, such as "independent spirit," "resilience," or "stick-to-itiveness" might actually turn into a Hook through an adroit presentation of skills on a résumé or through an essay.

And don't overlook your family's economic and ethnic background as the basis for a Hook. What you consider commonplace, such as speaking Urdu at home with your eighty-year-old Pakistani grandmother, caring for your little brother after school while your mom works at the grapefruit packing plant with other Haitian women, or helping to care for an uncle who has AIDS, can create a Hook that is anything but ordinary.

RECIPE FOR A HOOK: STEP 3

Once you've completed Step 1 with your list of activities and Step 2 with some input from your parents, it's now time to add to the mix a sense of who you are academically. This is a very important step in creating your Hook, because you may discover that the "one thing" that sets you apart from your peers is an unusual or unusually intense academic interest that you hope to continue in college.

For example, your enthusiasm for military history could be the start of a very compelling Hook. So could a passion for chemistry so explosive it leaves your mom shaking her head at the smoke filling the garage every weekend. If you are consumed by the field of intelligence as a future CIA operative, fascinated with Hindu art as a possible curator, titillated by meteorology as a budding TV weatherman, or mesmerized by time travel as a potential astrophysicist, you just might have found your Hook.

If you've responded to this questionnaire honestly, you may find that your answers bring to the surface a particular academic passion—with the scores and grades to support it. Perhaps your favorite subject is African history and you've been accepted to a selective summer program to work with the Masai in Tanzania. With a solid 3.5 GPA, you might establish your Hook as an African studies specialist aiming for a career with the United Nations or a nongovernmental organization.

Then again, you may be a whiz at Latin who is absolutely wild about Cicero. Your straight-A performance in the language over the past few years, coupled with the backpacking trip you took around Italy last summer investigating Roman ruins, could set you up nicely as a classicist. Throw into the mix a stated

Recipe for a Hook: Step 3
Academic Interest Questionnaire

Fill out the following questionnaire as honestly and accurately as possible:

- What are your favorite subjects? Why?

- List all Honors, AP, or IB courses.

- List any college-level courses (including on-line courses).

- What is your GPA? Weighted _____ Unweighted _____.

- What is your class rank?

- Give a rundown of your standardized test scores:

   - PSAT: (CR) _____ (M) _____ (WR) _____

   - SAT: (CR) _____ (M) _____ (WR) _____ Essay _____

   - ACT: Composite: _____ English _____ Reading _____
     Math _____ Science Reasoning _____ Essay _____

   - SAT Subject Tests 1. _____; 2. _____; 3. _____

- Indicate your special academic talents or interests.

- Describe any significant research papers or scientific studies you've conducted.

- How will you spend your summer?

- Describe any summer enrichment courses or programs in which you've participated.

- Where would you like to apply to college? Why?

- What are your possible areas of study in college? Why?

- Is there anything you'd like to add?

interest in majoring in Greek and Latin in college, and you may have found yourself a neat little Hook.

On the other hand, when you review the questionnaire, you might see an immediate disconnect between your dream major and your ability to follow through academically. If your SAT math scores are in the doghouse, it might not be smart to portray yourself as a future aeronautical engineer. This doesn't mean that you can't or won't come on strong in math in college. It just means that you haven't yet caught fire enough to set yourself up with a Hook in a math-heavy major for purposes of your college applications.

But don't give up yet. Everyone has a Hook. You just need to dig deeper to find it.

RECIPE FOR A HOOK: STEP 4

Now that you've done some preparation, it's time to look over everything you and your parents have jotted down in the first three steps and try to zero in on your Hook. Your goal in Step 4 is to find the "one thing" that jumps out and makes you distinctive.

This step calls for some creativity: What grabs you about you? What's funky, offbeat, funny, touching, or unusual?

This step also calls for some self-reflection: If you put a mirror up to yourself, what do you see?

Above all, this step requires you to think beyond high school to the world you'll be entering as a college freshman. Colleges want students who are independent thinkers and doers, people whose very presence will make a contribution to the campus.

They also want *diversity*—ethnically, experientially, and economically. What kind of unusual quality do you bring to the table? Keep asking yourself this question as you zero in on your Hook.

The best Hooks aren't necessarily the most obvious. But they tend to share some similar attributes—including passion, commitment, quirkiness, resilience, and recognition—that are included in the worksheet on page 23. Use them as guidelines when you're cooking up your Hook.

As you look over these guidelines, you'll inevitably see some patterns emerge that will serve as a guide to your Hook. For example, maybe you've spent every summer for the past seven years at a wilderness camp in the Adirondacks where you've hiked all forty-six of the High Peaks in New York State and you have a certificate to prove it. Compared to the other activities that have occupied your time in high school, perhaps your track record as a woodsman jumps out at you. That sounds like a good bet to be your Hook.

Or perhaps you've worked at a local restaurant for the past few years, starting as a lowly busboy. Because your work ethic and creativity so impressed the boss, he taught you the ropes as a chef. These days you wear a toque and stand behind the stove as second in command, or sous-chef, creating original dishes that wow the locals.

Then again, maybe you're an expert polo player who has spent every summer at a dude ranch out west. Last summer you worked as a wrangler—a real-

RECIPE FOR A HOOK: STEP 4
COOK UP A HOOK

Follow these guidelines to zero in on your Hook.

• *Pay attention to passion:* The strongest Hooks reflect a passionate interest in an activity, goal, or principle. What's yours?

• *Capitalize on commitment:* A significant track record in one area or related areas could signal a Hook. What has commanded your time and energy over the past three or four years?

• *Be open to the offbeat:* Sometimes what makes the most arresting Hook is the quirky thing that you keep hidden or that your mom yells at you about. What might you have missed?

• *Recognize resilience:* Overcoming a personal obstacle or crisis in your school or family life may be grounds for a compelling Hook. What has been your biggest challenge?

• *Revel in recognition:* A strong Hook tends to have something concrete to back it up, such as awards, a body of work in the arts, DVDs or CDs, or outside recognition. What does the recognition you've received say about you?

life cowboy who herded horses and led trail rides—and you've been asked back to do it again.

You may be thinking, *But I still don't get it! I'm not a wrangler, or a professional chef, or a woodsman. I've read over my questionnaires, and I have no idea what my Hook might be.*

It's normal to be overwhelmed at this stage of the game. Few of us can see ourselves as others see us, no matter how hard we try. If you find yourself reading over your questionnaires and seeing nothing but a confusing jumble of activities and interests, don't panic. Instead, call for help:

• Ask your favorite aunt or a close family friend to sit down with you for an hour or two to brainstorm about your Hook. An outsider's perspective may be just what you need to see yourself in a new light.

• Call four or five friends you trust and ask them to play the Hook game popularized by New York City college counselor Lily Trayes, who has worked with students at some of Manhattan's top private schools. Lily regularly asks her students to sit in small groups and identify one another's Hooks.

During one session a few years ago, everyone in the room found a Hook except Laura, who burst into tears and wailed, "I don't have a Hook!" Quickly perusing Laura's activities, Lily discovered that the young woman worked as a lifeguard.

"Being a lifeguard is a huge responsibility," Lily said. "People have to trust you. Have you ever had to rescue anyone?"

The answer was, "Yes."

"Laura, there's your Hook. You're responsible, trustworthy, and you care about people. And you are applying to the School of Nursing. You've found your Hook!"

Laura realized she did have experience that positioned her as a good applicant for the nursing school at a major university. She left smiling, and so will you, if you follow Lily's lead. So get your friends together—and find a Hook!

Now it's your turn. Have you found your Hook? Try to sum it up in a word or phrase, such as:

State-Ranked Swimmer
Aussie with a Diverse Cultural Perspective
Future Astrophysicist
Aerial Acrobat
Drum Captain of Nationally Ranked Marching Band
Entrepreneurial Graffiti Artist
Hispanic Achiever
Military History Expert
Veterinary Intern
French/Creole Linguist

By now you should have a pretty good idea of what your Hook might be. Or perhaps you have more than one viable option and you haven't quite settled on which one is paramount. Although many students will settle on only one Hook for all their schools, a number of you will find that you have one main Hook and one or more secondary Hooks, which may help you gain admission to particular schools.

The important thing at this juncture is to pick one Hook and start building on it. A good way to understand how your Hook can be developed is to review some of the most popular categories that define students in their college appli-

---

Your Hook:

cations. The Top Ten College Hooks (ordered this way for the sake of this book, not in order of colleges' preferences) include:

1. The Athletic Hook
2. The International Hook
3. The Music Hook
4. The Political Hook
5. The Technology Hook
6. The Humanitarian Hook
7. The Science Hook
8. The Writing Hook
9. The Drama Hook
10. The Multicultural Hook

Perhaps you can easily see yourself fitting into one of these categories as an athlete, a computer whiz, or an actor. Or maybe you're a musician, an internationalist, or a scientist. Then again, you might be a writer, a politician, or a humanitarian. Or maybe, just maybe, you fall into the hottest category of all these days, what I like to call "multicultural man/woman": a student whose ethnicity or cultural background is so compelling that the door to a top college swings wide open.

Right now you may be wondering, *What about legacies?* Although your position as a legacy, a child of a parent or grandparent who attended a particular school, can carry weight, it is unclear how much pull legacies can generate these days, particularly if there is no sizeable financial gift or celebrity status involved. Typically, you won't be considered a legacy unless your parent or a sibling attended the school as an undergraduate. Some schools are known to give legacies an edge only in the Early Decision pool. Others give little or no preference at all.

At one Ivy League school, for example, a student who was at the top of his class was deferred from the Early Decision round despite the fact that his ties to the school went back three generations. He was later denied. At Notre Dame, on the other hand, roughly 9 to 10 percent of applicants are legacies. Furthermore, 17 percent of admitted students hold legacy status, as do 22 to 23 percent of those who actually enroll, according to the admissions office. One recent applicant pressed her case by artfully drawing a Fighting Irish family tree filled with generations of Notre Dame graduates. The tree was a triumph; she was admitted.

Because the value of legacies differs so widely from school to school, this book has focused its Top Ten Hooks on those that are common to a wider universe of students. But if you think you might qualify as a legacy, you should make that known to the admissions office and inquire about the school's policies. It always helps to pick up the phone and speak to an admissions counselor directly.

This list of Hooks is certainly not exhaustive, and you may have created a Hook in a category that is all your own. But if you do fall into one of the Top

Ten categories, be forewarned: These categories are not marketable in and of themselves. In other words, it's not enough in these competitive times just to play the flute, or write poems in your journal, or play a sport. If you want to follow your dreams to a favorite college, you've got to live your dream now by taking your passions and interests to the highest level of achievement possible. Then you've got to strut your stuff so clearly on your application that your identity can flow from the lips of admissions committee members in a simple phrase:

"She's the Florida pole-vaulter."

"He's the Music Man."

"She's the op-ed writer."

In Part II, you'll meet students who have communicated their Hooks clearly and with great success. Each fits into a category that colleges might look for to round out a class. But as these students were filling out their applications, they made sure that every aspect of their presentation, from the activities list to supplemental submissions, screamed their Hook, so that their identity was loud and clear.

PART II

The Top Ten College Hooks

CHAPTER FOUR

The Athletic Hook

HOOK TIP

Athletics works as a Hook *only* if you are a recruited athlete. That's the cold, hard truth, but it could save you a lot of grief. You don't need to play a sport to get into college. But if you want to get into college by playing a sport, you have to be good enough to get recruited by a Division I, II, or III school. Otherwise, find another Hook. Some possible exceptions to this rule: You're a world-class athlete such as Olympic gold medalist Sarah Hughes, who skated her way to Yale, or you play a funky sport, such as women's wrestling or competitive wake-boarding, which may not involve intercollegiate athletics, but may make you stand out through sheer novelty.

CHELO CANINO: POLE-VAULTING TO PRINCETON

"Princeton was one of the only places I didn't think I'd get in," confessed Chelo Canino, a pole-vaulter from a large public high school in Tampa, Florida, who applied to a string of top-tier colleges, including Cornell and Stanford.

From the get-go, Chelo was ruthlessly honest with herself about her chances for admission. "I knew that these schools were incredibly competitive," she said. "I hoped that my pole-vaulting, a coach's push, and other factors such as my essays would get me in."

Ever since she was a freshman in high school, Chelo had set her sights on college. At the time Princeton wasn't even on her radar screen, but she was determined to prepare herself as well as she could to get the education that had eluded her parents. The daughter of a landscaper and a medical technician, Chelo wanted to be the first in her family to graduate with a four-year degree.

She chafed at the idea of doing what was expected in her conservative Hispanic community: "Staying at home until I got married."

Instead, Chelo poured herself into academics. "I took advantage of the Florida academic system, which added .16 to your GPA for every AP course," she said. "I was the only sophomore in the history of the county to take an AP course, and by the time I was a senior I had taken 12 AP courses and ended up with a GPA over 5.0."

Next she focused on activities, especially on initiating an environmental education program to teach elementary school students about the endangered Florida black bear. By the time she was a senior, she was leading teams of high school students who were giving lectures on the black bear in sixteen elementary schools around Tampa. "I remember being told in an eighth-grade gifted class that colleges look for students who lead organizations," said Chelo. "And so, I went out and tried to do it."

But the icing on the cake was pole-vaulting. Chelo started out in ninth grade as a runner in the 800 meters on the varsity track team. "But I was getting killed in workouts," she said, "and in races I never amounted to much."

One day she looked over at the pole-vault pit and saw the other kids sitting around having a good time. At the time, pole-vaulting had just been introduced as a sanctioned sport for women in Florida, and Chelo jumped at the opportunity.

But the coach took one look at her 100-pound, five-foot-six frame and said bluntly, "No! You're a runner."

Chelo didn't give up. Instead, she saved up the money she earned working at McDonald's to go to summer pole-vault camp at the University of Florida. On the day she was checking into camp, she knew she was in trouble when the coach asked, "How high have you jumped?"

"Everyone else knew what they were doing, but I had never jumped in my life," said Chelo. When she admitted this, she was saved from embarrassment when her friend interjected, "She means she's never jumped in a *meet* before."

With that, the coach checked her into camp. The coaches stuck with her "even though they thought I was skinny, uncoordinated, and unathletic," said Chelo. "Every night I was so upset that I cried to my mom on the phone. She was so supportive. If I had said I wanted to be in the circus, she would have been there reading books about becoming a better circus performer."

The next winter, a friend's dad paid for Chelo to attend pole-vault camp with his daughter in Miami, where she vaulted seven feet. When track season started sophomore year, Chelo was ready. She walked up to the coach boldly and said, "I'm a pole-vaulter. I've been to two camps, and I've vaulted seven feet."

The coach just smiled. "Okay, you can work out with the sprinters."

That was the beginning of Chelo's ride to the top of the college athletic recruiting lists. At one of her first track meets as a pole-vaulter, she vaulted nine feet while still training on her own. At another meet, ever eager for ways to improve, she spied a coach from Florida's east coast who was actually coaching half the athletes at the meet.

"I want to be coached by him," she told her mom.

"Are you crazy?" her mom said. "He's two hours away, and our car is always breaking down!"

Undeterred, Chelo headed across the state once a month to train with the coach, paying him with money she earned at McDonald's. When summer rolled around, she upped her training schedule to once a week.

"All the other kids were buying cars," says Chelo. "I was buying poles and paying for a coach."

By her junior year in high school, she was in top form. At a pole-vault competition in Reno, Nevada, that winter, she jumped 11' 4", which put her on the national list.

"It shocked everyone," she said.

During track season, she earned a berth at her first state championship, where she set a new state record: 11' 9". The records and the opportunities kept coming: Olympic Development Camp, Champion of the Nike Indoor Nationals, a second state title in the spring of senior year.

"I jumped twelve-six that year, which was the top mark in the state by about a foot."

Even before she had made her biggest jumps, the college coaches had started calling: Kansas, UCLA, Cornell, Georgia. Her room was stacked full of envelopes from hundreds of coaches from schools all across the country.

For Chelo, it was heady stuff. Methodically she weeded out the letters from the schools that interested her and put them in a binder. On each recruiting letter she made a list of questions to ask the coaches when they made their weekly phone calls.

But two schools weren't calling yet: Stanford and Princeton. She took the initiative to make the first contact, and before long they were calling back.

She started making "official visits" the fall of senior year. She went to Kansas, where one of the top coaches in the country held court. At Cornell, every student she met had been a school leader with SATs in the stratosphere. And then there was Princeton, which she loved best of all.

I don't know if I'm going to get in this place, she thought, after researching the school and its academics. *I just don't think I'm good enough.*

The coach was optimistic. "I want you to come here," he told her.

"But I can't get in!" she would protest.

"I have a good feeling about it," he said, trying to reassure her.

When April rolled around, Chelo's years of hard work paid off. Her mailbox was crammed with acceptance letters from some of the top schools in the country: Stanford, Cornell—and, yes, Princeton.

The coach's "feeling" had been right on the money. As a student at Princeton, Chelo went on to hold the pole-vault record for the school, for the Conference, and for the NCAA East Region. Ultimately, she finished as an NCAA All-American, one of only two women in Princeton's history to hold that title in a field event.

As for her Hook, Chelo credits pole-vaulting with taking her over the top. "Maybe I would have gotten into all those schools on my own," says Chelo, "but pole-vaulting guaranteed it."

Of course, Chelo stands at the top of the heap for the athletic Hook, but don't be discouraged if you're not nationally ranked or recognized in some sport. There are plenty of athletic recruiting slots open at many smaller, Division III schools, including elite colleges like Amherst, Williams, and Swarthmore. You just have to know how to "court the coaches" (see Chapter Twenty-Four). Also, if you have absolutely no athletic aptitude at all, there are countless other Hooks, such as an International Hook and the other Hooks in the pages that follow, that will work just as well for you.

BRIGHT IDEAS FOR ATHLETES FROM CHELO CANINO

In her freshman year at Princeton, Chelo teamed up with her old private coach, Mike Lawryk, to start a pole-vault club for high school athletes in a tri-state area. Today, through Vertical Assault Athletic Club, based in Bath, Pennsylvania, she not only creates training opportunities for pole-vaulters but also gives tips on recruitment at the Division I, II, and III level. Here's her advice for student athletes in all sports:

- **Take a hard look at the statistics of the top players on the college's Web site.** Ask yourself, "Will I fit in on this team?" If a school's athletes are ten times your caliber, then look elsewhere. Otherwise coaches will take one look at you and decide that you won't have an impact on the team.
- **Write a letter to the coach, once you determine that you can be competitive.** Explain who you are, your height and weight, your statistics, and something about your academics. Attach a résumé and a profile of your high school.
- **Send an e-mail to the coach.** Their addresses are all on-line. Include the same information you put in a letter.
- **Stop by the college athletic office and meet the coach.** At the very least you'll get some good information; at the most you might impress the coach with your persistence.
- **Ask questions about athletic scholarships, *if* you are being recruited.** Some coaches might say, "Here's what we can give you." Other coaches won't bring it up at all. At one school, the head coach sat me down after an official visit and said, "Do you have any questions?" For a while, I had the number one jump in the U.S. This was the time for me to say, "What can you do for me financially so that I can come here?" But I had no clue, and so I didn't have any money questions.

- **Understand scholarship realities.** A large number of students on every Division I collegiate team do not have scholarships. If you're lucky enough to have a "full ride," that's great. But keep in mind that the number of athletic scholarships on a team is limited. Coaches have to try to spread out their allotted scholarship money among the team members.
- **Don't count on admission until you get an official letter of acceptance.** I got my letters in April like everybody else. Many coaches wanted me to apply Early Decision. But because I wasn't sure where I wanted to go, I applied Regular Decision. Although no one told me for sure that I was "in," I got a letter from one coach that said, "I can't tell you that you're in, but there's a strong likelihood."
- **Don't worry if the college coach never contacts your high school coach.** In the recruiting game these days, coaches often bypass high school coaches completely. Typically, college coaches will call you at home or get you through your guidance counselor.
- **Use official college visits wisely.** If a coach wants you, you'll be invited to visit. You are permitted only five official visits to Division I and II colleges. (Check the NCAA Web site for regulations.) If you go on an official visit, you are sending a signal that the school is one of your top five choices. It's rare to get a scholarship if you haven't made an official visit. Coaches may talk about it or hint at it, but until you visit you won't get a concrete offer.
- **Steel yourself for a barrage of phone calls.** If you're a top athlete, coaches will call you regularly. The first couple of calls are very exciting. After that, you may find yourself trying to avoid the phone. But stick with it.

CHAPTER FIVE

The International Hook

HOOK TIP

If your passion is international affairs, being a member of your school's Model United Nations club can get you only so far. Find something extra and exotic to set yourself apart—but be sure to stop short of risky business, such as the secret trip to Iraq that earned international notoriety for one Florida teen a few years back. Instead, you might study Arabic or Chinese, spend a summer in Botswana, or get selected for a fully paid summer exchange program—and then write home about it.

ERIKA PAGANO: JAPAN TO GEORGETOWN IN TWO GIANT STEPS

For Erika Pagano, the route to Georgetown was paved with yen. Her selection as one of fifty students in the nation for the Japan United States Senate Exchange (JUSSE), a fully paid five-week program sponsored by Youth for Understanding, propelled her on a course toward a world-class Hook as an international communicator.

"I was interested in international affairs because of my involvement in Model United Nations," said Erika, who was president of her prep school's Model UN club. "But I had no idea of the speed at which the exchange program in Japan would send me in the direction of Georgetown's School of Foreign Service. Going to Japan was the catalyst toward clarifying what I wanted to study, where I wanted to go to school, and how I would position myself to get in."

Erika got her first taste of Georgetown the summer before her junior year in high school, when she spent five weeks on campus taking two college-level courses: one in Web site design and technology, and the other in anatomy and physiology. At the time, she was toying with the idea of a career in medicine, even as she was pursuing her passion for computers. Although the courses excited her, the school left her cold.

"The first two weeks, I hated it," says Erika. "There was just something about the place I didn't like."

Then one day during a break between classes, she found herself near the college chapel, and something compelled her inside to pray.

"A feeling of peace came over me," she said, "and I knew that this was where I needed to be."

From then on, her summer at Georgetown was golden. She aced her courses and started investigating what the school had to offer.

"The first major that caught my eye was the Science, Technology, and International Affairs major in the School of Foreign Service," said Erika, who had been a computer buff since eighth grade. Among her other exploits, Erika had devoted more than 2,500 hours to creating and maintaining an official fan Web site for Cirque du Soleil's Orlando production of *La Nouba*. The project had involved countless hours on the phone or e-mail with Cirque du Soleil's public relations staff in Montreal, giving her firsthand experience in technology and international relations. As Erika saw it, the major at Georgetown might be a perfect fit.

But still, she wasn't sure, and once back home in the fall of junior year, Erika filed the information away in her brain and started thinking about other pursuits: namely, how to get herself to Japan. The idea wasn't a calculated move to gain admission to Georgetown. Rather, she wanted to visit some summer camp friends who were living with their families in Tokyo.

"I had been to a Teen Writers Workshop on the subject of creativity, and the writer, Leslie McGuirk, told us to write down five goals," Erika explained. "Along with getting into Georgetown, going to Japan was one of my goals, and so I started writing it down in my journal every day."

Although her parents balked at the price tag of a junket to Japan, they gave her permission to go, on two conditions: "It had to be for educational purposes, and I had to pay my own way," said Erika.

With that green light, Erika turned to her computer and Googled the words "Summer Exchange—Japan." Up popped the Web site for the nonprofit group Youth for Understanding, where she found an application for the highly selective JUSSE program that was sponsored by the Japanese government.

Erika knew it was a long shot: only fifty students, one from each state, would be selected out of hundreds of applicants for the all-expenses-paid five-week program. Determined to see her friends in Tokyo, she gamely filled out the application, wrote the essays, and, without her parents' knowledge, sent it off.

Two months later, she learned she had been selected for an interview. Within a month after that, she had her ticket to Japan. When summer rolled around, she would be on a plane headed to the city of Akita on the Sea of Japan. There, she would live with a Japanese family, attend a Japanese high school, and speak at public events as a student "ambassador" of the United States.

Primed to go to Japan, Erika started thinking about her other goal: getting into Georgetown. Overnight, it seemed, she had the makings of a powerful international relations Hook that could set the stage for admission.

"JUSSE put me over the top," says Erika. "Now I had a Hook, a focus, which reinforced everything else I had done in the area of international affairs."

As it turned out, the JUSSE program was just her first giant step toward a Georgetown-sized College Hook. Erika had an ace in the hole that many students don't have: an ability to write, and write fast. Using contacts from the Teen Writers Workshop, she arranged to file regular columns from Japan as a "foreign correspondent" in the *Press Journal,* a local daily newspaper with a circulation of more than 80,000. The day before she left for Japan, the newspaper featured her in a front-page article. The headline said it all: "Planning ahead: St. Edward's Upper School junior snags scholarship to spend her summer vacation learning to live surrounded by Japanese."

As a kicker, the article quoted the intrepid Erika as saying, "The only thing I'm worried about is not wanting to come back home."

Her quote was prescient. Once in Japan, while her exchange student colleagues were adjusting to sleeping on *futon* and taking baths in *ohuro,* Erika was not merely living it—she was also writing about it in her "Letter to America" column. One article featured her struggles with the high-tech Japanese toilets. Another focused on the differences between Japanese and American high schools. Yet another described the bizarre questions she was asked on a regular basis by students whose knowledge of America came strictly from the movies. By the time she returned and started senior year, Erika had accumulated a lifetime of experiences and five published articles as a foreign correspondent. (See one of Erika's articles in Appendix B.) The result was an International-Hook-to-die-for. Erika was not merely a scholarship-winning exchange student with a background in international relations; she was an *international communicator.*

As a result, when she filled out her application to Georgetown, Erika included her newspaper clippings in a portfolio and highlighted her multinational communications experience through a résumé and essay. Her issue-oriented essay for the School of Foreign Service, for example, focused on her insights into a growing problem she had encountered among teenagers in Japan: the practice of *enjo kosai,* in which upper-middle-class teenage girls prostitute themselves with older men to receive classy consumer items such as Gucci bags or Hermès scarves. (See Chapter Seventeen.)

Erika hoped that her application sent a message to Georgetown: Across cultures and languages, she could communicate in a way that resonated with people around the globe.

As it turned out, Georgetown got the message. Of course, it didn't hurt that Erika had earned a 33 composite ACT with a perfect 36 on the English section, or that she was recognized as an AP Scholar with Honor, boasting scores of 5 on three AP tests and 4 on a fourth. She was accepted Early Action to the School of Foreign Service, which has a very low acceptance rate. Studying international affairs and technology, along with Chinese, she spent eight weeks in Beijing the summer after freshman year, and—you guessed it—she filed stories from China with her local newspaper, the *Press Journal.*

"Without a Hook, I might have fished around for a college and simply followed a general liberal arts program," said Erika. "But once I found my Hook, I knew what I wanted, and I chose a school where I knew I could pursue the interests I had already developed.

"My Hook pulled together all my assets with one clear focus. On my application, I tried to manipulate everything I had done to support that focus."

"Colleges have been at this game for decades," adds Erika. "But you're only in this game for one year. So you have to play the game the smartest way you can with the tools that you have. Make the most of what you have—and bait your Hook!"

BRIGHT IDEAS FOR INTERNATIONALISTS AND LINGUISTS

- **Apply for an exchange program abroad through Youth for Understanding.** This Atlanta-based nonprofit organization hosts dozens of exchange programs, many of them with sizeable scholarships attached. Note especially YFU scholarships to Finland and Japan, as well as special scholarships for minority students and Model United Nations participants.
- **Spearhead an exchange program with a high school in a sister city through Sister Cities International.** If your city is not affiliated with this nonprofit program, lobby with the mayor or city council to get connected to a sister city in Europe, Asia, or Africa. Then take steps to organize an exchange program through your school.
- **Create your own one-credit independent course in a hot language such as Arabic or Chinese, a dead language such as Greek or Latin, or an offbeat language such as Croatian or Turkish.** If your school permits independent study projects, find a mentor who would be willing to teach you once a week. If your school won't do it, then find a way to study on your own.
- **Indicate on your application that you'd like to major in international affairs and minor in a language.** Focus especially on languages that dovetail in some way with your Hook.
- **Spend a summer, or longer, perfecting your language skills in an intensive program abroad.** Aim to become fluent. Because so many high school students are involved in intensive language programs, you need to distinguish yourself by your linguistic virtuosity with the credentials to prove it.

- **Sign up for UCLA's Summer Language Intensive,** to study such languages as Yoruba, Japanese, Romanian, or Catalan, as well as Arabic, Hebrew, German, French, and Italian. These courses, which compress thirty weeks of college-level language into eight weeks, are "not for the fainthearted," says the program's coordinator. But you'll be rewarded with college credit and an official UCLA transcript. Students entering junior or senior year are best suited to the program, which offers some scholarships. Register early in the calendar year.
- **Rediscover your ethnic or linguistic roots.** If you have the financial wherewithal, take a trip to the country of your forebears and get to know the sights and sounds of your heritage. Spend a month studying the language. Then write about your experiences in an essay.

CHAPTER SIX

The Music Hook

Hook Tip

Even if you're not planning to major in music, don't hesitate to send a CD of your solo performance as a singer or instrumentalist to the admissions committee, band leader, or orchestra director. Although some large universities may not take time to evaluate such submissions, at other schools the leaders of the band, orchestra, or chorus may have clout with admissions.

At one Little Ivy, for example, the heads of the instrumental department and chorus routinely rated audio submissions and passed the information along to the admissions office.[8] Recruiting for the band or orchestra may not be on a par with athletics, but it often can give you an edge.

JEFF DANIELS: THE MUSIC MAN

Jeff Daniels never doubted for a moment what his Hook should be. A sax player with three school bands, he lived, breathed, and slept music, from Sousa to Saint-Saens.

In fact, everything about him rang out "Music Man." That's why, when he was filling out his college applications, he made sure to hit his Hook from every angle.

For starters, Jeff tackled the Common Application's activities grid titled "Extracurricular, Personal, and Volunteer Activities," which he hoped would tantalize the admissions readers with the depth of his musical accomplishments and commitment. He led with the following information:

Symphonic Band: Grades 9–12—1st Chair Sax/Carnegie Hall Concert 20 hours/wk; 20 wks/yr

Marching Band: Grades 9–12—Sax Section Leader 25 hours/wk; 20 wks/yr

Jazz Band: Grades 10 & 12—Excellent/Superior Rankings 6 hrs/wk; all year

Church Instrumentalist: Grades 9–12—Weekly performances 1 hr/wk; all year

Private Piano Lessons: Grades 9–12—Since Grade 5, 2 hrs/wk; all year

Next he filled in the section on "Work Experience," where he included professional musical gigs for local theater productions.

But the highlight was his résumé, which he planned to include as a supplement to his applications. Because the short format of the Common Application's activities grid could only hint at his accomplishments, he knew he needed something more explicit. With a detailed résumé, he could expand on his activities and unleash on the admissions committee everything he had done musically over the past four years.

For easy readability on the résumé, Jeff arranged his activities by category rather than by year of involvement. There was a category for his honors, called "Academic Achiever"; another for his church work, titled "Church Volunteer"; yet another for his travels abroad, called "Overseas Student Experience"; and one for his jobs, called "Work Experience."

But Jeff's Hook took center stage. His résumé led with a headline that summed up who he was in two simple words: Music Man. The very first page of his résumé looked like this:

MUSIC MAN

Saxophone First Chair, Vero Beach High School Symphonic Band

- First chair out of 15 saxophone players in this elite band at Vero Beach High School—band has been ranked "Superior" at state level 18 years in a row.
- Member of Vero Beach High School Symphonic Band, Grades

9–12—only one of three freshmen to be chosen for this top instrumental group.
- Plays both alto and bari sax.
- Carnegie Hall National Band Concert participant, Grade 10.
- Band ranked "Superior" at district level, Grades 9–12.
- Personal "Excellent" solo ranking, Grade 11.
- Personal "Superior" solo and "Excellent" ensemble, Grades 9 and 10.

Sax Section Leader, Vero Beach High School Marching Band
- Member (Grades 9–12) and Section Leader (Grade 12) of this top-rated band, which has been ranked "Superior" at district marching festival 24 years in a row.
- Grand Champions out of 8 bands competing at the Fernandina Beach Marching Festival, Grade 9.

Musical Gigs
- Paid appearances at Central Florida polo games and shopping mall.
- Performances in orchestra pit for local theater productions of *Bye-Bye Birdie*, *Wizard of Oz*, and *Chicago*.
- Instrumental roles in several church cantatas.
- Weekly performances at worship services.

Vero Beach High School Jazz Band
- Band ranked "Excellent" at district level, Grade 10; "Superior," Grade 12.

Band Camps
- Attended one-week marching band camps to learn and practice drills in Tampa and Haines City, Florida, Summers, Grades 9–12.

Sax Teacher
- Teaches sax to a 5th grader weekly, Grade 12.

Private Sax Lessons
- Took private sax lessons from a professional jazz musician, Grade 11.

Private Piano Lessons
- Studied both classical music and jazz since Grade 5.

With his résumé ready to go, Jeff handed a copy to his guidance counselor, who was so taken by his accomplishments that she picked up on his identity as a Music Man and wove the nickname into her recommendations.

"I have known this talented young man, who is known by his peers as Mr. Music Man, for three years," she wrote glowingly (See Appendix B).

Jeff's musical exploits weren't all his guidance counselor had to brag about. He was ranked in the top 2 percent of a class of nearly 600 students. And with a curriculum laden with eleven AP courses, Jeff was at the top of his game not just musically, but also academically.

A solid 28 composite on the ACT put him in the mid-50-percent range of admitted students for most of the colleges on his list, but he was counting on his academics and his Hook to give him an edge at such schools as Boston College, University of Michigan, and Lehigh.

Every aspect of his application, from his activities list to one of his essays, played to his Hook. But still Jeff wasn't satisfied. He was a musician, after all, and he reasoned that his music needed to be *heard* and not just seen.

"My Hook was obviously music," said Jeff, "but I felt I needed something that could provide concrete evidence of my interest beyond what I wrote in my application. And so I recorded a CD."

Jeff lined up a professional recording studio, spent hours practicing, and stepped into the sound booth to make his very first recording. On the alto sax, he played two jazz pieces, "Moon Glow" and "Harlem Nocturne." And then, he said, "just to show that I could play more than one instrument," he threw in three piano pieces: "Misty Melody," "Big City Blues," and two excerpts from the "1812 Overture."

"It was a cool experience to have a CD with me playing," said Jeff. "It was my first time in a recording studio. I had never done anything like that before."

Jeff sent his CD to the admissions offices and band directors of all the schools to which he was applying, along with a cover letter explaining how much he wanted to play in the band. He also made sure that his band director sent a recommendation letter. He followed the first CD with a second one geared to the requirements of a special band scholarship that he was applying for at Boston College.

"I sent in the CDs not expecting any response at all," said Jeff.

At the end of March, he got more than he had bargained for: an acceptance to Boston College from a pool of nearly 24,000 applicants *and* an invitation to join BC's Wind Ensemble, the university's highly selective new concert band. The band invitation came with a $1,000-a-year renewable band scholarship.

Jeff sat back amazed as the acceptance letters rolled in—Lehigh, Michigan, Syracuse—all schools that were at the top of his list.

"I was a little anxious while I was waiting for the acceptances to come in, wondering where I'd end up," admitted Jeff. "Making a choice was tough, too." What made his decision even more difficult was a personal lobbying effort by one Michigan alumnus, who showed up at the restaurant where Jeff worked to compliment him on the strength of his application and résumé.

"You're a very impressive young man," the man told him. "I hope we'll see you at Michigan."

But in the end, it was the personal recruiting for BC's band that won Jeff over. "I felt comfortable, because I knew I would be in the band and might even major in music," said Jeff, who is toying with a double major in music and science. "Before I even set foot on campus, I was already involved. It made me feel at home."

Jeff hit the ground running the minute he arrived at Boston College as a freshman. "I'm in every possible band thing you could be in," said Jeff, who finds himself at practice almost every night. "I'm in the marching band during football season, the Wind Ensemble playing three or four concerts a semester, and the pep band for basketball games. Over spring break, we'll be in North Carolina playing for the ACC women's basketball tournament."

The list of Jeff's musical exploits doesn't stop there. There's the liturgical band he plays in for Mass every Sunday at one of three chapels on the Boston College campus, the private sax lessons he's taking from a member of the Boston Pops, using money from his band scholarship, and the informal sax lessons he gives to fellow students who are transitioning to the band from orchestral instruments such as clarinet or flute.

But rather than being overwhelmed by all the demands on his time, Jeff is energized.

"It's exciting and fun," said Jeff, who is known around campus as the Actor because of his Hollywood namesake. "A lot of kids have trouble adjusting to college," Jeff adds. "It's hard to leave your old friends behind and meet new ones. But because the band arrived early for band camp, I met a lot of new people before classes even started. Most of the friends I have now are in band. We're a tight group. We hang out together, eat together, and travel together. Everywhere I walk, I see someone I know. The band helped make my transition to freshman year a lot easier."

But the band did even more for Jeff: It gave him a platform to showcase his talents as a leader. As the year went on, he found himself emerging as the go-to guy in the band because of his vast experience in high school. By the middle of sophomore year, he had cemented a leadership role by being named assistant drum major for the marching band.

Ultimately, said Jeff, "My Hook gave me confidence in what I could do."

When it comes to finding your Hook, Jeff has this advice: "Go with your gut instinct. Choose a Hook that is something you enjoy doing and your passion will come through on your application."

BRIGHT IDEAS FOR MUSICIANS

- **Make a CD or audio tape of you playing your instrument.** Send it to the admissions office and music department at all the colleges on your list. Get your private teacher to help you select pieces to perform.

- **Use your expertise to get recruited, just as an athlete is recruited for a team.** Call the band, orchestra, or choir director of each school and ask: 1. What it takes to be a member and how you might get recruited; 2. Whether they need a CD; 3. If being recruited can help with admissions; 4. If they offer special scholarships, and how to apply. Follow up with a letter, your résumé, and a CD or tape, along with any relevant breaking news about your musical achievements.
- **Audition for music programs, if you want to major in music.** Check specific audition deadlines and requirements for each school. Some schools require live auditions on campus or in major cities, while others accept tapes or CDs. At many colleges, the audition is the major factor in admission.
- **Start a band.** Instead of merely jamming with your friends, give yourselves a cool name, develop a repertoire, make up some business cards, and start getting your name around to get gigs.
- **Perform solo at local coffeehouses.** Talk to the owner about letting you come in a couple of times a month for a free gig. Emphasize that you can attract a younger crowd. Make up flyers and distribute them around school and hangouts where teenagers congregate.
- **Volunteer to perform at local fund-raising events.**
- **Volunteer to play your instrument or sing at your house of worship.**
- **Perform at music festivals in your area.** Many communities have regular jazz, rock, or folk festivals that are open to local musicians. Call to see if you can audition and how you might get on the roster of performers.
- **Take a music course in the summer after junior year from a well-known musician or at a top college program.** For example, if you're a jazz musician, check into special programs or courses at The New School for Jazz and Contemporary Music in New York City.
- **Start a music program at the local Boys and Girls Club or other youth center.** Perhaps you could get people to donate instruments.
- **Compose your own music.**
- **Establish yourself as an original artist by recording and performing your own work.** Make a video of yourself performing, book several gigs, create a three-song demo to show your diversity, and put together a portfolio with a photo, bio, and sample recording. Then send them around to potential agents and try to get discovered.

CHAPTER SEVEN

The Political Hook

HOOK TIP

Each student body president has something special to offer. That's why it's important to distinguish yourself as a politician by being specific in your application.

For example, if you come from a large public high school with a student body of 2,000, be sure to emphasize the size of your school on your application. If you attend a small private high school, include details of your accomplishments, such as "met with headmaster and dean of students weekly," or "initiated school spirit rallies before all sporting events."

Better yet, use your political know-how to catapult yourself to prominence at the county, state, or national level. Teens at the top of the political rung can score big in college admissions.

KAITLIN CONNELL: POLITICKING HER WAY TO HOPKINS

Before Kaitlin Connell was out of diapers, she knew her way around the Florida State Capitol building. Her grandmother, or "Ya-Ya," as Kaitlin called her, was a legislative aide to a succession of state legislators, and once a year, Kaitlin made the seven-hour trek to Tallahassee to get a front-row seat on the political process.

"I was captivated by the hubbub of men and women in business suits carrying their briefcases and cell phones, scurrying around outside the legislative chamber to push for their bills to be passed," said Kaitlin, who followed her grandmother on her rounds in the Capitol. Even more exciting for Kaitlin was sitting in the gallery of the state legislature, watching a session in action.

"At the time, I had no idea about parliamentary procedure or how a bill becomes law," said Kaitlin. "But I enjoyed watching the heated debates that took place on the chamber floor. Even at a young age, I had fallen in love with politics."

Ultimately, it was politics—not high school politics in the traditional sense, but rather a lifelong track record of political action and leadership—that propelled Kaitlin to Johns Hopkins University. She even won a highly competitive Bloomberg Scholarship, which is given to only 150 students in the school per year who are destined to "make a difference."

"Until I sat down to put my résumé together at the end of junior year, I hadn't really thought about all the things I had accomplished," said Kaitlin. "But I realized that I had a passion for politics that had developed over a long period of time—and a track record to support it."

By the time Kaitlin entered kindergarten, she had her sights set on political office. When her teacher asked what she wanted to be when she grew up, Kaitlin didn't hesitate: "I want to be president of the United States!"

"I bet she could," her teacher wrote in a follow-up note to her mom.

Kaitlin took her first real step toward her goals in junior high, when her grandmother invited her to work as a page on the floor of the legislature during spring break.

"I was only running drinks and papers back and forth," said Kaitlin, "but I adored the job because I was able to talk to the representatives personally and watch as they made important decisions. From them, I learned the importance of strong but fair leadership and the power of standing up for a belief."

Three years later, she graduated to the role of "messenger," which involved doing errands all over the Capitol building. From this experience, she learned the "less glamorous side of government—the multitude of letters, phone calls, meetings, appointments, and decisions that stress both the legislators and their staff."

But to Kaitlin, this taste of real-world politics served to warm her to the challenge. Back home at Sebastian River High School, a large public high school in Sebastian, Florida, she threw herself into academics as an International Baccalaureate student, where she consistently earned top honors. By the time she applied to college, she was number one in a class of nearly five hundred students, graduating as valedictorian.

In high school, she also plunged into such political activities as student council, where she was selected every year as a representative, and Teen Court, where she honed her debating skills. Every few weeks through Teen Court, Kaitlin served as a prosecutor or defense attorney in real cases in the Indian River County Court system, where she helped adjudicate sentencing for teenagers found guilty of misdemeanors.

"Teen Court was not only fun and taught me a lot, but it was an important service to the community," said Kaitlin. "What I love about politics is the idea of helping people who don't always get a voice, and teenagers in trouble with the law are among them. This was one small way that I could make a difference."

Although Kaitlin never threw her hat in the ring to run for a class or student government office, she was known around school as an organizer who could rally others and get things done. When her International Baccalaureate Program needed someone to put together an awareness project about land mines for the entire school, it was Kaitlin who stepped up to the plate and put it into action. When Teen Court lost its funding and was threatened with extinction, it was Kaitlin who initiated the letter-writing campaign and fund-raising effort that got the program reinstated.

Kaitlin's leadership abilities—and her passion for making a difference—didn't go unnoticed. She was named Citizen of the Month by the school administration—not just once, but twice. And in her junior year, she got the nod as her school's nominee for Girls State, the American Legion program that propelled an Arkansas teenager named Bill Clinton to fame in its counterpart program for boys back in 1963. After a rigorous interview, Kaitlin was selected as one of two girls from her county to attend the Girls State convention in Tallahassee the following summer. She was one of 120 girls from around the state at the weeklong political fest, which involved drafting a bill, participating in committee meetings, and running for elective office.

Once at Girls State, Kaitlin decided to go for broke and run for justice of the Supreme Court. But before the final balloting, she first had to win a primary election and then give a speech to the entire convention.

"I was nervous," Kaitlin admitted. "There wasn't much time to prepare, and it was hard to convey in a short time who you are and why you're so passionate. But because I had done a lot of public speaking before, I figured, what's the worst that can happen?"

Kaitlin stepped up to the podium for a rousing speech that focused on how her Teen Court experience nurtured her love for the law, and when the ballots were counted, she found herself elected to the Supreme Court as one of six justices. The election sealed her Hook as a politician and gave her a state-level credential on her college applications.

"Supreme Court justice was a strong leadership role that built on my Hook," she said.

But that wasn't all. Following Girls State, Kaitlin headed for Durham, North Carolina, where she had been selected for the Duke Global Dialogues Institute. The high-powered summer program brought together twenty-three students for two weeks to focus on a single issue: international security. In one stroke, Kaitlin had jumped from state politics to the international political arena, where she could put her debating and leadership skills on display.

"For the first time, I developed an interest in international politics," said Kaitlin, who was so enthralled by the experience that when she filled out her college applications, she indicated "international relations" as a major.

With a solid political Hook—and bragging rights to political involvement at the highest level—she confidently attacked her activities list and résumé:

Girls State: *Chosen as one of 120 girls in the state for American Legion program; elected as 1 of 6 Supreme Court Justices.*

Duke Global Dialogues Institute: *Selected as one of 23 students for 2-week symposium on International Security.*

Legislative Page and Messenger, *Florida State House of Representatives: Worked on floor of legislature and in Capitol from grades 6 to 12.*

The list continued: two-time Citizen of the Month, Teen Court, IB landmine project organizer, student council.

"All of these experiences built on my Hook," said Kaitlin, who made sure that a state representative who knew her well wrote one of her college recommendations.

To showcase her Hook even further, she wrote her main essay on the political saga that took her "from wearing diapers to the robe of a Supreme Court Justice." She reinforced the Hook in the Common Application's "most meaningful activity" essay by focusing on her accomplishment reviving Teen Court. And she gave a hint of her global interests in answer to a quirky essay question for Johns Hopkins: "What would you do if you had $10 to spend for an entire day?"

"I wrote about 'geo-caching,'" said Kaitlin. "It's a kind of global treasure hunt, where people all over the world hide boxes of treasure and give coordinates on-line."

Kaitlin found her own treasure when the mail came in April: A fat envelope arrived from Johns Hopkins with a hefty financial package—including the Bloomberg Scholarship. "That came as a complete surprise," she said. Clearly, Hopkins wanted her, and she wanted Hopkins. When September rolled around, she showed up on the Baltimore campus ready to take on the world—literally.

Immediately she signed up for a course titled "Global Security Politics."

"It's a 'manly' course—about blowing things up and nuclear weapons and missiles—all of these concerns that we haven't yet figured out," she said. "These are issues that are going on right now, and I think it's fun.

"My professors are the ones who are writing the books and doing hands-on research," she added. "They're at the top of their fields.

"But learning is not just in the classroom," said Kaitlin. "It also comes from those who surround you. My fellow students have lived all over the world, and they bring a global perspective to the clubs and the recreational opportunities. I'm trying to take advantage of all the diversity on campus."

For Kaitlin, that meant "trying things I had never done and might never do in other places," such as joining a belly dancing troupe and taking an enrichment course in Indian classical dancing during January term. She also tried out for the co-ed Indian Bhangra folk dancing team, where she won a spot as the only non-Indian member. The team competes in gauzy, bejeweled costumes against teams at such schools as Cornell and George Washington.

As for politics, Kaitlin is deeply involved in College Democrats, a group that holds voter registration drives and meets regularly with state and national officials to network and discuss current issues. But for now, she is taking a wait-and-see attitude toward running for political office—both at Hopkins and in future venues.

"I'm thinking of doing some sort of government or humanitarian aide work abroad and then going to law school," said Kaitlin, who as a college freshman was already starting to shape her Hook for law school.

"From what I've read, law schools like to see people who have taken a year off and gotten experience of some kind, or who have something unique they can bring," said Kaitlin.

To that end, she sensed Africa beckoning: "There's a program in Senegal that interests me." She also felt drawn to Capitol Hill. "We're so close to Washington, I'd love to get an internship on the Hill or in an agency."

As for a future run for the U.S. presidency, Kaitlin is noncommittal. "That's a lofty goal," she said judiciously. "I don't know if that's seriously what I want to do." But you can bet that she hasn't ruled it out.

And remember: All this got started with a college Hook focusing on politics.

BRIGHT IDEAS FOR POLITICIANS AND DEBATERS

- Campaign for your local congressperson, governor, or senator.
- Ask your guidance counselor or assistant principal if you could be considered for Girls State or Boys State, sponsored by the American Legion. It's a great honor to be selected for this elite leadership program, held the summer after junior year. It never hurts to ask.
- Apply for a summer institute sponsored by Duke University's Talent Identification Program (Duke TIP). In the past, Duke has sponsored a Global Dialogues Institute, a Great Debates Institute, and a Leadership Institute. You don't need to be a Duke TIP scholar to apply for these two-week programs, but you should apply early to get a leg up. Check the Duke TIP Web site in January for new summer offerings and applications. Need-based financial aid is available for these programs.
- Ask a teacher or guidance counselor to nominate you for Tomorrow25, a leadership program sponsored by Bentley College. Bentley selects twenty-five high-achieving juniors for an all-expenses paid trip to a one-day Leadership Forum with top business execs on its campus outside of Boston. The twenty-five winners will be honored at the event and featured in an advertisement in *Time* magazine.

- **Apply for the Junior Statesman of America Summer School.** Held on the campuses of Princeton, Yale, Northwestern, Georgetown, and Stanford, this four-week program will give you a chance to take two college-level courses in government and politics, as well as hone your skills as a debater during nightly congressional debate workshops. The program also provides you with opportunities to rub shoulders with guest speakers in the field of politics and international affairs. Rising juniors and seniors are eligible to apply with an application, transcript, and teacher recommendation.
- **Become a congressional or legislative page.** Check with your local U.S. Congressperson to get the details.
- **Take a shot at being accepted to Northwestern University's National High School Institute in Debate.** Experienced debaters only should apply for this summer program, which offers three- and four-week sessions on the college's Evanston campus. If you're one of the forty-eight students selected on the basis of a lengthy application and teacher recommendation, you'll focus on a specific debate topic selected for the coming year by the National Forensics League. The program is open to rising sophomores, juniors, and seniors.

CHAPTER EIGHT

The Technology Hook

HOOK TIP

With the hot market for technology around the globe, students who have spent their spare time tinkering with computers could have the beginnings of a ready-made Hook. But to get an edge at colleges with top technology programs, you've got to do more than just tinker. You've got to take your tech talent to the highest level possible by starting your own computer consulting business, working for your school's computer department, or bolstering your skills through special college courses or programs. And of course, while you're tinkering, don't forget to ace your math grades.

RYAN ALLIK: MEMOIRS OF A TECHIE

"A long time ago, I foresaw that everyone would be depending on technology," said Ryan Allik, who got his first personal computer when he was four years old. "I knew the field was rapidly growing and that it was the area people needed to be involved in. These days, it's the best Hook of all."

Ryan's journey to Purdue University as a computer technology major, one of the leading programs of its kind in the country, started modestly enough with a passion for video games as a child.

"I was always playing video games," said Ryan, who became so immersed in the technology that he started staying after school in third grade just to spend time with the computer teacher.

"Computers fascinated me, and in my spare time I started messing around with them on my own. I spent so much time messing around that when the new Windows came out, I was able to teach myself everything on the system."

From there, he said, "I taught myself how to program. Building computers? I did that, too. I've always been motivated to do things myself. I think my entrepreneurial drive comes straight from my father. We're always looking for the next best thing.

"Computers were the only thing that was moving at my pace, and it's still the case. The changing technology keeps me going. I can never get bored. Next week, there will always be something bigger and better than you have this week. When I was younger, my parents knew more about computers than I did, but by junior high—whoosh! I zoomed past them, and I was the one teaching them."

But despite his expertise, Ryan's obsession with computers sometimes got him in trouble at home, especially when he started running an Internet radio show that consumed endless hours in ninth grade.

"I did the show from a downstairs storage room across from the laundry room," said Ryan. "It was the only place I could plug in my computer and get a high speed.

"My parents finally made me move my computer down there permanently, because they thought I was using it too much in my room. They were always on my back about how much time I was spending on the computer.

"I would tell them, 'You just wait!'" he said.

Ryan's parents didn't have to wait long. Once he arrived at boarding school, he immediately started a computer club, as well as a small business building computers for other students in the dorm. In the club, he and his fellow techies spent hours in the school basement, building computers with scrap parts given to them by the school's computer department.

"We loaded the computers up with Linux, an operating system that's an alternative to Microsoft products," said Ryan. "I taught myself the fundamentals of Linux, just as it was becoming more mainstream. It was a viable alternative to Microsoft because it was free."

Ryan became so enamored of Linux that he convinced his school to let him use the new system to reconfigure the school's "firewall," or the gateway server through which all the school's computers were filtered.

"I was trying to show them how easy it was to use and how much money they could save," said Ryan, who got paid for the project. As a volunteer, he then supervised and maintained the entire dorm network, running the server, maintaining network connections, and troubleshooting individual computer problems.

"I was a big nerd," admitted Ryan.

The summer before his senior year, Ryan took another leap forward in the field when he attended a Young Technology Leaders Conference in Austin, Texas, sponsored by a company called Envision. The conference brought together more than 1,000 teenagers from around the country who had been nominated by their schools.

At the conference, Ryan not only attended brainstorming sessions on Linux with other young computer experts but also had a chance to hear firsthand from some of the gurus of the industry, including Michael Dell, CEO of Dell Computers.

"When you come up with these great ideas and wonder if they're any good—and then you hear Michael Dell—you realize you're on the right track," said Ryan.

Inspired by Dell and new friends such as a teenager from Connecticut who held a Cisco Networking License and owned a string of computer companies, Ryan returned home pumped up for more. He was so excited he even wrote an article about the convention, which was picked up by the South Florida *Sun-Sentinel.* Titled "Jocks Play Games While Techies Tackle Future," the article gave Ryan an impressive credential for his college applications, which he began filling out in earnest in early August. (See Ryan's article in Appendix B.)

When it came to picking colleges, Ryan knew what he wanted from the start: a school where he could build upon his Hook, possibly as a computer engineer.

"At the time I was applying, I didn't realize that computer engineering just dealt with circuits," said Ryan. "I thought it included working with networks, which is where I had experience and what I wanted. And so I went ahead and applied for a major in computer engineering."

Purdue was high on his list, along with Georgia Tech, Virginia Tech, University of Michigan, and the University of Central Florida (UCF), among others. With a 29 composite on the ACT, SAT Subject tests of 720 in math I and 680 in physics, and a B average, he felt ready to handle the pressures of a top-level engineering program. He sent off his applications by early September and spent the first part of senior year focusing on his courses and continuing his work with the school's computer network.

Purdue was one of the first colleges to return a thumbs-up. Both UCF and Virginia Tech also gave him a yes.

In the end, a trip to Purdue in West Lafayette, Indiana, sealed his decision. "When I went there on spring break, I really liked the campus," said Ryan. "Plus, its engineering program was one of the top ten in *U.S. News & World Report*'s rankings."

But once at Purdue, Ryan realized quickly that he was in the wrong major. "Computer engineers are those who are designing the computers and circuit boards," said Ryan, "while computer science is straight programming.

"I wanted to look at a broader picture, to take technology and apply it to real-world situations in business. I got lucky because Purdue offered a major in computer technology, network engineering, and information systems, which was exactly what I wanted."

But there was a catch: In order to transfer into the highly competitive computer technology major, which was even more demanding than computer engineering, Ryan needed a B average. At the end of first semester freshman year, the realities hit home during his first meeting with the computer technology adviser.

"I was ten minutes late, I had on a baseball cap, and I didn't have the right paperwork," said Ryan. "She was really mad."

"Good first impression," the adviser told him, with more than a hint of sarcasm. Then she handed him a sheet that spelled out the department's evaluation of his potential for switching majors.

When Ryan looked down at the paper, the first thing he saw was the word UNLIKELY splashed in big red letters across the top.

"It was underlined," said Ryan. Scribbled on the side was a note: "Will wait until the end of the semester."

"The evaluation was basically saying that if a miracle came along and I got really high grades, then I could be in the program," said Ryan. "I needed a cumulative 3.0, a B average, to switch."

Ryan took one look at the evaluation, flashed a smile at the adviser, and took up her challenge: "Okay," he told her. "I'll look forward to seeing you at the end of the semester."

The end of the story is that Ryan aced his grades, finishing second semester with a 3.8 out of a perfect 4.0. Just after his grades came out, he got an e-mail that said, "Welcome to the School of Technology."

He jumped into the program and never looked back. "I've had great grades ever since," said Ryan, who has juggled a course load heavy with computer labs and such subjects as wireless networking and network administration.

"I just finished a class in network administration," said Ryan. "We had several different types of operating systems, including Linux, Unix, and Windows, and we had to get them all to work together. With eight computers and two different networks, our job was to integrate them and get all the services to talk to each other."

Such courses, says Ryan, are on the cutting edge of technology applications in business.

"Purdue is one of the leaders in this right now," he said. "Most colleges stick to rudimentary computer majors. But here, we're taking the software and putting it together with the hardware to organize the whole system.

"What's happening now in industry is that companies have invested a lot of money in software and hardware but they have no clue how to integrate it. Data integration, data warehousing, and business intelligence—these are all big needs in the market that companies are just starting to become aware of. These companies could be taking all their historic data and data mining it, which means looking into years and years of their own data and discovering trends, discovering patterns, and studying behavioral factors. The opportunities are unlimited."

If Ryan sounds breathless, it's because he's moving up fast. As a result of his top grades and computer experience, he was hired on at Purdue during sophomore and junior year as an assistant network engineer, maintaining the school's fiber-optic infrastructure. The summer before senior year, he landed job offers for coveted technology internships at three of America's corporate giants. He was so thrilled by his achievement that he posted the letters on the door of his room at his frat house, Phi Delta Theta, which boasts astronaut Neil Armstrong among its former members.

"There's no ceiling to the field of computers," said Ryan. "It's taking off like a rocket."

Ryan is taking off along with it—thanks to his Hook, which opened doors at Purdue and continues to shape his future.

"It's important to establish your goals in life as early as possible," said Ryan. "Then you can focus all your actions on achieving them.

"The thing about a Hook is that you've got to be building on it constantly once you reach college. People are always having higher expectations of you, especially potential employers. You can't ever let your Hook get stale."

BRIGHT IDEAS FOR TECHNOLOGY JUNKIES

- **Start your own computer consulting business.** Give yourself a catchy name, make up business cards, and circulate them around the community. Before you know it, you'll have more business than you can handle.
- **Create a computer service organization to help senior citizens.** Line up a team of teen computer experts who are ready to serve low-income seniors. Get in touch with senior centers and churches to let them know you're available. Then dispatch your team to install computers, troubleshoot problems, and teach seniors how to use e-mail and navigate the Internet.
- **Volunteer to troubleshoot problems in your school's computer labs.** This could establish your credentials as an expert and also might lead to a job on campus in college.
- **Get a sales job at a computer store.** A background in sales could set you up for a variety of internships and jobs later on.
- **Design Web sites for nonprofit organizations.** This will underscore both your computer expertise and your service orientation.
- **Start a computer graphics and film editing business.** Produce DVDs using still photos, film clips, and sound tracks for weddings, family reunions, and other events.
- **Apply for the National High School Game Academy (NHSGA) at Carnegie Mellon University.** Modeled after Carnegie Mellon's graduate program in entertainment technology, this six-week summer program will give you hands-on experience in interactive digital game development. Check the college's Web site under "Pre-College Programs."

CHAPTER NINE

The Humanitarian Hook

HOOK TIP

It's great to do good, but loading up on random community service hours is not the key to an admissions committee's heart. To set yourself apart, find one area of service where you can be a standout and give that project or organization your undivided attention. Then look for creative ways to package your interest and promote your project and yourself.

The *Wall Street Journal* reports that because so many high schools are mandating community service, "its value as a way for students to boost their admissions chances may be decreasing."[9] Let's face it: A laundry list of hours devoted to well-meaning activities, from walkathons to Habitat for Humanity to Students Against Drunk Driving, will appear to be just that—a list of items neatly stacked up on your application but virtually undistinguishable from that of other worthy students.

JAMES PANGILINAN: WOOING WESLEYAN WITH A FILM FROM THE HEART

When it came to community service, James Pangilinan had done it all. There were Catholic Heart Work Camp trips to rural South Carolina and suburban Atlanta two summers in a row to refurbish houses for the poor, Habitat for Humanity building projects three to four hours every Saturday in junior and senior year, Red Cross hurricane relief work caring for the victims of Hurricane Jeanne, and several hundred hours of volunteer work since sixth grade for such causes as the Salvation Army and the American Cancer Society.

To top it off, the summer before his senior year, he even took a trip to Africa, where he taught English to elementary school students in Tanzania.

But strange as it may seem, James was almost *too* good in the area of service. His heartfelt focus on the poor and downtrodden, and his years of commitment to service projects, might have played to a deaf audience at colleges if he hadn't found a way to focus their attention. In fact, when he tried to discuss his trip to Tanzania during one college interview, he could see from the glazed eyes of the admissions staffer that the topic was evoking "little more than a yawn," as James recalled.

"At the places I was applying, it was standard fare to be involved in such things abroad," he said.

But James had something going for him beyond merely doing good deeds. He was also a budding filmmaker on a quest to awaken other teens to the needs around them—especially the needs of the homeless. What had triggered his passion was the example of his aunt, Marya Delia Javier, an actress and masseuse known as "Mama D," who had started her own feeding program for the homeless in Los Angeles.

"My aunt has been an inspiration to me for as long as I can remember," said James.

At reunions of his large Filipino family when he was quite young, for example, James eagerly got involved in his aunt's campaign to pick up pennies on the ground and get everyone's pocket change. "I had a little cup, and I would go around and get the family to dig in and give up their change," said James. "It was a token amount—what most people call 'unimportant.' But it was amazing to hear about the things she could do with all of that for the homeless."

At the time, James was too young to understand the details of her work in L.A., which he knew about only secondhand. Nor was he completely conscious of the poor surrounding him in Manila, which he visited in junior high on a trip to see his extended family in the Philippines.

"I saw slums, but it wasn't a reality to me," he said. "It was part of the atmosphere, part of the landscape."

But little by little, as he traveled the world on family vacations and started volunteering on mission trips with his church, he began to feel a yearning for something beyond his "pampered life," as he called it.

"After traveling quite a bit, I felt weary of going for my own pleasure's sake," said James. "Whenever you travel as a tourist, you're always missing another world. I wanted to do something that would expose me to that other world and help that world, too."

By his junior year in high school, fueled by his growing desire to serve, James decided to plunge into the world of the homeless in L.A. by trying to make a film. During spring break, while his friends were off on cruises to the Caribbean or treks in Switzerland, James flew to California, where he shot footage of the homeless in and around Hollywood and at Mama D's Kitchen, the soup kitchen run by his aunt. As a first-time filmmaker, he hoped to lay the groundwork for a documentary that could be shown at an upcoming charity fund-raiser at his school.

That trip "put a human face on homelessness," said James. It also awakened him to the magnitude of his aunt's sacrifice and commitment.

"She's a woman of humble means, and yet she transformed her entire life to help the homeless," said James.

"The film was my small way of helping my aunt," said James. "I wanted to do more than just have a dress-down day at school or sell ribbons to raise money for her program. I wanted to transport the experience, the image, the reality, to my friends."

Back home after spring break, James worked feverishly, poring over how-to books on filmmaking and experimenting with a new editing program for his computer in order to pull the film together in time for the fund-raiser. The stark contrasts he had witnessed in L.A. and a sense of urgency to communicate the message drove him forward.

Slowly, his vision began to take shape in the editing, as he juxtaposed posh images of Rodeo Drive and Beverly Hills with gritty street scenes of Hollywood's homeless on skid row. In one sequence he zeroed in on the famous white letters spelling out HOLLYWOOD on the hills behind the city. In the next, he honed in on homeless men rummaging through garbage cans at night and mothers with strollers standing in line to get bags of free sandwiches provided by his aunt and her volunteers.

James capped off the film with an interview featuring his aunt, who gave an impassioned plea for helping homeless children. As he pressed her for details during an interview on camera, he learned that she had found her moment of truth in her twenties, when she was working on a movie set as a designer.

"One day she had to put together a street scene," said James. "As she was collecting a bunch of rubbish for the set, she spotted a group of homeless people. As a fairly recent immigrant, she was immediately taken aback by such a sight in the U.S.—the land of opportunity—and so she hired a few of them to help her.

"Once she got to know them and saw their humanity, from then on she started a crusade to help them." As James explained it, his aunt gathered together friends and started delivering food to the homeless from a van on weekends. Eventually, some Buddhist monks she knew offered her use of a warehouse, and Mama D's Kitchen was born. Typically, he said, she distributed food on Sundays, and worked the rest of the week at various jobs to keep her operation afloat.

"She used her own money, along with private donations," said James. "In my film, I wanted to emphasize her idea that you can do a lot with a little. Small acts of kindness can be amplified into great things."

The result was a stark, thirteen-minute documentary he called *An American Childhood*, a name that evoked for him the plight of the lost and forgotten.

From the very start of the project, he said, "I challenged myself to craft this into something that would really touch my peers. Most of the people I know are pretty spoiled. They're driving BMWs, Audis, or Mercedes. They may think of themselves as humanitarians, but they're not getting their hands dirty or truly seeing the realities of the way people live. They're doing their little charity and giving their money, but that's it.

"I wanted to take some of real life to them. That's the act of creating a documentary and presenting it. That was my motivation."

With his film finally ready to roll, he held a screening at school that brought in more than $300 for his aunt's program. But what mattered to James wasn't the money. Rather, it was the opportunity to plant seeds of the humanitarian spirit that had been sown in him as a child.

As for James, his experience making the film not only deepened his own humanitarian instincts, but also served as his turning point, eventually setting him on a different course for college.

"When I started filling out my applications, I was focusing on international studies and political science," said James, who applied to schools such as Tufts, Georgetown, and George Washington University because of their reputations in these areas. "But by Christmas of my senior year, my orientation was starting to shift toward the arts, film in particular."

To keep his options open, he quickly sent off a Common Application to one of the "Little Ivies," Wesleyan University in Middletown, Connecticut, which was known for its film program. "It was the last school I applied to," said James. "I checked it out on the Web and it won me over."

To help win over Wesleyan's admissions committee, he included with his application a DVD of his film on homelessness, along with a résumé that detailed both his humanitarian work and his experience making the film. He followed up at the other colleges on his list with DVDs and résumés as well, hopeful that his humanitarian/filmmaker Hook would give him an edge on top of his strong grades and scores. Academically, James clocked in with a 3.8 weighted GPA, a combined SAT score of 1440 in Critical Reading and Math, a Writing score of 780, and SAT Subject Tests that topped 700 in Math I, Biology, and Chemistry. Added to that, he had earned an award as his school's best student in Chinese, along with the Bucknell Book Award, which was given to twenty students in the country.

With his applications finished before the New Year, James flew to London's West End for a ten-day intensive course in digital filmmaking at King's College, which coincided with his high school's senior internship period. As one of only two teenagers in a course filled with aspiring British filmmakers, he was hooked.

"After that, film seemed a lot more exciting than international relations," said James. "It grabbed me." He returned from London with a new film under his belt, *100 Seconds of Solitude,* a dialogue-free, guy-meets-girl-loses-girl story, which he created as actor and director. Once again, he sent off the DVDs to colleges, with a letter explaining his newest achievement.

By the time James started hearing from colleges, he was completely focused on film. And although he was accepted to Tufts and George Washington, he was determined to hold out for Wesleyan, where he had been put on the wait list.

"It's a place that's very intellectual and also very passionate," said James.

In May of senior year, he was delighted to find his own passion rewarded, when he won his prep school's humanitarian award—*and* got the nod from Wesleyan for admission to the class of 2009.

These days, when he's not running to classes or working on an independent film project, James can be found tutoring children at the local middle school or elementary school near the Wesleyan campus in Connecticut three or four days a week.

He's considering a stint with the Peace Corps after he graduates from Wesleyan. "But whatever I do, I'll always be involved in some kind of volunteer work," said James, who, after the recent death of his aunt, is carrying on her legacy. "My aunt taught me that you don't have to become a missionary or be out of the loop to help others."

BRIGHT IDEAS FOR DO-GOODERS

- **Ask someone to nominate you for the Daily Points of Light Award,** sponsored by the Points of Light Foundation. If you've started a significant outreach program or have accumulated hundreds of hours as a volunteer in a particular organization, you might just be tapped as a "Daily Point of Light." Initiated by former president George Bush, the POL Foundation chooses 365 honorees each year, many of them teenagers. You could be one of them.
- **Ask a teacher to nominate you for Mount Holyoke College's Take the Lead program.** This program selects forty outstanding sophomore girls for a weekend at the country's oldest women's college, where they are mentored by students and faculty. During the weekend, which is held in the fall of a student's junior year, each girl develops an action project to address an issue she cares about.
- **Start your own organization.** Although it's important to have a leadership position in groups such as Operation Smile or to be a regular participant in walkathons such as Walk for the Cure, it's even better to find your own niche by creating a service project and recruiting volunteers to make it happen. If you're a tennis player, start a tennis program for kids in the inner city. If you live in an agricultural area, initiate a tutoring program for migrant children. If you're an environmentalist, create a grass-roots program to save an endangered species. You get the idea.
- **Publicize your exploits.** Don't wait for your good deeds to be discovered by the local media: make up a press release and promote yourself.

- **Apply for the Global Issues Seminar at Notre Dame.** Peace and justice issues are the centerpiece of this fully paid, one-week program for young Catholic leaders. If you have a passion for the poor or for resolving international conflict, take a shot at being selected as one of the forty students invited to attend. You must be a junior to apply for this seminar, which is held the summer before senior year. Check the Notre Dame Web site under Pre-College Programs.

CHAPTER TEN

The Science Hook

HOOK TIP

When you're choosing a science fair project that could pave the way to a selective college, consider focusing on hot topics that are in the news, such as global warming, stem-cell research, or avian flu.

According to the *Wall Street Journal*, savvy science students are discovering that the "best route to a prize is to delve into politically charged subjects."[10] What's more, such topics, which tend to be less obscure than other fare at science fairs, can provide fodder for a compelling college essay and for lively "talking points" during interviews.

SUMMER NIAZI: THIRD-WORLD RESEARCHER

"I always knew I was interested in medicine," said Summer Niazi, who banked on her Hook as a medical researcher in Pakistan to gain entrée to pre-med and accelerated medical programs. "If you know what you want to do and have no doubt in your mind, then it's important to choose your activities during high school to fit your goals."

The savvy Summer started actively shaping her Hook back in ninth grade by throwing herself into science fair projects focused on health and medicine. But her passion for research actually began much earlier, in sixth grade, when she developed her first research project, an analysis of tessellations, or repeating mathematical patterns, that she dreamed up and executed all by herself.

"I wanted something I could do on my own without my parents' help," said Summer, who, inspired by the drawings of M. C. Escher, used a computer to create basic and complex tessellations of five geometric shapes to see which would make patterns most quickly. Once she had gathered her data, written a research paper, and created a backboard display, she stood in front of a mirror to practice her pitch to the judges.

"I rehearsed not just once, but three or four times," said Summer.

Her practice paid off: On the day of the Science and Engineering Fair, Summer bowled over the judges with her verbal agility and earned a place at the regional science fair.

"I still have a picture of myself standing wide-eyed next to my display board in a calico pinafore," said Summer. At the regional competition, she went on to earn first place in the math division, along with a special Discovery and Scientist Challenge Award.

"I was excited," said Summer. "I was the first of my sisters to do a science fair, and my success paved the way for the others." What's more, she said, the accolades ignited in her a passion for research that has remained unabated.

"I realized that there was power in research," said Summer. "It was a way that I could stand out and make a difference."

Once she had caught the research bug, Summer couldn't be stopped. In ninth grade she won first place at the regional science fair with a study on the effects of water intake and test-taking. Her conclusion: Subjects who drank water before and during tests performed better than those who didn't. (SAT takers, take note!)

But it was a cholesterol study in tenth grade that put her on the map—literally the map of the world. Together with her older sister, Anum, Summer came up with a project to study cholesterol levels of factory workers in Pakistan, where the sisters traveled every summer to visit their extended family. As it turned out, the project not only tested Summer's mettle but ultimately forged her Hook as a Third World researcher.

The idea for the research project was simple: Take blood samples and test cholesterol levels of young male factory workers in a village near Lahore to understand the risk factors for heart disease, which was running rampant in Pakistan.

The execution was another story. First there was the matter of organizing the testing. After months of correspondence by e-mail and cell phone to a contact in Lahore, Summer and her sister arranged to test one hundred factory workers, who were instructed to fast for twelve hours the night before the blood tests.

"We figured that a factory would be the ideal place to do the tests because variables such as exercise and diet could be controlled," said Summer.

The next hurdle was equipment. To do the cholesterol tests, the girls needed a machine that would evaluate blood samples on the spot. What's more, to keep things simple for themselves and for the men who would be tested, they wanted a machine that could run lipid profiles using nothing more than a drop of blood. After identifying a portable cholesterol testing machine that fit their specifications, they prevailed upon the manufacturer, Cholestech, to donate the equipment. Out of their own savings, they threw in $1,100 to buy cassettes that would hold each blood sample.

With the project designed and ready to go in June 2003, Summer and her sister waved goodbye to their parents and hopped on a plane for the sixteen-hour trip to Pakistan. In their carry-on luggage was the cholesterol-testing machine and a lipid/glucose control sample that had to be refrigerated during the flight to calibrate the testing machine properly once they landed.

"The stewardesses cooperated," said Summer. "But the immigration officials in Pakistan looked a little perplexed when I attempted to explain what the equipment was for and the purpose of my visit. Finally, they let us through."

Once in Lahore, where they were staying with relatives, Summer and her sister didn't waste a minute. Immediately they called the factory officials to confirm the dates for the testing and review a checklist of requirements:

- Remind test subjects to fast for twelve hours
- Have a nurse available to obtain blood samples
- Require test subjects to sign consent forms
- Provide breakfast to test subjects after the testing

On the appointed day, Summer and her sister awoke at 5 A.M. for the drive to the factory. As the hired car pushed and swerved its way through the teeming masses on the road, Summer could feel the adrenaline pumping.

"There were no lines on the road for any sort of organization into lanes," said Summer. "Cars, trucks, buses, donkey carts, motorcycles, and pedestrians were all moving helter skelter on the same road."

The girls arrived without a hitch, set up their testing stations and equipment, and set to work. Three days and one power outage later, Summer and her sister had accomplished the seemingly impossible: 7,500 miles from home, speaking their second language, Urdu, the two teenagers had succeeded in testing cholesterol levels of one hundred young men who had never even had a medical test in their lives. On their own the girls had taken health histories, obtained consent forms, tested blood pressure and heart rate, supervised the collection of blood samples by the nurse, run the samples through the cholesterol testing machine, and recorded the data. Out of 110 tests they had run, only four couldn't be used.

"The testing machine stopped during the power outage, and so we had to eliminate those samples," said Summer.

But the girls still weren't finished. With their results in hand, they followed up the tests by scheduling personal meetings with each participant, during which they explained the outcome—in Urdu. If any test appeared abnormal, Summer and her sister alerted the factory manager to make sure the man would be seen by a doctor.

"For most of these men, it was the first time that anyone had ever taken an interest in their health," said Summer. "Most of them had never even been to a doctor before."

With their mission accomplished beyond their wildest dreams, Summer and her sister headed home to prepare for the round of science fairs the following spring. The girls weren't disappointed. The project earned them second place in the medical division at their school's science fair, first place in the regional science fair, and a spot as an alternate in the state science fair. At regionals, they won the U.S. Army Science Fair Award.

Although they didn't make it to the very top of the science fair ladder, the research in Pakistan produced an unexpected payoff: admission to several leading colleges and combined B.S./M.D. programs—*and* a huge merit scholarship from one university—for Summer's elder sister, Anum.

Spurred on by this success, Summer decided to repeat the cholesterol testing the following year, this time with female factory workers. She dubbed the study, "Evaluating Lipid Profile in Young Healthy Females of a Developing Country: Year 2." Once again, she organized the study long distance. During winter break of her junior year, she found herself on a plane to Pakistan along with her elder sister, Anum, her younger sister, Faraze, and her cousin, Zehra.

Summer thought she was ready for anything. After all, she was now a seasoned Third-World researcher who had surmounted such physical challenges as transatlantic flights with sensitive equipment, wild car rides, and power outages to complete a clinical study of cholesterol in men successfully.

But as she discovered, testing young women in Pakistan posed challenges of a more *human* sort. Although eighty-two young women, most of them teenagers, had signed up to be tested, many of them were afraid. What frightened them was the needle that would prick their finger to draw out a single drop of blood.

One nineteen-year-old was so scared that as she approached the table where a nurse sat ready to take a blood sample, tears cascaded down her face. Feeling the girl's anguish, Summer immediately ran to her side, took her hand, and held it as she spoke to her teenager to teenager.

"It's okay to be afraid," Summer told the girl gently. "I don't like needles either."

As she continued to hold the girl's hand, Summer tried to deflect her attention from the nurse and the needle by complimenting her beautiful gold earrings.

"Ear piercing is probably more painful than this," Summer told her reassuringly.

At that very moment, Summer saw the girl wince as the nurse jabbed her finger and collected the blood in a tiny glass capillary tube. "Then she broke into giggles, realizing that the finger prick was over," said Summer.

Three days later, Summer was smiling, too, as her second research project in Pakistan came to an end. Just as she had done with the men, she presented follow-up reports to each of the young women who had participated. As it turned out, one of them had high blood pressure, while two others had elevated cholesterol levels.

"The women were happy to hear the results," said Summer. "I could tell that it made them feel good to know that someone cared about their health."

Back home in Georgia, Summer turned her attention to the science fair that was just two months away. To increase the impact of the cholesterol project, she and her sister Faraze compared their findings with the women to those of the men the year before. That small twist appeared to up the ante at the school science fair, where Summer and her sister walked away with the Grand Prize. From there, the awards came rolling in: Fulton County Science Fair—Grand Prize; Georgia State Science Fair—Second Place, Medicine and Health Division.

To top it off, the cholesterol project was one of only two in the state of Georgia selected to go to a regional competition in Nashville for the prestigious BioGENEius award, which focuses on biotechnology. Two winners from the region would be selected to compete for top prizes at the national level.

Once in Nashville, however, Summer's run of awards came to an abrupt halt. The Pakistan cholesterol study was beaten out for the national BioGENEius Challenge by two projects with heavy ties to universities.

"I realized that once you're at this level of competition, you can't be doing a project on your own as my sister and I did," said Summer philosophically. "You need to be working in someone else's lab, preferably with a connection to a university."

"Our cholesterol project was performed at a very basic level," said Summer. "We didn't find a new device for breast cancer, or a vaccine for avian influenza. But we did discover something: that there is a problem with cholesterol in developing countries. Ultimately, though, because we chose a project that we could execute and analyze completely on our own, we limited how far we could go. At the highest levels of science fairs, a project like ours won't compare to one done by a student who is sitting alongside a professional researcher with a Ph.D."

Summer ultimately finalized her Hook by working in the cardiology research lab at Emory University the summer before senior year. There, she assisted in a study aimed at increasing the longevity of human cardiac cells. Although the lab experience offered a powerful addition to her college résumé, it came too late in her high school career for her to fashion a sophisticated science fair project worthy of the highest awards.

But Summer has no regrets. "The cholesterol projects were much more than just science," she said. "They required the ability to establish contacts with the factory, to create and execute a detailed plan, and to be ready to make quick decisions on the spot. I learned a lot."

What's more, her scientific achievements paved the way to a host of highly selective schools, including Emory, Wellesley, and Mount Holyoke, as well as to an accelerated B.S./M.D. program at Rensselaer Polytechnic Institute and Albany College of Medicine and an eight-year medical program at Union College and Albany College of Medicine. She ultimately chose Emory, where as a pre-med student she continues to move forward with her research.

Developing her Hook, Summer said, helped reinforce her choice of career: "By doing research with the men and women in Pakistan and then working in a lab one summer, I could see that medicine was definitely something for me."

BRIGHT IDEAS FOR SCIENTISTS AND ASPIRING DOCTORS

- **Enter science fairs.** The more sophisticated and timely your project, the better your chances of winning top prizes at the local, regional, state, or national level.
- **Enter the Young Epidemiology Scholars Competition sponsored by the Robert Wood Johnson Foundation and the College Board.** This scholarship contest for high school juniors and seniors gives away $456,000 in prize money, including two top awards of $50,000 each. Check in the summer before junior and senior year for contest requirements.
- **Include an abstract of your scientific research with your applications.** For some visual interest, consider including a photo of you doing the research. (See abstract of Summer Niazi's cholesterol research in Appendix B.)
- **Volunteer at the local hospital.** Keep in mind that accelerated medical programs will ask you why you want to go into medicine, and the answer can't be "Because my parents are doctors." You need to have an independent interest of your own in the medical area, and working at a hospital over a long period of time will give you some credibility.
- **Become a summer volunteer with a medical or scientific program abroad.** If you have contacts overseas, see if you can spend a month or two doing volunteer work at a research center, hospital, or satellite medical clinic in impoverished areas.
- **Apply for a summer scientific field study sponsored by Duke University's Talent Identification Program (Duke TIP).** In recent years, the two-week programs have included tropical medicine and ethnobiology in Costa Rica; marine biology and neuroscience in Florida; and astronomy, physics and astrobiology in North Carolina. Applications and information on new summer field studies are posted in January on the Duke TIP Web site. Need-based financial aid is available, but only for domestic programs.
- **Land a summer internship at a local pharmaceutical company, engineering firm, marine science institute, or university laboratory.** You may start out washing test tubes, but if you show initiative you could end up working alongside a scientist on a significant piece of research or developing your own science fair project.
- **Get published.** It's not beyond the realm of possibility for your name to be included on a professional paper, along with a scientist under whom you

have worked. Don't be afraid to ask. A little chutzpah could pay off with a weighty credential for your college applications.

- **Get a scientific mentor.** Ask your teachers or family friends for connections to working scientists at local universities or corporations who might be willing to take you under their wing.
- **Invent and patent your own device.** If your mind is filled with as many creative ideas as Leonardo da Vinci's, don't just think about them: put them into action by applying for a patent. To learn how to do it, check out the book *The Inventor's Guide to Trademarks and Patents* by Craig Fellenstein (Pearson Prentice Hall, 2005).

CHAPTER ELEVEN

The Writing Hook

HOOK TIP

Stretch yourself beyond your high school newspaper or literary magazine to enter writing contests and submit articles to local and national publications. Working as a columnist for your hometown weekly or daily newspaper or having several prominent newspaper or magazine articles to your credit will underscore your level of achievement and serve as impressive proof of your abilities. Be sure to send copies of your published "clips" along with your applications.

NICOLE DUBOWITZ: HITTING THE JACKPOT WITH OP-ED

"Before I began the college application process, I never realized that my writing made me unique," said Nicole Dubowitz, who parlayed a lifelong interest in writing into a Hook that snagged Trinity College and earned her hefty merit scholarships at two other schools.

"I always thought of my writing as a hobby, and not something that I could use to market myself to colleges. I thought you needed to be an athlete or play an instrument to get into a good school."

So certain was Nicole that writing was a dead-end street that when her mom suggested that she sign up for a journalism class sophomore year in high school, she protested.

"I remember thinking that I wanted some consistency in my classes to demonstrate to colleges that I was interested in something," said Nicole, who at the time was considering a major in psychology. "Journalism just didn't seem to fit."

Succumbing to pressure from her mom, Nicole signed up for the course, and at the same time she joined her school's award-winning literary magazine, *Chips*. With that, the seeds of a Hook were sown—even if Nicole remained unaware of the potential impact of her choices. All she knew was that writing was her passion.

"From the time I could pick up a pencil, writing has been my outlet of choice," said Nicole. "It was something that came naturally, and I was always good at it."

By fourth grade, she was keeping a journal to record her daily musings, and by sixth grade, she had discovered essays and poetry. "Once I started, I couldn't stop." She wrote poems about New York, poems about relationships, and poems about her travels, building a body of work that numbered more than fifty by the time she applied to college.

Poets such as Billy Collins, the earthy, Brooklyn-born former Poet Laureate of the United States, became her idols.

"I loved his writing style and the creative way he used words," said Nicole, who found herself captivated by his poem "The Last Cigarette," about his life as a chain smoker. "He could take a subject like smoking that most people think is gross and turn it into something beautiful," she said. "I wanted to be able to write like that and live up to his standard."

With her finely tuned ear for poetic language, Nicole also found herself drawn to the lyrics of folk, rock, and punk music, especially the work of Conor Oberst, whose anti-war political bent dovetailed with her own.

"Listening to someone who is moved by the world he lives in inspires you to be the same way," said Nicole. "He made me appreciate all kinds of writers."

By the time she reached high school, Nicole was sending her poems to on-line contests and seeing her work appear on national Web sites and published in anthologies. But still, she never regarded her writing as particularly significant— or worth mentioning to anyone.

"Poetry was a personal thing, something I did for myself. I would never have considered starting a poetry club or showing off my accomplishments, not even for college."

Almost in spite of herself, over the next two years Nicole started building her credentials as a writer, even as she was feeding her interests in politics and community service. A longtime peace activist and feminist, she attended the Million Mom March for gun control, demonstrated in two anti-war rallies at the Washington Monument, and worked on the Kerry/Edwards presidential campaign. She spent hours during the school year doing volunteer work for the homeless, and weeks during the summers volunteering at a summer camp and interning for nonprofit groups designing brochures and doing research on women's issues. By senior year, her activism had earned her a place as one of forty students in the county selected to serve on the Youth Advisory Committee of Montgomery County, Maryland, where she could make her concerns known on issues ranging from school safety to driving restrictions on teens.

But it was her writing that consumed most of her energies. Every day she pored over her journals, logging in "whatever was going on in my head." Some days she'd spend twenty minutes writing an anecdote about a crisis with a friend. On other days, she'd write for an hour and a half, "ranting" with observations about some political topic that pushed her buttons. Every couple of months, she turned her rantings into letters to the editor that she'd send off to newspapers or teen magazines.

"One magazine had an article on teenage drinking that I didn't agree with," said Nicole. "I sent the editor a letter. It wasn't published, but that didn't stop me."

As her confidence in her opinions grew, so did the opportunity to write about them. In her junior year, a national writing assignment dropped in her lap when her mom invited her to co-author a chapter of a college-level book on feminism and the media for the American Psychological Association. The chapter, "Clash of Cultures: Women and Girls on TV and in Real Life," was right up Nicole's alley.

"I wrote about how the female characters on *Friends* and *Sex and the City* portrayed the American dream for young women," said Nicole. "Because the characters had good careers going and seemed to be on top of all aspects of their lives and relationships, girls looked up to them.

"I watched these shows all the time with my friends," said Nicole. "I knew I could speak for a lot of girls my age."

With the book chapter under her belt, Nicole felt emboldened to sign up for an elective in creative writing senior year. And by the time she started filling out her college applications, all of her writing experience suddenly started to gel. As she reviewed her activities, pastimes, and academics, she couldn't ignore a clear and overwhelming trend:

- Co-author of a book chapter
- Published poet
- Creative writing editor of the school literary magazine
- Journalism class
- Creative writing class
- Journal writer
- AP English score: 5

"That journalism class turned out to be a good thing," admitted Nicole, who also gained a new perspective on her daily journal.

"Once I focused on writing as my Hook, even my journal writing made sense as something to put on my application," said Nicole. "Because a lot of teenagers keep journals, I didn't think mine was terribly unique. But I figured that since I was going with the whole writing thing, why not include my journal as an 'activity'?"

Fueled by her newfound Hook, Nicole got even more creative: she started looking for ways to ratchet up her writing to a professional level by getting a few articles published in nationally recognized media outlets.

She knew that admissions competition was fierce at some of the colleges that interested her: Penn, Emory, Trinity, Pomona, and the University of Maryland, which had rejected several top-notch students from her public high school the previous year.

Nicole knew, too, that it was anybody's guess how her test scores would play out with admissions. With a 204 on the PSAT (comparable to a 2040 on the SAT), she had been recognized as a Commended Student on the National Merit Scholarship Qualifying Test. What's more, she had earned a perfect 5 on the English AP, and a 31 composite on the ACT, with scores of 33 and 34 on the English and Reading sections respectively.

Do I stand a chance? she wondered.

Despite a program heavy with AP and Honors courses, Nicole sensed that if she wanted a shot at the top schools on her list, she needed something big to call attention to her writing talent. As she assessed herself honestly, she reasoned that a book chapter written with her mom, a few published poems, and a role as creative writing editor of the literary magazine might not be enough to achieve her college goals.

But how could she make a name for herself as a writer—and do it quickly?

She found the answer at an anti-war rally she attended in the fall of senior year. As the Iraq war had heated up, so had the protests, and Nicole was among those who thought America should pull out. With one of her friends, she had shown up with 100,000 others at the Washington Monument on September 24, 2005, to let her voice be heard.

She was so moved by the experience that a week later she whipped off an op-ed piece titled, "A Teenager's Take on the War in Iraq," and sent it to the *Baltimore Sun,* the *Washington Post,* and the *Hill Rag,* a newspaper for staffers working on Capitol Hill. Two of the papers, the *Baltimore Sun* and the *Hill Rag,* snapped it up. The *Baltimore Sun* printed it on October 5 under the headline, STUDENT MOVED, ENCOURAGED BY ANTI-WAR RALLY, and the *Hill Rag* published the piece in November (see Appendix B).

But that wasn't all. Unbeknownst to Nicole, the *Sun* had published several opinion pieces by a high school student the previous year. Nicole's article on the Iraq rally was so good that the editor tapped her to write a few more articles during her senior year. Her assignment: Write an op-ed article on any topic of interest, no more than every three months.

Overnight, Nicole Dubowitz wasn't just a teenager writing in her journal. She was a regular writer for the op-ed section of one of the country's most prestigious newspapers. She added this new recognition to the activities and honors sections of her college applications and included a copy of the article with her résumé.

Three months later, as the *Sun* had suggested, she followed up with an article on the agonies of applying to college, including sitting for new SATs. As if that weren't enough, she managed to get herself quoted on the SAT in *Parade's* "Fresh Voices" column and churned out an article on her childhood nannies that was accepted for publication in *Nanny* family magazine.

Nicole was on a roll, and she knew it. Just as her mid-year grades came out, she dashed off letters to all the colleges on her list along with copies of her second op-ed article. Whenever she went for a college interview, she made sure to hand the alumni or admissions interviewer a copy of her résumé, saying casually, "I thought you might also want to take a look at the articles I've written for the *Sun*."

Then she sat back and waited.

One of the first colleges to respond was the University of Maryland, which invited her to become a University Scholar, the school's honor program. Next came Pitzer, which offered her a $5,000-a-year Trustee Community Scholarship, the highest honor given to an entering freshman. Northeastern came through with an $11,000-a-year Dean's scholarship, which was also the highest award given. Altogether she received good news from seven colleges, including Trinity, which was one of her top choices.

But as thrilled as Nicole was by her college acceptances, she was at least as gratified by the practical experience—and confidence—she had gained as a writer. By pushing her Hook to a professional level, she had actually *become* a journalist, setting the stage for a possible career.

"After my first article for the *Sun*, I became a much better op-ed writer," said Nicole. "It was cool to get to work with editors. We'd go back and forth, and he would tell me what he wanted changed, and I'd put my foot down or give the okay. Even though we disagreed some of the time, it was a useful experience to get a taste of real-world journalism."

By the second article, she said, "I had figured out what the editors were looking for and tailored my writing accordingly."

She also discovered what the public was looking for: a passionate young writer whose voice resonated with every word.

"God bless you for raising this issue," one fan wrote on a Web message board following her Iraq article. "Just hang in there," wrote another, giving words of encouragement in response to her angst-ridden piece on the college application process.

"I didn't think I'd be taken seriously as a young person," says Nicole, "but I realized that it's precisely because I'm young that people are interested in what I have to say. The responses I've gotten have made me want to continue writing and receiving feedback.

"The college application process took me to a new level as a writer," said Nicole. "I think I might just have a chance in this business."

BRIGHT IDEAS FOR WRITERS

- **Try to get published.** Write short stories or poems and try to submit them for publication. A good source for publications is *Writer's Market* or *Poet's Market,* both published annually. Check your local library.
- **Enter writing contests.** Two of the most prestigious writing contests for teens include: *Guideposts* Young Writers contest, which has a top prize of $10,000; and the annual playwriting contest sponsored by Young Playwrights, Inc.
- **Submit your writing to the Scholastic Art & Writing Awards.** Sponsored by the Alliance for Young Artists & Writers, the nonprofit arm of Scholastic, this program offers recognition for writing portfolios and individual works in eleven categories, including poetry, personal essay/memoir, journalism, and science fiction/fantasy. There's even a $10,000 Gold Award for five seniors whose writing portfolios are exceptional. Check the Internet under "Scholastic Art & Writing Awards" in early fall for on-line entry and deadline information.
- **Apply for and attend the Young Writers Workshop at the University of Virginia (UVA).** Every summer, UVA offers two-week and three-week programs in poetry, short stories, creative nonfiction, etc. Check the college's Web site for application deadlines.
- **Become a writer for your local daily or weekly newspaper.** Many daily newspapers have sections written entirely by students. Typically, student writers will have a chance to be mentored and edited by the editorial staff. *Florida Today,* for example, has a competitive program called "the Verge," which is restricted to thirty students a year. At other newspapers, slots for student writers go begging, and so if you sign up, the sky could be the limit for your development as a professional writer.
- **Attend the Sewanee Young Writers' Conference.** Fiction, poetry, and creative nonfiction are the focus of this two-week summer workshop at the University of the South. The program draws faculty from up-and-coming writers featured in such venues as the *New Yorker* or Oprah's Book Club. Classes are limited to ten students. The program, which requires a recommendation and writing sample, restricts enrollment to fifty students entering tenth through twelfth grades. Admission is rolling, so apply early. Some scholarships are available.
- **Apply for Northwestern University's National High School Institute in Journalism.** Held at Northwestern's prestigious Medill School of Journalism, this five-week program will immerse you in the rigors of writing and reporting for the print media. Only eighty-eight rising seniors are chosen on the basis of writing samples, a personal statement, teacher recommendations, and a résumé. An application and fee are also required.
- **Write for your school newspaper.** This will give you valuable writing, reporting, and editing experience. If your school doesn't have a newspaper, start one.

- **Keep clippings of your published writing to submit to colleges in a portfolio along with your application.** (See sample clips from real students in Appendix B.)
- **Write "Fan Fiction."** You can write your own story lines for various popular TV shows, movies, manga, and books and post them on the Web. It's a good way to develop your writing skills and fire your imagination.
- **Publish a "chapbook" of your poetry and submit it with your applications.** Chapbooks are small, handmade booklets that offer poets a time-honored way to publish their work. If you have a sizeable body of work, pick a dozen poems and put together twenty to thirty copies of your own chapbook. Then see if local bookstores will carry it for sale.
- **Take a creative writing class at a university.**
- **Improve your skills as a creative writer at A Writer's Art: Creative Writing, sponsored by Duke University's Talent Identification Program (Duke TIP).** Held at Ghost Ranch in New Mexico, this field study is bound to expand your vision as a poet or writer of short fiction simply by virtue of the environment. Check the Duke TIP Web site in January for details. Need-based financial aid is available for this program.

CHAPTER TWELVE

The Drama Hook

HOOK TIP

Your skills as an actor could get you a foot in the door at a school that might otherwise be out of reach academically—*if* your audition is off the charts.

At some schools, the audition weighs more than grades and standardized test scores—up to 70 percent in some cases. At Julliard, for instance, the audition is practically the only thing that counts: SAT scores aren't even required. An audition could also land you a generous scholarship, such as the Presidential Arts Scholarship at George Washington University.

But many colleges and universities with top drama departments, such as Yale or Northwestern, don't offer auditions. At others, it's not an audition but rather the sum total of your credentials that can pave the way to a drama-related major such as film production or criticism. In such cases, it will be up to you to set the stage for your Hook by packaging yourself creatively on the pages of your application.

MICHAEL MACCOOK "MACK" ELDER: HAMMING IT UP—STRAIGHT TO HOLLYWOOD'S DOORSTEP

Mack Elder never had the lead in any school plays. Nor did he have a track record as a professional actor. Nonetheless, he used his drama experience and vast knowledge of film history as a Hook to snag colleges, specifically the University of Southern California's top-rated School of Cinema-TV.

"Way before high school I knew film was 'it,'" said Mack, who as a boy of ten displayed such an encyclopedic knowledge of cinema that he could recount details of almost any classic or current film at the drop of a hat.

Name any film and Mack could recite such arcane facts as a director's filmography, along with the film's aspect ratios, principal actors, musical score, screen writer, production costs, number of cuts, and more. By the time he entered high school, his knowledge base had grown so great that he could barely contain his passion for the subject.

"Have you heard of 'six degrees of Kevin Bacon'?" Mack quipped, referring to a running joke among film cognoscenti. "It's said that every actor that ever lived could be linked to Kevin Bacon in six movies or less."

With that, Mack rattled off a list of actors and their films in rapid-fire succession: "Robert De Niro was in *New York, New York* with Liza Minnelli . . . who was in *Cabaret* with Joel Grey . . . who was in *Remo Williams: The Adventure Begins* with Fred Ward . . . who was in *Tremors* with Kevin Bacon."

With such a command of movie trivia, it's no wonder that when it came time for Mack to apply to college, he turned his sights toward L.A. and USC, where the likes of *Star Wars'* director George Lucas and *Back to the Future* director Richard Zemeckis once studied.

"It was the oldest and the best film school in the country," said Mack, who hailed from New York City. "I wasn't sure that I could get in, but I said, 'Let's do it!' I wanted someplace where I could get real hands-on experience."

Mack's own practical experience in the field had come primarily through drama, both as an actor in school productions at Manhattan's elite Hunter College High School and as an active theatergoer.

"Theater was the first means I had of deconstructing the elements of film," said Mack. "Because there was so much theater in New York, by the time I was applying to college I had seen over 200 productions. And as an actor in high school, I had already lived it.

"Drama was storytelling in a way that I could get my hands on," he explained. "Without having to buy a $7,000 camera, a Moviola, or sixteen-millimeter film, I understood the elements in the process."

Mack started building his acting credentials beginning in junior high, when he got his first walk-on role as "G-man #2" in his school's stage version of George S. Kaufman's *You Can't Take It with You.*

"The film won Best Picture in 1938," Mack recalled. "It was one of Jimmy Stewart's big breakouts."

As for Mack, he said his role could have led to a break of a different sort. "My first line was, 'Yeah,' and the second was, 'Hey, you crazy broad, get off me!' Then they threw me down a flight of stairs. But I was pretty chubby back then, and so I could sort of bounce down the stairs without hurting myself."

Next came high school, where Mack was cast in a succession of character and ensemble roles in productions ranging from *Guys and Dolls* to *Noises Off.*

"I was in all the plays—nine in a row," said Mack. "I had one of the longest streaks in the history of my school."

Mack even did a stint as a director in eleventh grade, leading middle-school students in a series of one-act plays. He topped off his theater career senior year when he played the part of Algernon Moncrieff, the foil in *The Importance of Being Earnest,* and Moonface Martin, the featured comic relief in the musical *Anything Goes.*

"In *Anything Goes* my character was in nearly every scene," said Mack. "I had to sing and dance and do a huge pratfall sequence. I can sing, and I can kind of dance. I'm a vaudevillian, but I'm not hugely talented. Luckily, they used a version of the script that gave me the fewest musical numbers.

"But I was good at hamming it up. I had a solo at the end of the show and got a standing ovation three out of four nights. I held a note for thirty seconds. It was awesome."

As he was developing his skills as an actor, Mack was also bolstering his credentials as a playwright and film critic. For three summers running, he attended the University of Virginia's highly selective Young Writers Workshop, where he immersed himself in playwriting and fiction. At school, he churned out monthly movie reviews for one of the school newspapers and also wrote and edited a humor magazine. In his spare time, he put together a twelve-minute film celebrating the work of sci-fi writer Philip K. Dick, who wrote the books that gave rise to the films *Blade Runner* and *Total Recall.*

Finally, the summer before senior year, Mack landed an internship at the Museum of the Moving Image, the country's leading film museum, which brought together all of his talents as an actor, writer, and film buff. Writing program notes for screenings of five classic movies a week, he excerpted movie reviews, wrote plot summaries, and gave background on the cast, director, cinematographer, and writer. In addition, he edited transcripts of seminars with actors, directors, and writers for reproduction on the Web site.

"I had two months of unlimited access to the largest film studies archive in New York City, if not in the Western Hemisphere or the world," said Mack, relishing the memory.

With such a background, by the time he started filling out his college applications, Mack felt confident that he had the credentials necessary for a major in cinema studies, a program that focused on film analysis rather than production. What's more, he expected that his 1480 on the verbal and math sections of the SAT, a B+ average (his school didn't compute GPA), and honors as an AP Scholar with Honor might position him well academically. The only hitch—and it was a big one—was that the cinema studies program had spots for only fifty students.

But Mack was determined to be one of them. From the start he knew his essays could make or break him, and so he made a deliberate choice to set himself apart.

"I wanted to pick a topic that was completely off the beaten path," said Mack. For one question about a favorite movie, for example, Mack turned to his all-time favorite, *Blade Runner,* rather than to something more current.

"I felt I needed to differentiate myself from the hundreds of kids who were going to write about something like *Gladiator,* which was pretty recent," said Mack. "*Blade Runner* was a film I'd been associated with for most of my life. I had watched it on TV since I was four." (See Mack's *Blade Runner* essay in Appendix A.)

When it came to his main essay, Mack plunged in with a topic he was sure would tug at the emotions: his experience living through the World Trade Center disaster on 9/11, which had unfolded just a few weeks earlier.

"I was applying at a very specific time in history," said Mack. "There was never ever going to be another class of students like mine. We were all starting our applications at the end of September. At that point, planes were still grounded, schools were closed, subways were closed, and we were all sequestered.

"I did draft after draft of the essay, and then I just gave up. I didn't want to write about the subject, and my essay reflected that feeling. Although I didn't want to open up about it, I had felt compelled to try to write the essay because it was a hot-button topic. I thought, 'Maybe they'd take the kid from New York because he's an anomaly.'"

And so, instead of spilling his guts about 9/11 for the admissions committee, Mack took a boldly creative tack. He decided to write a page from a screenplay, starring himself as the main character. In the essay, his character, Mack, was sitting in a bathtub pondering what to write for his college essay (see Appendix A).

"I took a risk," said Mack. "I decided that if I was going to get in, I would do it on my own terms. 'Don't do exactly what they expect you to do,' I told myself. 'Write about what feels right.'

"I figured, writing about the art of writing an essay hadn't been plumbed before, and so I would try that.

"What college admissions people are really looking for is that person who is going to create the next eBay, or be the next George Lucas—the guy who is going to give back. I wanted them to think that I might be that person."

Once Mack's essays were done, he turned his attention to the interview. "I couldn't get out to California, because I had no intention of flying right after 9/11," said Mack. As a result, because USC had roaming interviewers, he met an admissions rep at a hotel in Manhattan.

"It didn't hurt my comfort level that my interviewer was in her mid-twenties," said Mack. "We were able to talk the same language. We got into the realm of important movies that needed to be seen. There was an Italian movie she liked, *The Conformist,* and although I hadn't seen it, I was aware of it. I knew enough about the film to talk about it, but I also tried to look eager to learn."

After the interview, Mack sent off his application in a red folder, USC's colors. Attached were a résumé geared to USC's specific format, and a portfolio of his movie reviews. He intentionally did not include a DVD of his short film on *Blade Runner.*

"I was told that it would be better not to send a film, because the cinema studies department would rip it apart," said Mack.

A few months later, when Mack was in London studying drama for three weeks at the Globe Theater, he got news of his acceptance to USC. Davidson admitted him as well, but for Mack, there really was no choice.

"USC is exactly what I needed," said Mack. "I wasn't going to wait another four years to study film in grad school. USC offered the single best film education anyone could have, and I needed to be there."

Once at USC, Mack flexed his media muscles at every opportunity. He served as executive producer of several shows for the campus TV station, *Trojan Vision,* where he won a major promotion award in 2006; he published an award-winning paper in *Depth of Field,* USC's journal of cinema studies; and he held internships at MTV and Miramax. In his spare time, he even wrote his first full-length screenplay.

"The final revisions are almost done," he said. "I'm hoping to shop it around."

From the moment he stepped on campus Mack lived his Hook, and you can bet that wherever the future leads, he'll continue on the same path. "I'm doing exactly what I've wanted to do my entire life," said Mack. "With USC, I hit the jackpot," he said. "Don't give up on your dreams."

BRIGHT IDEAS FOR ACTORS

- **Start a Thespian troupe.** If your school isn't a member of the International Thespian Society, ask a teacher to be a sponsor and register your club with this well-known organization. Thespian chapters around the country hold regular festivals and conferences where you and your acting buddies can showcase your talents. You can also earn awards for individual monologues and ensemble acting and singing. Teen actors who qualify can also perform at an international festival held annually.
- **Get involved in community theater productions.** To broaden your repertoire, audition for community theater. You'll not only give yourself a valuable résumé item, but you'll also learn to work with people of all ages who share your passion.
- **Apply for Northwestern University's National High School Institute in Acting.** This highly competitive five-week summer program admits 160 rising seniors for an intense, seven-day-a-week immersion in theater arts. "This is no camp," says the program's coordinator. "There are no tennis breaks." Students ready for such rigor must fill out an application, write a personal statement, and provide a résumé, letters of recommendation, and an application fee. Check the National High School Institute Web site for details and deadlines.

- **Turn pro.** Try to get jobs doing voice-overs or commercials for local ad agencies to develop your professional credentials and expertise. Even better: Land an acting job with a professional children's theater group that might be touring in your area. Often, such groups reserve parts for teens from the city or town in which they're performing.
- **Spend two weeks producing films at Reel Expressions: Filmmaking, a field study sponsored by Duke University's Talent Identification Program (Duke TIP).** This California-based program will expose you to all aspects of filmmaking in front of and behind the camera. Log onto the Duke TIP Web site in January for information and applications. Need-based financial aid is available for this program.
- **Try out for local and state beauty pageants.** These days, many pageants have eliminated bathing suit competitions in favor of evening gowns, talent competitions, and public speaking. Such pageants can be a way to demonstrate your poise and talent and put some scholarship money in your pocket. So go for it!
- **Audition for the Rutgers Summer Acting Conservatory for High School Students.** A four-week intensive program taught by working theater professionals may set the stage for your own acting career in college and beyond. Along with honing your skills through daily classes on acting, movement, and speech, you'll get real-world exposure to the craft through seminars with Broadway and film actors and trips to Broadway shows. To audition for the program, which is open to students in grades 9 to 12, send a videotape or appear in person at the school's New Brunswick, New Jersey, campus on designated dates. Thirty students are selected. Some need-based scholarships are available.

CHAPTER THIRTEEN

The Multicultural Hook

HOOK TIP

Multiculturalism is the name of the game in college admissions these days. So if you've got it, flaunt it.

For example, if you are African-American or Hispanic, don't be afraid to let your ethnicity shine forth from every page of your application. If your forebears are from the Indian subcontinent, you might highlight your linguistic abilities and your passion for Indian drumming or "Bollywood" movies. By celebrating your roots, you'll give admissions committees something to consider seriously.

KIRA GESELOWITZ: OUT OF AFRICA TO NORTHWESTERN

By a strict dictionary definition, Kira Geselowitz could have legitimately claimed to be African-American. But she didn't check that box under "ethnicity" on her application because her African heritage is of a different sort: she's a Caucasian South-African-American.

Nonetheless, when she applied to college, Kira brought to the table a unique background that she hoped would add to the diversity on campus.

Born in Walkerville, South Africa, on a farm near Johannesburg, Kira immigrated to the United States with her parents and older brother when she was nine years old. Kira and her family were forced to leave their rural "paradise," as she called it, when a band of robbers "barged into the house in a mass of yelling and waving guns."

It was two years after the end of apartheid, and although the South African blacks "finally had the freedom they deserved," said Kira, many found themselves forced to live hand-to-mouth in squatter camps—including a new one that was set up right outside of Walkerville. "With such desperation, crime was inevitable," said Kira, remembering the day in 1996 that changed her life.

The armed intruders threw her father on the floor and hustled Kira, her brother, and her mom into a spare bedroom, where they tied them up and left them paralyzed with fear.

"I heard them kicking my father in the head . . . while they took any possession they wished," Kira wrote in her college essay. "As I lay there, I thought I was going to die. As my short life flashed before my eyes, I had the sure feeling that I was living the last minutes of my life."

An hour later, the men took off in the family's Volkswagen, leaving Kira and her family miraculously alive. Six weeks later, Kira and her family were on a plane to America. Having sold nearly everything they owned to pay for the trip, they carried nothing but four suitcases, two teddy bears, and a lifetime of memories.

"I was afraid, because it was such a big change," said Kira. "But all I really needed was the three people sitting on the plane beside me."

Once in the United States, the family ended up in Florida, where Kira's father had some business acquaintances, and before long, they put down roots. "The cost of living was cheap, and the lifestyle was laid back," said Kira. Even though "it wasn't always easy," she said, "the life we've lived here has been exciting."

It was a life that has been anything but ordinary. Steeped in the philosophy of Ayn Rand, Kira's family always seemed to find themselves involved in offbeat, creative ventures, such as raising snakes for a venomous snake "theme park" that her dad hoped to start. For a while, the family even had a spare room filled with more than twenty cages for cobras and other venomous snakes. Later on, her dad put the snake park idea on the back burner and used his talents as an artist to become a popular muralist throughout Florida. But the influence of these myriad ventures on Kira and her brother was clear: Follow your passion. Anything goes.

As for Kira, from the time she was a child in South Africa, she had developed her own passion for snakes, an interest that continued through high school. Attending monthly meetings of the local herpetological society, she was exposed to lectures by some of the top snake experts in Florida.

Once she hit high school, Kira also discovered sailing. Ever adventuresome, she became a member of Sea Scouts, which met once a week for such outings as sailing on the nearby Indian River, camping, and canoeing. Before long, Kira's enthusiasm propelled her to the head of the group as boatswain, a leadership post she held from sophomore to senior year.

Then there was swing dancing. As with everything else, she took up that pastime with a vengeance, dancing weekly with people of all ages, including a group of adults who were competition-level dancers. After that came a position with Masterminds, a Jeopardy-like academic competition where Kira advanced to captain as early as tenth grade.

With everything she did, Kira seemed to have the golden touch—including academics. In a demanding International Baccalaureate (IB) program at Sebastian River High School, she threw herself into her studies, ending up as the top Spanish student in tenth grade. By the time she graduated, she had a 4.5 weighted grade point average and a rank of 14 in a class of nearly 500 students.

"I was at the top of the heap," said Kira, who wrote her 4,000-word IB Extended Essay on "The Use of Snake Venom Proteins to Cure Cancer."

When it came time to apply to college, Kira focused first on schools such as the University of Southern California, which were engaged in snake-venom research.

"But then I thought it would be good to look at schools where the research was more broadly based," said Kira. "I knew I wanted one of the top schools, and so I started looking at Web sites of the top one hundred schools in the country. Rochester looked cool, and Cornell had some interesting aspects, but Northwestern seemed to be the place that had everything I wanted. I did the search and made the choice all by myself."

Throwing herself headlong into the application process, she applied Early Decision to Northwestern, despite the fact that she had never even set foot on the Evanston, Illinois, campus. Although she sensed she had a lot going for her with her IB credentials and her powerful personal story that she recounted in her essay, she also knew that her combined SAT score of 1290 for Math and Critical Reading could be a problem.

"The average SAT score at Northwestern was way above mine," said Kira. In fact, at the time she was applying, the SAT range for the mid-50 percent of admitted students at Northwestern was 1310–1480, according to rankings in the 2005 edition of *America's Best Colleges,* by U.S. News & World Report.[11] By the following year, the range had increased to 1320–1500.[12]

Despite her qualms about her chances, less than a decade after Kira left South Africa, she found herself on another plane—this one headed for Chicago, to start her freshman year at Northwestern. She had been admitted Early Decision with a financial aid package that covered all but about $6,000-a-year in government loans.

"After I was accepted, Northwestern sent me a thank-you note and a nice little present, a leather key chain. It was the greatest feeling to find my dream school and be finished with the application process while others were still applying."

Northwestern is all about diversity, said Kira, and as one of the few South Africans on campus, she knows she has added something significant to the mix.

"My culture was my Hook," she said matter-of-factly. "I learned that if you take the initiative and let the school know how much you want them, you can go farther than you could ever imagine."

BRIGHT IDEAS FOR MULTICULTURAL STUDENTS

- **Start a multicultural club at school.** This is a good way to draw attention to your ethnic or cultural background and make a statement at school about the importance of diversity. As part of your club activities, organize a multicultural fest, with foods from around the world and entertainment such as Indian Bhangra dancing or Latin American salsa. Involve club members in service projects aimed at various ethnic constituencies in your community. For example, you might provide Thanksgiving baskets for migrant workers' families, offer weekly tutoring for inner-city kids, or plan recreational activities for children of newly arrived immigrants or refugees.
- **Organize a school assembly focusing on the issue of identity.** Invite guest speakers from various ethnic groups in the community to serve on a panel to discuss the question, What constitutes identity? This could be a provocative way to open up a discussion about the issue and create bridges of understanding in your school. Your efforts could establish you as an activist on multicultural issues.
- **Emphasize your ethnic or cultural roots in one of your college essays.** What better way to underscore your background than an essay about your experience with racism, for example, or how you were influenced by your mother, who was one of the last refugees to escape from Vietnam when Saigon was falling in 1975? (See samples of multicultural essays in Appendix A.)
- **Apply for diversity weekends on campus.** Many colleges offer special weekends or even weeklong programs on campus—some of them fully paid—to heighten their multicultural recruiting efforts.

   For example, the University of Notre Dame, which was named one of the top 25 colleges for Latinos by *Hispanic* magazine in 2006,[13] hosts two weeklong, all-expenses-paid seminars, Latino Community Leadership Seminar and African American Scholars at Notre Dame. The seminars, which are held the summer before senior year, offer students one college credit. The only cost is a $125 confirmation fee for those who are selected. Check the school's Web site for pre-college programs in the fall of junior year so that you don't miss the application deadlines. (See additional programs and ideas for multicultural students in Chapter Twenty-Three, "Romancing Admissions.")

You've just read the stories of ten students whose Hooks helped launch them on successful college careers. For these students, packaging their Hook clearly through the pages of their applications was a key factor in achieving their college goals. Step-by-step, through their essays, activities lists, résumés, and supplemental submissions, they marketed their Hooks to admissions committees until they ultimately "closed the sale." By following the guidelines in Part III, you'll find that these marketing skills can be yours as well.

PART III

Packaging Your Hook

Your College Application Marketing Plan

HOOK TIP

Play up your Hook every chance you get. That's the key to packaging and selling yourself to colleges.

Whether you're filling out your activities list, work experience, honors and awards, résumé, or essays, your Hook should be the first thing that catches a reader's eye on your application. You may think it's cheesy to promote yourself, but when it comes to winning at college admissions, some subtle boasting is best.

Although at first the comparison may seem harsh or even crass, the bald facts are that the college application process is a marketing game—and it's a game you can win. But to succeed at this game, you have to be willing to become a marketing expert and to see yourself as a "human product" that can actually be "sold."

Perhaps an even more helpful analogy would be the job application process, where the applicant does all he or she can to put the best foot forward with prospective employers. So from the moment you start surfing college Web sites or visiting campuses, you have to see yourself as the colleges see you: a kind of prospect on the admissions market, with potential strengths that can benefit a given college. The colleges are doing the buying, and you are doing the selling. It's as simple as that.

Despite all this talk about "selling" and "marketing" yourself, don't automatically assume that this view of college admissions is dehumanizing. Rather, understand that both you and the college must benefit in some way from the process. The challenge for you is to convince your favorite college that it will in fact be better off, with a more interesting student body, if you gain admission.

Your job, through your application, interviews, and recommendation letters, is to become a master sales rep at the height of the game. As a savvy salesperson, you need to use all the marketing tools at your disposal to increase the odds that your "product,"—i.e., *you*—comes out on top of the "admit" pile at every college to which you are applying.

But how exactly do you start promoting yourself? How can you cut through the overwhelming application information and requirements to begin to market yourself to colleges?

Like every good salesperson, you need to start with a marketing plan, a simple, step-by-step strategy for making yourself a winner.

MARKETING YOUR APPLICATION PACKAGE

When it comes to marketing yourself to colleges through your application, you have at your command seven simple selling points, most of which are *under your control:*

> *Selling Point 1: PSAT/SAT/SAT Subject Tests/ACT*
> *Selling Point 2: GPA/Class Rank/Difficulty of Courses*
> *Selling Point 3: Résumé, including Honors/Activities/Jobs*
> *Selling Point 4: The College "Hook"*
> *Selling Point 5: Essays*
> *Selling Point 6: Teacher/Guidance Counselor Recommendations*
> *Selling Point 7: Supplemental Material (Portfolios, Music CDs, Scientific Abstracts, etc.)*

These seven selling points add up to the total "package" you will submit to colleges through your application. To increase your chances of admission to your favorite colleges, you must max out on as many selling points as you can.

Take Selling Point 1, for example. PSAT, SAT, and ACT scores are like money in the bank: The higher your scores, the better your chances for admission. Although some colleges reported significant drops in average SAT scores among applicants in 2006,[14] the bar for the test scores of admitted students has been inching up higher and higher, not only at highly selective colleges, but also at some second- and third-tier schools. This is the reality, and if you were on a reality show, you'd be busting your chops to come out on top. So why not give yourself the best shot at the SAT or ACT by prepping? (See more on standardized tests in Chapter Eighteen.)

The same principle holds true with each successive selling point: If you put everything you've got into each selling point, from your grades to your essays, you'll succeed in creating an application package that could carry you further than you've ever dreamed.

The point here is not to add extra pressure that will make your life miserable. Rather, the idea is to lower the stresses in your life by getting started early with the admissions process, formulating a comprehensive plan, and increasing your odds of getting into the school or schools of your choice. Also, spending time working on your marketing plan early will give you options—lots of options—at admission time.

In the next few chapters of Part III, you'll learn specific ways to create an effective application package, including tips on résumés, activities lists, essays, and portfolios—all focused on your Hook. Then, in Part IV, "Selling Your Hook," you'll go beyond the application itself to learn how to sell yourself by mail, e-mail, and face-to-face interviews with admissions officers and coaches. This section will also help you formulate an overall strategy for deciding when and where to apply, as well as a back-up plan for "working the wait list" if you've been deferred or wait-listed.

But before you plunge into the packaging and sales techniques that will help you mold your own powerful marketing program, take a look at how the process worked for one Ivy League hopeful, whose experience finding and marketing her Hook might serve as a model.

AMANDA'S STORY: MARKETING A BROADWAY BABY

Amanda was in a quandary. She had her heart set on applying to Dartmouth Early Decision, but she wasn't sure she had the right stuff.

"Nothing about me seems special," she moaned.

The good news was that her grades were strong, with As and a smattering of Bs in AP and Honors courses. Even better news was that she was a National Merit Semifinalist, which meant that her PSAT scores had put her in the top 0.5 percent of all students in the country who had taken the test. With SAT scores of nearly 750 in each section and SAT Subject Tests that topped out in the high 700s in Math, Writing, and Chemistry, she appeared to have the numbers Dartmouth was looking for.

The bad news was that she had tanked in English junior year, and her GPA was hovering around 3.3. Also, there were seven other students applying early to Dartmouth from her suburban Westchester, New York, high school. Finally, she was the only one of the seven who had opted to go the "non-traditional" route and attend the alternative school offered by her high school. The alternative school had given her more flexibility with scheduling, along with smaller classes that opened the door to a more personal relationship with her teachers.

But Dartmouth had never accepted anyone from the alternative program, and how Amanda would fare against her more traditional peers was anyone's guess. Would she be perceived as offbeat and somehow less serious about academics? Or would she be applauded for her boldness as a self-starter? The answer wasn't clear.

Nor was it clear to her how her extracurricular activities would come across. When she reviewed the school activities that she had listed on a form provided by her guidance counselor, nothing seemed to pop off the page—except, perhaps, her stint as manager of the football team.

That's quirky enough to get some attention, she thought.

To Amanda, the rest of her school activities seemed fairly prosaic, even though she had poured her heart and soul into them: Drama Club, Peer Adviser, county Drug Awareness Representative, School Fairness Committee. She had listed them as the guidance counselor had asked, in order of importance to her, as follows:

Activity	Year	Position Held
Drama Club	Grades 9–12	Character Roles; Tech Crew
Peer Adviser	Grades 10–12	Counseled Fellow Students
Varsity Football	Grade 11	Manager; Recorded Statistics
Fairness Committee	Grade 12	Mediator
County Anti-Drug Team	Grades 10–12	School Rep

As for jobs, she had listed her summer job as a counselor in a day camp one summer:

Position	Employer	Dates
Camp Counselor	Camp Ah-wha-ne	Summer: 8 weeks

But what this list didn't capture—and what Amanda had failed to report to her guidance counselor—was her secret life, a life she had kept hidden from most of her teachers and classmates for four years.

Amanda's secret was that she was a professional actress. She wasn't just a wanna-be, but rather was a full-fledged member of Actors' Equity who as a ninth-grader had landed a major singing role in an Off-Broadway musical called *Violet*. Not only that, she had garnered rave reviews—by name—in the *New York Times*.

For six months during her freshman year, she had appeared in eight shows a week—two on Wednesdays and Saturdays—without missing a day of school. In order to perform this juggling act, she had rearranged her school schedule so that she was free right after lunch on Wednesdays. The minute her classes were over, her mother appeared at school and drove her to the city in time for her 2 p.m. matinee performance. She had kept up this pace—*and* maintained a straight-A average—for the entire run of the show.

Despite her professional success, Amanda knew better than to flaunt her Off-Broadway credentials to anyone at school. In the culture of her competitive high school, academics came first, and she had gotten strong hints from a couple of teachers that anything that might appear to interfere with schoolwork, even an acting job Off-Broadway, could work against her.

"We don't give special favors for celebrities," one teacher had sniffed.

Also, among her friends, Amanda didn't want to set herself apart. A typical teenager, she wanted to be viewed as just one of the crowd. And so, while she was performing Off-Broadway, Amanda had stayed mum, keeping her professional and school lives separate.

Once the run of the play was over, she decided to let her acting take a backseat to life as an ordinary high school student. For the next three years, except for weekly voice lessons and occasional performances in commercials or staged readings, she concentrated exclusively on her schoolwork, social life, and standard extracurricular activities. She did keep her hand in theater as a member of the school Drama Club, but, rather than take a chance on upstaging her peers, she worked as a stage hand or member of the tech crew or took smaller character roles in productions.

By the time she was ready to apply to Dartmouth, her Off-Broadway run seemed like a distant memory, and her professional career seemed hardly worthy of mention on her college application. At least that's what she thought. But she was dead wrong.

A High-Performance Hook

Amanda's persona as a professional actress was her Hook—not just any hook, but a major-league Hook that could help her hit a home run in the Ivy League. Despite the fact that her last major stage role had been as a high school freshman, Amanda had the professional credentials that could make colleges sit up and take notice—*if* she packaged herself properly. What she needed was an overall strategy, one that involved communicating her credentials as an accomplished actress at every stage of the application process.

With the help of an adviser, Amanda came up with a packaging plan that would communicate a single, powerful message to the Dartmouth admissions staff: Amanda is an Off-Broadway actress.

Amanda's Packaging Plan
Step 1: Bolstering the Hook with a Portfolio

For starters, Amanda bolstered her image as a professional actress by submitting, along with the college application, her professional portfolio, which included:

- A professional black-and-white head shot
- Her agent's name and contact number

- Her music coach's name and contact number
- Her membership in Actors' Equity and SAG
- A listing of the plays in which she had appeared, focusing especially on her Off-Broadway show, and also on her Broadway/Off-Broadway staged readings.
- A listing of her commercials and voice-overs
- A listing of her recordings
- Clips of her reviews, including one in the *New York Times* that described her by name

As part of her portfolio, Amanda also had something to offer Dartmouth that many other professional actors don't have: a CD of the cast album of her Off-Broadway show, which featured her singing two important solos. She planned to send her CD with her portfolio to Dartmouth as an artistic supplement.

With her portfolio and CD as her secret weapons, Amanda was poised to complete her application.

Amanda's Packaging Plan
Step 2: Hooking the Application

When it came to the application, Amanda understood that her packaging strategy was to "sell" her Hook every chance she got in the limited space available. In four areas of the application, Dartmouth provided opportunities for her to communicate her expertise as a seasoned actress subtly but effectively:

1. Honors and Awards
2. Extracurricular Activities List
3. Work Experience
4. Essays

In each of these areas, Amanda focused on making her Hook a centerpiece, so that the members of the admissions committee would immediately recognize who she was and what she had accomplished.

The Hook as an Honor The application's first packaging opportunity was in the Honors and Awards section, where Amanda applied a little original thinking. Rather than merely listing her stellar academic achievements, such as National Merit Semifinalist and AP Scholar, she also included her selection for Northwestern University's competitive summer program in theater. She wrote:

Northwestern University, National High School Institute, Theater Arts Division. Selected as a junior for this five-week acting program, which is usually reserved for seniors.

With her acting Hook now actively in play in the application, Amanda made the message even stronger in the next section of the application: the extracurricular activities list.

Packaging the Activities List Having her packaging strategy uppermost in her mind, Amanda immediately revised the activities list she had given to her guidance counselor—a list in which she had focused exclusively on *school* activities.

Now, instead of looking at the list through the narrow lens of high school activities, Amanda approached the list much more broadly as a tool to communicate her Hook. Accordingly, the very first activity she mentioned on her revised list was "Professional Actor." With her professional expertise and Off-Broadway role on the top line, it couldn't be overlooked by admissions readers. On the second line, she listed "Private Voice Lessons," which further reinforced the depth of her commitment to her craft. Then she added the name of her singing coach and professional CDs to underscore her high level of accomplishment.

Amanda's revised activities list looked like this on her application:

Activity	Year	Positions Held
Professional Actor	Grades 9–12	Featured Off-Broadway singing role; Cast Album
Private Voice Lessons	Gr. 9–12	Coached by (name of vocal coach); Professional CDs
Peer Adviser	Gr. 10–12	Selected by faculty to counsel peers
Fairness Committee	Gr. 12	One of four students chosen to work with faculty as mediator
County Anti-Drug Team	Gr. 10–12	Only student rep on community-wide committee
Varsity Football	Gr. 11	Team Manager; kept stats
Drama Club	Gr. 9–12	Character roles in all major school productions; stage hand; tech crew

Working the Hook Under work experience on the application, instead of leading with her summer camp job, Amanda emphasized her freelance work doing voice-overs and songs for commercials and audio tapes. She also added some volunteer internships she had held during a special January term:

Type of work	Employer	Hours/wk	Dates
Commercials/ Voice-overs	Della Famina	Up to 10	Grades 9–12
ESL Voice-overs	Macmillan Pub.	Up to 10	Grades 9–12
Camp Counselor	Camp Ah-wha-ne	40	Summer: 6 weeks
Clinical Trials Assist. (Vol.)	Pharmaceutical Co.	35	January, Gr. 10
Teaching Intern (Vol.)	Westchester Elementary	35	January, Gr. 11

Résumé A résumé is an absolute *must* for all students. (See Chapter Sixteen.) Amanda submitted two: 1.) her professional acting résumé, which accompanied a portfolio with her photo and reviews; and 2.) an activities résumé, which simply reprinted her activities in the order in which they appeared on Dartmouth's activities list. This second résumé provided an expanded description of her accomplishments.

She recognized that without such a detailed explanation of her achievements, the activities list in the Dartmouth application would come across as little more than a Western Union telegram. In other words, the standard activities list would send an abbreviated message, but it wouldn't tell the whole story. Consequently, she elaborated on her activities on a separate sheet and attached it to her application (see Appendix B).

The Essay as a Sales Pitch As part of her college packaging program, Amanda made her professional acting Hook the focus of her main essay. She understood that the essay was in a sense her "sales pitch," through which she could communicate her Hook persuasively and also go deeper into her psyche as an actress.

But which essay topic would best serve her needs?

To jump-start her thinking, she turned to the questions on the Common Application and started brainstorming.

An obvious choice would have been for her to write on the Common Application's Question 1: *Evaluate a significant experience, achievement, risk you have taken, or ethical dilemma you have faced and its impact on you.* Amanda could simply have given readers a flavor of what it was like to be in an Off-Broadway play and described how the experience had changed her.

But Question 3 was potentially more provocative: *Indicate a person who has had a significant influence on you, and describe that influence.*

After brainstorming for twenty minutes or so, Amanda opted for Question 3. The person she chose to write about wasn't a real person, but rather the character she played Off-Broadway. Her essay about her relationship to her character, and the influence of the character on her, was a winner.

The essay involved Amanda's imaginary conversation with the girl from North Carolina—a girl who was, in fact, the character she played onstage. The essay concluded with insights she gained from this new "friend." But most important of all, the imaginative essay told a bigger story about the boldness and creativity of Amanda herself. (See her complete essay in Appendix A.)

As a counterpoint to this main essay, Amanda addressed her position as manager of the football team in her "most meaningful activity" essay, and her role as a peer counselor in an essay on what she could contribute to Dartmouth. In this way, she could communicate other aspects of her personality and other talents or secondary Hooks without diminishing the impact of her professional acting Hook *or* running the Hook into the ground.

Amanda's Packaging Plan
Step 3: Selling the Hook

Amanda's marketing program didn't stop with her application. Once the application was finished, she made some important personal contacts at her high school and at Dartmouth to reinforce her Hook.

The first person she contacted was her guidance counselor. Because her counselor was in the dark about her theatrical experience, Amanda's mother made an appointment to bring the woman up to date. Leaving nothing to chance, her mother brought to the meeting a CD player and a copy of Amanda's Off-Broadway cast album. The minute the guidance counselor heard Amanda's show-stopping solos, she was sold.

"She's astonishing!" said the guidance counselor. "I had no idea."

By the time Amanda's mom left the meeting, the guidance counselor was wholeheartedly behind Amanda's application to Dartmouth. This was critical because it was the counselor's job to write one of Amanda's letters of recommendation, in which she would explain what distinguished Amanda from her peers.

With the guidance counselor firmly in her camp, Amanda next contacted Dartmouth's music department to learn more about opportunities she might have to continue her private voice lessons. She was lucky enough to touch base with one of the professors personally, and she immediately followed up the phone call by sending the professor a copy of her Off-Broadway cast album.

The Early Bird Sometimes Gets the Worm

Amanda didn't have long to wait. Just before Christmas, she received a big fat envelope in the mail welcoming her to Dartmouth—Early Decision. But not every applicant from her school was so lucky. Although all seven of the early applicants were exceptional students, only two besides Amanda were accepted.

"The secret to my success was my Hook," says Amanda. "There's no doubt about it."

Amanda may have had a ready-made Hook as a professional actress, but if she hadn't first identified her Hook and then taken steps to market it, her story might not have ended so happily. Instead, through some deft packaging of her Hook through her activities, honors, essay, portfolio, and CD, and through her willingness to "sell" herself and her achievements to her guidance counselor and influential people at Dartmouth, she came out on top.

Part of the secret to packaging yourself effectively is to find ways to bolster your Hook. In the following chapter, you'll discover that by strengthening your Hook creatively through activities, portfolios, and other submissions, you can take your application to still another level.

Chapter Fifteen

Bolstering Your Hook

Hook Tip

In these times when competition for admission is hotter than ever, it's essential that you take your Hook to a professional or semiprofessional level.

So if you're in a band, get some paid gigs. If you're an artist, enter community art shows. If you're a photographer or writer, get published. If you're a fashionista, become a model, intern at a fashion magazine, or create your own line of purses or skirts. And by all means, accentuate your achievements with a portfolio to accompany your applications. Bolstering your Hook isn't hard. All it takes is willingness to work and a little dose of extra creativity.

I t's not too late to shore up your Hook with a few "extras" that could have big payoffs. Whether you are a senior who is staring applications in the face, a junior with room to run before deadline time, or a freshman or sophomore just starting to develop your interests, you have time to buttress your Hook with eye-catching internships, courses, projects, or adventures.

Look especially for activities *outside* of school that can give you "quick hits" for big results, such as publications, contests, or special programs that could serve as honors or awards on your applications. And of course, don't hesitate to start a club. By taking the initiative, particularly in an area related to your Hook, you'll position yourself as a go-getter.

But these suggestions are not a license to lie. You *must* follow through and actually start that club or write those articles; otherwise don't even think of including them on your applications and résumé.

Your personal integrity is more important than any college acceptance. And if your own honor isn't enough to hold you back from fudging on your application, keep in mind that some schools, particularly some in the University of California system, are known to do random checks of application information. According to one report, a student who indicated on his activities list that he worked several hundred hours at the local library discovered that one college actually called the librarian to check up on him.

There are plenty of legitimate, and life-enhancing, ways you can build up your Hook and make an impact, not only on your college applications but also on your growth as a person. The more you step out of your comfort zone to try new experiences and test yourself, the more confident you'll become. Consider these success stories:

- A senior with her sights on a fashion career proposed a teen fashion column to her local paper. Samples of her biweekly column, which read like a sophisticated tip-sheet from *Glamour* magazine, ended up in a portfolio with her applications.
- A science-oriented senior who had developed a passion for salsa dancing as an exchange student in Spain started a salsa club at the start of senior year. Even he was surprised by the response: More than sixty students showed up for the first meeting. His zeal for salsa played against type, and he danced his way to admission at seven leading universities, including Northwestern, UNC–Chapel Hill, and Washington University in St. Louis. (See essay in Appendix A.)
- A junior with a passion for the underdog led a yearlong lobbying and fund-raising campaign to support the Save Darfur Coalition, founded by the American Jewish World Service and the Holocaust Museum. With part of the $6,000 he raised, he organized a bus trip that carried a group of Darfuri Muslims, members of his synagogue, and his fellow high school students to Washington, D.C., for a rally in the spring of his senior year. His compassion and chutzpah earned him national media coverage.[15]
- A sophomore at a large Catholic boys' school hoped that basketball would be his Hook for a Division III college. Sensing that he needed some "cultural enrichment" to round out his activities, he signed up for the Asian Society as the only Caucasian member, and by the time he was a senior he was club secretary. With his basketball stats and cultural connections, he was a slam dunk at Amherst.
- A student who invented a video camera stabilizer while working on a movie set the summer before junior year not only entered science fairs but also applied for a patent. He topped out as one of forty finalists in the Intel Science Talent Search and was admitted to Stanford, NYU, Harvard, and USC.[16]
- A junior who loved jamming on the guitar with friends every weekend put together a CD and some business cards and lined up paid jobs as a musician and guitar teacher. His CD and his professional persona played well at one of the hottest music schools in the country, Belmont, which was his top choice.
- A junior who worked as a lifeguard built on his rescue expertise by taking

a course to become an emergency medical technician. Although he was also a varsity swimmer, his meet times weren't good enough to get him recruited, but he created his own waves with a special Hook as an emergency responder.

- A seventh-grader who had struggled to read as a child started a program called Project Books and Blankies to encourage local children to read. She solicited book donations and made cozy quilts, which she gave to homeless shelters and schools. The program, which she continued to build throughout high school, landed her on the cover of *Time for Kids* and earned her national recognition as a Daily Point of Light from the Points of Light Foundation. She was accepted at Stanford, Princeton, MIT, and the University of Southern California, which named her a Trustee Scholar.[17]
- A junior whose Hook was nature photography submitted a photo of a wild pig and an accompanying story to a national wildlife magazine. He became the youngest photographer ever published by the magazine, earning him bragging rights—*and* a unique portfolio item—for his college applications.

These real-life examples are just a taste of how you can expand your Hook to deepen your level of experience and expertise and communicate your passion. Colleges look for commitment to an activity or interest not only over time, but also by the magnitude of your involvement. In the case of the nature photographer, Zach Kappel, his published photograph and article were just the crowning touch of a freelance interest that had been developing since junior high.

For years, Zach had been taking nature photographs at his summer home in New England. By the fall of his junior year, he had amassed several thousand photographs on environmental subjects, mostly of birds, which were his specialty. In addition, he had held a position as a raptor photographer and volunteer at a local environmental center where he also had served for three summers as a camp counselor. Added to this list was his track record as the only teenager in a local photo club, which served to further underscore his Hook. He could express these pursuits on his application through the activities list as follows:

Activity	Years	Positions Held
Freelance Wildlife Photographer	Grades 9–12	Nationally published; museum shows
Raptor Photographer, Environmental Ctr.	Grade 11	Web site/promotional photos
Professional Photo Classes	Grade 11	Mentored by *National Geographic* photogs
County Photo Club	Grades 10–12	Only teen member/local awards
School Photo Club	Grades 11–12	Founder/teaches photo techniques
Environmental Counselor	Grades 10–12	Taught children aged 10–13

Zach bolstered his Hook even further by selling his photographs professionally in a local coffee shop frequented by artists, and at the gift shops of a local botanical garden and environmental institute where he had volunteered. And, of course, he made sure to write about photography in at least one of his essays, so that there would be no doubt in the minds of admissions readers about his passion or his abilities.

Now take some time to meditate on *your* Hook and on ways you might strengthen it for your applications. Get your parents and friends in on the act to bounce around ideas. Once the ideas start to flow, you'll find they won't stop.

HOOK-BOLSTERING BRAINSTORMS

To jump-start your thinking, refer to the "Bright Ideas" at the end of each chapter in Part II, or look over the following additional Bright Ideas covering additional categories below. Use your local library and the Internet to find out even more information on these and other resources.

Bright Ideas for Historians

- **Submit a history research paper to the** *Concord Review*. This highly regarded history journal for high school students selects the best history papers submitted by teens around the globe for publication four times a year. The $40 submission fee earns you a subscription to the journal, plus a chance to be published and win the *Review*'s Emerson Prize. Admissions officers at leading colleges routinely give the *Concord Review*—and its writers—thumbs-up.
- **Start a history club through the National History Club (NHC), created by the founder of the** *Concord Review*. With 248 chapters in forty-two states, the NHC seeks to encourage historical scholarship and discussion at the high school level. There is no fee to charter a club chapter at your school.
- **Submit a history research paper to the National Writing Board for evaluation.** This service, offered by the *Concord Review*, offers a chance for you to have your writing evaluated by an independent panel of experts. Results of the evaluation, which costs $100, can be forwarded at your request to colleges in support of your application. According to the founder of the *Concord Review*, dozens of top colleges, including Amherst, Claremont McKenna, Stanford, Notre Dame, Harvard, and Yale, welcome this service as a tool in the admissions process.
- **Videotape oral histories of old-timers in your city or town.** You could donate copies to the library archives and also try to have the films aired on

local television. Once you get a series of films under your belt, hold a film festival to celebrate your town's roots—or enter a film contest or two.

Bright Ideas for Photographers and Artists

- **Submit a portfolio of your photographs or artwork with your applications.** A portfolio demonstrates a strong commitment and talent in an area, regardless of whether you plan to study art or photography in college. Check portfolio requirements for each school. It wouldn't hurt to indicate on your applications that you want to minor in fine arts, no matter what your intended major.
- **Hold an exhibition at school and have an "opening."** If you schedule the exhibition for the spring of junior year or the fall of senior year, the timing will be perfect for your application. For the opening, you can invite the press and public.
- **Get a booth at various art shows in town to sell your work as a fund-raiser for your favorite charity.**
- **Get an artistic or photographic mentor.** Find someone well known locally with whom you could work once a month in your medium of interest.
- **Intern one summer for a prominent artist or photographer.** Use whatever connections you have to land a position working with a pro.
- **Develop your expertise in digital media.** Animation and graphic arts are hot these days, and you should do your best to be at the cutting edge. Check into summer courses at local colleges.
- **Take a series of photos on specific themes.** For example, if you're a surfer, you might shoot a series titled, "A Day in the Life of a Beachcomber." If you attend a large, multicultural high school, you might do a series called "A Day in the Life of an Urban High School."
- **Send some of your funky photos to the photography editor of your local paper.** Better yet, pay a visit to the newsroom and meet the photo editor, bringing some samples of your work. Ask if you can become a "stringer," someone who sends in photos as a freelancer. You never know where this might lead.
- **Enter photo or art contests.** Magazines such as *Parade* as well as local museums and organizations have regular contests. Pay attention to deadlines and specifications, and enter as many contests as you can.
- **Enter your photos or artwork in the Scholastic Art & Writing Awards program.** With fourteen contest categories to choose from, you're likely to find one that fits your talent, whether it's painting, animation, ceramics, photography, or video/film. What's more, if you're a senior, you may be one of five artists and two photographers chosen to receive a $10,000 Gold Award. Look for the program on the Internet under "Scholastic Art & Writing Awards," administered by the Alliance for Young Artists & Writers. Enter and submit your work on-line in early fall.

- **Create a calendar of your photographs.** If your specialty is nature photography, perhaps you can work with a local environmental center to develop a calendar as a fund-raising project.
- **Produce a book of photographs.** Although it would be pricey to publish a book on your own, put out feelers at regional publishers who might have an interest in photos with a local angle.
- **Make greeting cards of your photographs or artwork and see if local museums or bookstores will carry them for sale.** If you live near a botanical garden, for example, take photos of the flowers and ask if the bookstore will carry framed photos or cards of your work.
- **Take an art or photography class at a local community college or museum.**
- **Start a business to sell your photographs or artwork.**
- **Take courses in AutoCAD at a local junior college or university.** These computer-based design programs will give you skills essential to a possible career in architecture, engineering, or interior design.

These ideas are just the tip of the iceberg. No matter what your Hook, you can use these bright ideas to stimulate your thinking. Keep in mind that as you are pondering practical ways to enhance your own particular passion, nothing is too over the top. Your only limits are your own imagination—and your ability to generate opportunities to put your inspiration into practice.

Once you've expanded your Hook with a few salient activities, achievements, and honors, it's time to package yourself—beginning with a résumé and the all-important application grid known as the activities list.

CHAPTER SIXTEEN

The Résumé Power Play

HOOK TIP

Supplementing your application with a résumé is essential. Without one, you simply won't have ample running room to describe the full extent of your achievements in the standard list of activities required by most applications, including the Common Application. That's why a résumé that highlights your Hook is a key weapon in your packaging arsenal.

Send a résumé to every college on your list. If you've applied on-line and there's no space to include it, then send it by mail. Don't forget to give it to your teachers and guidance counselors *before* they write recommendations, and bring it along on interviews, especially with alumni. You won't regret the extra effort.

Packaging your Hook with a résumé will do more than merely help you sell yourself to colleges. It will also help you sell yourself to your teachers, your guidance counselor, your parents, and, most important of all, to *you*.

The college application process can be a confidence-building experience, and a résumé can go a long way toward helping you see how much you truly have to offer. But in order to put together a résumé that has maximum readability and impact, it's critical that you adjust your thinking about how to present your strengths. Résumés, particularly job résumés, are often sequential, with the most recent experience or achievement listed first. But this is the kiss of death for a college résumé. So is a résumé that merely lists everything you've ever done in your life, including the one day you spent working on a Habitat for Humanity building in sixth grade, or the one year you spent playing JV golf.

First and foremost, a college résumé is a communication tool, a way for you to convey your Hook and other strengths as clearly as possible. Your goal isn't to impress admissions readers with the sheer *quantity* of activities in which you've been involved. Rather, it's to capture their imaginations with the quality and originality of your main Hook and secondary Hooks.

ORGANIZE ACCORDING TO CATEGORIES

The easiest way to write a memorable college résumé is to lump your activities together in clearly defined categories, with subheads that sum up each category. A good place to start is the Activities Questionnaire that you filled out in Chapter Three. Using the categories in the questionnaire as guidelines, put your activities in order on a résumé, starting with your Hook. Follow up with categories that communicate your passions or most exciting experiences in descending order of importance.

For example, let's say your Hook is Future Astrophysicist with an interest in time travel, but you've also been deeply involved in varsity sports, competitive break dancing, and volunteer work. You might arrange the categories on your résumé as follows:

Aspiring Astrophysicist
Competitive Break Dancer
Varsity Athlete
Volunteer

Or perhaps your Hook is Freelance Artist and Designer, and you've also devoted your time to life-guarding, along with a new interest in robotics after a summer program. You might create headings for your résumé such as these:

Freelance Artist and Designer
Professional Lifeguard
Robotics Experience

If your Hook is Mentor for the Mentally Disabled, and yet you're also a state-level musician, varsity athlete, and school leader heavy with academic and personal honors, you could configure your résumé this way:

Academic Achiever
Mentor for the Mentally Disabled
All-State Singer and Pianist
School and Community Leader

You'll note that Academic Achiever was placed first, before the student's primary Hook, Mentor for the Mentally Disabled. The reason for this order is that academic achievements and high standardized test scores will almost always be your first selling point with colleges—even before a strong Hook. (See the 7 Selling Points in Chapter Fourteen, "Your College Application Marketing Plan.") Good grades and high scores position you to make the most of your Hook with admissions committees.

Then again, you might be a state-ranked athlete with strong leadership skills, outstanding church and volunteer credentials, and a creative edge. Here's how you might play up those attributes on a résumé:

State-Ranked Soccer Player
Award-Winning Volunteer
Set Designer and Photographer
Church and Community Leader
Work Experience

Even your ethnicity can be projected on a résumé as one of your main categories. Consider the subheads you might include if you're a Hispanic student with a track record in school leadership and a Hook as a Marching Band Drum Major.

Marching Band Drum Major
Hispanic Heritage
School and Community Leader
Commitment to Service

If military history is your Hook and you have aspirations as a physician and the experience and academic honors to back it up, you might want to play it up like this:

Academic Honors and Awards
Passion for Military History and Strategic Analysis
Varsity Athlete
Medical Work and Service

Suppose you're a technology junkie, with a passion for architecture, literature, and a variety of sports. With Technology as your Hook, you could get a little creative and arrange your résumé in categories like this:

A Talent for Technology
A Passion for Architecture
A Mind for Literature
A Heart for Athletics

Finally, take a look at the way you might play your Work Ethic Hook, along with interests in volunteering, engineering, and water sports:

Committed Restaurant Employee
Dedicated Volunteer
Engineering Enthusiast
Florida Water Sportsman

These examples only hint at the categories and subheads you can use to organize your résumé. Without such organization, you might drown your Hook

and other accomplishments in a sea of detail. But with clear subheads and categories, you can tell your story to overworked admissions readers quickly and
easily. Admissions officers are inundated with literally thousands of applications, so the more organized you can be on your résumé, the easier it will be for
them to understand you and your Hook at a glance.

For example, in the case of the budding astrophysicist on page 110, a reader
could see instantly from the categories that he was an intriguing guy. Not only
did he have an esoteric career interest, but he also had a fun side as a competitive
break dancer. Added to that, his background in sports and volunteering suggested that he was someone who didn't just sit behind a telescope all day looking at the stars. He was out there doing and engaging in a very down-to-earth
way, even as he was dreaming of a world beyond our own.

As you are organizing your résumé, let the categories and subheads sum up
your personal story. Then you can flesh them out with specific details that will
bring the résumé—and you—to life.

Dramatize the Details

Although it's important in any résumé to dramatize the details, that does not
mean you can pad your résumé with fabricated credentials. If there's one car-
dinal rule, it's this: *Never, ever put on a résumé a lie or a half-truth.* Such shabby
practices not only are unethical, but also could destroy your chances for admission, as at least one well-known coach discovered after being sacked from his
job after his doctored résumé was exposed.

Still, since your goal in a résumé is to package your legitimate accomplishments, especially your Hook, in a way that jumps off the page, it is essential that
you explain each achievement in glowing detail. Now's your chance to explain
the significance of what you've done and subtly *puff yourself,* a practice that is
anathema to most high school students.

Colleges actually want you to highlight your strengths. That's the only way
admissions readers know how to distinguish one student's chemistry award
from another's. The University of Virginia (UVA) application, for example, asks
students to list any significant awards or honors, both academic and extracurricular. But UVA invites students to be specific:

"Please explain any award that we are not likely to understand. For example,
if you earned all-region honors in band, a brief explanation of 'all-region'—'one
of three flutists chosen from twenty schools'—would help us better understand
your achievement."

Following UVA's lead, don't hesitate to emphasize the scope of your accomplishments. All you have to do is play it straight and the details will speak
for themselves, as they did in the following résumé by Sara Gore, who successfully packaged her Hook as a School Leader/Communicator. To emphasize her
Hook and further underscore her get-up-and-go, she included a line with her
entrepreneurial career goals.

SARA MARIE GORE

*Future Goal: To run a business
in the field of fashion or communications*

School Leader & Communicator

Student Body President (Name of public high school), Grade 12

- Elected to lead student body of 1,900+ students.
- Responsible for planning Homecoming; Shark Frenzy; major fund-raising drives for Dollars for Scholars; and Thanksgiving baskets for underprivileged families.

Junior Class Vice President, Grade 11

- Elected by class of 495 students.

Principal's Leadership Award, National Association of Secondary School Principals (NASSP), Grade 12

- Nominated by principal and selected by NASSP as one of 150 student leaders out of 5,400 nominees across the country for this national award.

Co-Captain, Varsity Cheerleaders, Grade 11

- Captain JV, Grade 10.

Teen Court Lead Advisory Council/Prosecutor and Defense Attorney, Grades 9–12

- Helped adjudicate sentencing in the county court system for teens convicted of minor crimes.
- Interviewed defendants; argued cases before jury of peers.
- Member of leadership team that plans and organizes Teen Court program.

National Honor Society, Grades 11–12

President, Model U.N., Grade 12

- Named president of this new school club.

Varsity Swim Team, Grade 12

continued

Vice-President, Multicultural Club, Grade 12; Member, Grade 10

- Helped promote awareness of diversity on campus and sponsored float at Shark Frenzy.

Fashion & the Arts

Teen Fashion Columnist, *Press Journal*, FL, Grade 12

- Wrote a biweekly teen fashion column for local Scripps daily newspaper with a circulation of 80,000+ readers.

International Baccalaureate Extended Essay Topic: "Impact of World War II on Fashion History"

- Writing 4,000-word essay for history category based on primary sources such as *Vogue* magazine and interviews with editors in the fashion press.

Photography Editor, School Yearbook, Grades 10 & 12

- Responsible for photos and copywriting.

Art Camp Counselor, Museum of Art, Grades 10 & 11

- Volunteered 196 service hours as counselor for children aged 3–5, Summer, Gr. 10.
- Volunteered 80 service hours, Summer, Gr. 11.

Teen Writers Workshop, Grade 12

- Member of a group of young working writers who are aiming for publication.
- Met in half-day sessions with professional poets, journalists, novelists, and nonfiction book writers in a program supported by the National Endowment for the Arts and the State of Florida's Division of Cultural Affairs.

Experienced Equestrian

Award-Winning Equestrian, Grades 7–12

- Won more than 50 awards and trophies in local equestrian competitions in such categories as: English, Western, hunter, and dressage.
- Trained horse "Gallant Heart," an Appaloosa, for competitions starting in Grade 7.
- Trained horses beginning in Grade 5.
- Rode three times a week for three hours throughout the year.

Work & Other Interests

Law Office Intern, Summer, Grade 11
• Worked as assistant in office of solo practitioner.

JV Lacrosse, Grades 9 & 10

As you can see, the full range of Sara's achievements come across boldly in her résumé, both because of the categories she chose to highlight, but also because of the rich detail. Any reader could get a snapshot of Sara's strengths simply by reading her résumé. Here was a young woman with recognized leadership abilities who could get things done. With her well-documented fashion interest, she demonstrated flair. With her equestrian exploits, she showed guts and persistence.

In the résumé, Sara's image was sharp and clearly in focus, all because of the details. Coupled with a rank in the top 10 percent of her class, an essay that described her triumph over defeat in a class election, and a portfolio of her fashion columns, the résumé helped open doors for Sara at Virginia Tech, Rollins, Villanova, and Southern Methodist University, which awarded her a merit scholarship. She ultimately matriculated at Villanova.

Similarly, a student with very different interests, David Fell, elaborated on his many musical gigs in New York City in order to highlight his Hook as a professional rock musician. He followed suit in other areas of his résumé, which couldn't help but overwhelm a reader with his accomplishments. Obviously, New York University was duly impressed: David was admitted Early Decision to the Gallatin School, where he may just find himself studying side by side with one of the Olsen twins.

DAVID FELL

Professional Rock Musician

Rock Musician, Robbin' Spectre Band, Grades 11–12
• Composes and performs in an urban Jewish rock/jam band coached by an opera singer from the Metropolitan Opera.
• Plays guitar, piano, drums, and bass.

continued

- Professional CD in production for national distribution.
- Plays a Gibson SG61 Re-Issue.
- Band practices four hours on weekends.

Professional Gigs at New York/New Jersey Venues, Grade 11–Present

- Wild Spirits, 96th Street & 1st Avenue, NYC, October, Grade 12.
- The C-Note, East Village, Summer, Grade 11. (Selected by club as a result of band performance on "Indie Music Explosion," a music Web site.)
- The Lion's Den, Greenwich Village, March, Grade 11.
- The Knitting Factory, Greenwich Village, December, Grade 11. (One of 3 bands chosen by audition.)
- N.J. United Synagogue Youth, Feb., Grade 11 (One of 3 tri-state bands selected.)
- Jewish Community Center, NYC, March, Grade 11. (One of 6 bands selected to perform at convention of 200 students.)

Drummer, School Jazz Band, Grades 10–12

- Meets twice a week after school.
- Focuses on early 20th century jazz and bossa nova.
- Paid performance at private party, Grade 11.

Guitar Teacher, Grades 11–12

- Paid weekly job as guitar teacher to eighth-grade student.

Composer, "Ode to Eliahu," Grade 10; "Ode to La Florida," Grade 10

- Composed four pieces on the computer inspired by the story of the prophet Eliahu for a sophomore project.
- Composed song inspired by summer exchange program in Costa Rica.

Piano/Guitar Practice, Grades 9–12

- Private guitar lessons, Grades 9–10.
- Private piano lessons, Age 4 to Grade 7.

Multicultural Perspective

Exchange Student, Costa Rica, Summer, Grade 10
- Lived with Costa Rican family for five weeks in rural town of La Florida.
- Built community center, working 6–7 hours per day.

Six-Week Israel Immersion, Summer, Grade 11
- Exposed to in-depth lectures and debates by Palestinians and Israelis.
- Panel discussions/small group meetings with young Israeli Arabs during an Arab-Jewish encounter program titled "Minorities and Co-Existence."
- Studied the archaeology of the ancient Talmudic city of Tzippori.
- Hiked 4 days from sea to sea, from Kinneret to the Mediterranean.

Israel Adventure, December, Grade 11
- Spent two weeks in the Negev and Dead Sea regions with high school class.
- Lived in a Bedouin tent; visited several Kibbutzim.

Hebrew/English Dual-Curriculum Academic Program (Name of Jewish Day School), Pre-K–Grade 12
- Rigorous academic program includes Talmud, Hebrew, and Tenach, along with a demanding high school honors curriculum.

Speaks Spanish and Hebrew

Jewish Youth Group Leader/Expert Torah Reader (Name of Synagogue), NY, Grades 7–12
- Reads Torah monthly at teen minion.
- Reads Torah in synagogue annually at Simchat Torah festival.

School Leader & Volunteer

Co–Vice Chairman, Student Senate, Grade 11
- Class Representative, Grade 9.

continued

- Helped establish most of the academic and social rules of the school beginning in freshman year, as a leader of school's first graduating class.

National Youth Leadership Retreat, Grade 9
- One of 15 students chosen to represent school at a national conference.

Captain/Co-Captain, School Basketball Team, Grades 9–11
- Captain, Grade 9; Co-Captain, Grades 10–11.

As David and Sara discovered, a résumé served as a powerful vehicle to package their Hooks and supplement their applications.

But the résumé also played an important role in helping them fill out the applications themselves. Once their résumés were ready to go, it was an easy next step for Sara and David to attack their applications, particularly the all-important "activities list" that is standard on the Common Application and others.

HOOKING THE ACTIVITIES LIST

Almost every application includes an "activities list," a grid of about eight to ten lines that offers you a chance to summarize your most important extracurricular experiences, hobbies, and summer adventures. The grid lets you designate not only the activity but also the years in which you've been involved, the hours per week and weeks per year of your involvement, and the position you've attained. The Common Application's activities list* is arranged like this:

Activity	Grade level or post-secondary 9 10 11 12 PS	Approximate time spent Hours per week	Weeks per year	Positions held, honors won, or letters earned
_____	❑ ❑ ❑ ❑ ❑	_____	_____	_____
_____	❑ ❑ ❑ ❑ ❑	_____	_____	_____
_____	❑ ❑ ❑ ❑ ❑	_____	_____	_____
_____	❑ ❑ ❑ ❑ ❑	_____	_____	_____
_____	❑ ❑ ❑ ❑ ❑	_____	_____	_____
_____	❑ ❑ ❑ ❑ ❑	_____	_____	_____
_____	❑ ❑ ❑ ❑ ❑	_____	_____	_____

* © 2007 The Common Application. Reprinted with permission.

Regardless of whether you are including a résumé with your application, the activities list is an absolute must to help admissions readers size you up at a glance. But like everything else on your application, this list should package your Hook! To that end, when you're ready to fill out your applications, pull out your résumé and replicate the individual line items as closely as possible on the activities list. The very first item on your list should be an activity that communicates your Hook. If possible, the second or third items should be Hook-related as well.

You can follow up with other activities as they appear on the résumé, leading with your secondary Hook or other dominant interests you want to communicate, as well as those that have occupied your time over several years. Note that because applications typically provide separate spots for honors and work experience, you should restrict this list only to school and outside hobbies and pastimes unless otherwise specified.

To give you an idea how this works, take a look at how Sara Gore transposed her résumé to her activities list.

Activity	Grade level 9 10 11 12				Positions held, honors won, or letters earned
Student Council Pres				✓	Elected head of student body
Junior Class Vice-Pres			✓		Elected position
Teen Court					
Prosecutor/Defense	✓	✓	✓	✓	Lead advisory council
Competitive Equestrian	✓	✓	✓	✓	50+ local awards
Multicultural Club		✓		✓	Promotes campus diversity
Newspaper Intern/Yrbk		✓		✓	Fashion columnist/Photo editor
Art Camp Counselor		✓	✓		275+ hours at art museum

On the activities list, Sara led clearly with her main Hook: her role as student body president. Then she hit the reader over the head with her other leadership accomplishments one by one, including her role as junior class vice-president and as a prosecutor and defense attorney with Teen Court. The result leaves no doubt about who Sara is and why a college would want her.

Now consider how David Fell's Hook comes across on his activities list. Keep in mind that as a professional musician, David could highlight his Hook in two places: the activities list *and* the section of the application called "work experience." Here's how he played them both.

Activity	Grade level 9 10 11 12				Positions held, honors won, or letters earned
Urban Jewish Rock Band			✓	✓	Professional gigs in NY & NJ
Guitar/Piano	✓	✓	✓	✓	Private lessons
School Jazz Band		✓	✓	✓	Drummer: Jazz & bossa nova
Composer		✓	✓	✓	Computer & band compositions

Costa Rica/Israel	✓	✓	Built community center
Foreign Exchange			
Student Senate/Class Rep	✓	✓	Co-vice chair student senate
Basketball	✓ ✓	✓	Captain/co-captain, 3 yrs.

With his Hook in play in his activities list, David became more specific under the work experience section of the application, listing the clubs and conventions in New York and New Jersey where his band had performed.

Work Experience

Specific Nature of Work	Employer
Professional Music Gigs	Knitting Factory—Greenwich Village
Professional Music Gigs	The C-Note, East Village, NY
Professional Music Gigs	NJ United Synagogue Youth
Professional Music Gigs	Jewish Community Center

Both David and Sara focused relentlessly on their Hooks when filling out their activities list, and you should too. You don't want to leave anything to the imagination of admissions readers, who sometimes have less than five minutes to skim through an application.

Remember that when it comes to résumés and activities lists, keep it clear and simple: Play to your Hook!

Once you've completed your résumé and filled out your activities list, there's another important area of your application where you can package your Hook: your essays. You can use one of your essays to take your Hook beyond mere description in a list or résumé to a realm of feelings and personal growth.

Sometimes, if you pick the right topic, the essay itself can be your Hook, as your words and emotions connect the reader deep inside to the real you.

CHAPTER SEVENTEEN

Hooking Your Essay

HOOK TIP

Make sure that at least one essay—either your main essay, a "most meaningful activity essay," or a supplemental essay—focuses clearly on your Hook. This is a fundamental strategy in packaging your Hook. And because admissions folks have only a few seconds or minutes at best to read your peerless prose, grab them right from the start with a catchy lead—one that sums up not only the essay, but also your Hook.

When Florida teenager Farris Hassan made a clandestine trip to Iraq in December of his junior year to see for himself how the war was going, he scared his parents, taxed the military, and put his life in imminent danger.

But when he walked in to the Associated Press after two nights at a hotel in Baghdad, the first thing on the lips of one Florida TV anchor reporting the story was: "He's got the makings of a great college essay!"

In one respect, the anchorman had it right. No matter how many apologies Farris made for his reckless act, the truth is that the teen's risky business had the stuff of a winning essay, an essay that had the potential to carry him all the way to his dream schools. However, there's a cautionary note: No student should follow such a dangerous path, and no responsible guidance counselor would suggest this kind of risk-taking is appropriate for beefing up a college application. But putting the dangers aside for a moment, let's examine how an incident like this might play out in an application.

From a college adviser's perspective, Iraq clearly was his Hook. All the student had to do to package it was to tell his story in an essay—and explain the lessons he learned from his experiences and how he might profit from his mistakes and questionable judgment.

His story, as the *New York Times* reported, was simple: Using money saved from stock investments, Farris hoped to write a man-on-the-scene editorial for an immersion journalism class. So he flew to Kuwait, where he took a taxi to the Iraq border. Unable to slip through security, he ended up in Lebanon with family friends, and from there he got a visa for Baghdad. Two days after his arrival, the six-foot teen walked into the Associated Press office to report that he was interested in doing research and humanitarian work.

"I would have been less surprised if little green men had walked in," Patrick Quinn, an editor for the AP, told the *New York Times*.[18]

The AP immediately called the American embassy, which had been alerted by Farris's parents, and soldiers were dispatched to get him. Three weeks after he left Fort Lauderdale, he arrived home, miraculously unscathed.

"My worst fear was that I'd turn on the TV and see my brother and hear someone was killed—a U.S. kid," Farris's twenty-three-year-old brother, Hayder, told the *Times*.[19]

The danger notwithstanding, Farris's Middle Eastern adventures play out like a real-life, international version of *Ferris Bueller's Day Off*—and what admissions officer wouldn't like to read about them? Who wouldn't want to find out what it was like for Farris to sip tea with Kuwaitis in a tent in the desert, or order food from a street vendor in Baghdad using an Arabic phrase book, or interview Christians in Lebanon? Who wouldn't want to feel as though he were right there with him as he tried to get across the Kuwait/Iraq border or as he met with the soldiers who picked him up and put him on a plane for home?

And who wouldn't be moved by his passionate exclamation of love for his native America and the privileges he has here, after seeing what he called "the worst place in the world"?

"When you go back home you have such a new appreciation for all the blessings you have there, and I'm just going to be, like, ecstatic for life," he told the Associated Press before he left Baghdad. All he wanted to do, he said, was "kiss the ground and hug everyone."[20]

If Farris managed to capture even a hint of this spirit and spunk in his main college essay, he would probably have impressed at least some college admissions committees.

But you don't need a life-threatening trip to Iraq to put you over the top in your essay. In fact, some of the best college essays have celebrated small, ordinary things: street basketball, a job as a pizza deliveryman, or a secret obsession with Broadway musicals.

What you do need is passion—and an honesty that lets the reader believe that, for a brief moment, he has peered deeply into your soul. Good college essays have a confessional quality that makes them intensely personal. That doesn't mean you should air all your dirty laundry or give the details of some sordid, sophomoric experiences, such as the girls you dated on a Spanish immersion trip to the Costa del Sol. Rather, you have to reveal who you are in those moments when no one is looking. You need to get inside your own head and heart to reveal on paper your true self.

But how do you find the topic that will let your real personality and interests come through to tantalize admissions committees? The best place to begin is with your Hook.

START WITH YOUR HOOK

Since your goal through the college application process is to communicate your Hook every chance you get, an essay is a critical vehicle for presenting it.

To get started, take a look at the personal essay questions in the Common Application and see which one might best showcase your Hook. The six Common Application personal essay topics* include:

1. *Evaluate a significant experience, achievement, risk you have taken, or ethical dilemma you have faced and its impact on you.*
2. *Discuss some issue of personal, local, national, or international concern and its importance to you.*
3. *Indicate a person who has had a significant influence on you, and describe that influence.*
4. *Describe a character in fiction, a historical figure, or a creative work (as in art, music, science, etc.) that has had an influence on you, and explain that influence.*
5. *A range of academic interests, personal perspectives, and life experiences adds much to the educational mix. Given your personal background, describe an experience that illustrates what you would bring to the diversity in a college community, or an encounter that demonstrated the importance of diversity to you.*
6. *Topic of your choice.*

As you look over the list, ask yourself which of these questions fits your Hook. In the case of Farris Hassan, the Florida teen who risked his neck in Iraq, Question 1 would have fit the bill perfectly, with an emphasis on the risks he had taken.

If your Hook is International Communicator, as it was for Erika Pagano, whom we met in Chapter Five, you might go for Question 2, an issue or "hot topic" essay, where you can demonstrate your virtuosity dealing with newsworthy international topics.

---

*© 2007 The Common Application. Reprinted with permission.

Erika's Hot Topic Essay

Teen Prostitution in Japan

Conflict diamonds, human trafficking, and the proliferation of weapons of mass destruction—all are matters of the utmost concern to the international community. Yet, in the age of the global War on Terror, our focus has shifted toward global matters of defense and protection and away from regional humanitarian issues of special concern to me, such as the protection of vulnerable young women. In particular, on an exchange student program to Japan last summer, I became deeply disturbed by the practice of *Enjo Kosai,* or "compensated dating."

Enjo Kosai, also known as *Enko,* is the twenty-first century's high-tech answer to traditional prostitution. Originating in Japan during the late 1990s, this dangerous and growing trend is taking root worldwide from Leeds, England, to Minneapolis, Minnesota, facilitated by the rapid boom of mobile phone technology.

While *Enko* is, at its most basic level, nothing more than a modern form of prostitution, it differs greatly from its historical predecessors in that most *Enko* participants are school-aged girls from ages 14 to 21. Furthermore, a majority of these young women maintain high grades and pursue advanced levels of education. Unlike traditional sex rings, there is no pimp; girls operate independently, arranging appointments through an intricate web of cell phone–based text messaging. Potential customers and *Enko* girls submit and review profiles on specialized Web sites and contact one another by mobile phone. The typical customer is a middle-class businessman, and the services performed range from a dinner outing to sexual intercourse.

Enjo Kosai is anything but cheap. Girls typically make anywhere from $30 to $800 per night, based on the services performed. With this extra cash, girls can satisfy their increased demand for luxury goods promoted by the pressures of a heavily materialistic society. During my tenure as a participant in the Japan-U.S. Senate Exchange program in Akita, Japan, I asked girls why they chose to do *Enko.* The answer was simple and consistent. "I like the extra cash and the freedom to buy things that I want," stated one peer, a second-year high school student. "It makes me feel important, and it makes me feel accepted." Shock and pity surged through my veins.

Because family members are spending less time with one another, parents often simply aren't aware of their children's actions. When questioned on their whereabouts, girls reply that they have been working, hanging out with friends, or participating in an extracurricular activity. As for parents, they may be lying to themselves, saying that the new designer bag carried by their beaming daughter is no more than "a gift from her high school boyfriend."

Enjo Kosai is such a new phenomenon that world governments are dumbfounded about how to combat the problem. In fact, many law enforcement agencies choose simply to ignore the issue. Since *Enko* is an individual activity as opposed to an organized crime, it is nearly impossible to track, arrest, and prosecute participants. As a result, the grave consequences of *Enko* are overlooked and even disregarded.

Aside from its clashes with conventional morality, the continuation of *Enko* practice worldwide will certainly contribute to the long-term spread of sexually transmitted diseases and HIV/AIDS. *Enko* practice will also result in a higher teenage pregnancy rate, creating an unnecessary, unsafe, and avoidable social burden.

Educational initiatives and stricter prostitution regulations alone may prove powerless against social pressures to obtain luxury goods. I plan to expose the *Enko* crisis both in my senior project video documentary and also in essays and materials I am sending to the media. By increasing awareness of *Enjo Kosai,* perhaps we can force parents and government at the local and national levels to own up to the problem. Only then can we expect meaningful research and real progress toward eliminating this scourge, which threatens increasing numbers of ordinary teenage girls worldwide.

—Erika Pagano, Georgetown, Class of 2008

The key to an issue-oriented essay like Erika's is not merely to discuss an issue as you would for a school essay, but to frame your response in light of how it impacts you *personally.* For example, if your Hook is your passion for the homeless, then be sure to insert not only your intellectual opinions but also your experiences and feelings with respect to the homeless issue. A college essay, even an issue-oriented essay, must still be a deep revelation about *you.*

That principle also holds true if you choose the Common Application's Question 3, which asks you to write about a significant person in your life. Take the case of Amy Smick, a Chinese-American adoptee, who chose to write about her inner struggles searching for her Taiwanese birth mother. The poignant essay, which won her *Guideposts* magazine's Grace Award and a $250 prize, said much more about Amy than about her biological mother. The essay also succeeded in implanting her Chinese ethnic Hook indelibly in readers' minds: She was accepted at almost every college to which she applied, including Trinity, Bates, and the University of Richmond, where she ultimately matriculated with a minor in Chinese.

Because Amy tugged at the heart strings, her essay falls into a category we'll call the "Essay from the Heart." (See Appendix A for additional sample essays in a range of popular categories.)

Amy's Essay from the Heart

SAFETY DEPOSIT

The most influential person in my life I keep locked in the bank. She is safe there, and always available. I think about her often. I wonder if she ever thinks of me or if she still cares.

That person is my biological mother. She was my age, seventeen, and unmarried when she became pregnant with me. Her name was Chiu-Lan Chen. She had many choices over my future, and yet I like to imagine that she lovingly chose the path she thought best for me. She could have kept me as her daughter, but if she had, I would not be who I am today. I would be Chih-yun Chen. And Chih-yun Chen would live in Taiwan, be poor, and speak Chinese.

Or, she could have taken the easy way out and had an abortion. My life would never have even started. By the grace and guidance of God, she decided to carry me for nine months and make another couple's dreams come true. She not only gave my adoptive parents the gift of a child whom they could never have had on their own, but she also gave me a life of endless possibilities. By her act of selflessness in a complicated situation, she gave me the chance to make something of myself. She gave me a new beginning. Chiu-Lan Chen is my hero.

Ever since I was capable of logic I have wondered exactly who Chiu-Lan Chen was, where she lived, or what she would look like face-to-face. I have wondered if I ever passed her accidentally in a crowded store or at the airport. If I did run into her somewhere, would I recognize her?

A simple black-and-white head shot is all I have left of her. It was taken right before I was born. Because it is so priceless to me, I keep it in a bank vault, in a safe deposit box where people usually lock up expensive jewelry, documents, or valuables for safekeeping. When I was young, from the time I was four years old until I was ten, I ventured into the bank once a month with my adoptive mom just so I could stare at the picture. I looked at my mother's face and I imagined over and over again what it would be like to meet her. I would dream that she would be so happy to see me that she would cry and embrace me, as though she had been searching for me since she gave me away.

Those were my fairy tale dreams. Now that I'm seventeen and more realistic, I'm not sure I want to meet her—not right now. I'm simply scared to know the truth. I have no idea if she was raped, or simply careless. I don't know if she really wanted a good life for me or didn't have the money to have an abortion. Whatever the answer, I prefer just to look at her photo and think about her sacrifice. My mother carried a child out of wedlock as a teenager with no money in a traditional society that offered her only unbearable humiliation, shame, and pain. I feel nothing but compassion for this woman whom I love and admire from a distance.

Although I am reluctant to meet Chiu-Lan Chen, my attachment to her photo only grows. I no longer go to the vault and open the safe deposit box, but instead, I photocopied the picture and placed it in my wallet, in the smallest, tightest pocket, where it is nearly impossible for a mother to fall out.

—*Amy Smick, University of Richmond, Class of 2007*

Although Amy's essay fit clearly within a specific essay category, not every essay topic is so clear-cut. If you have a story to tell and are undecided about how to position it, go with Question 6: *Topic of Your Choice.* That was a perfect choice for David Blake to showcase both his Hook as a freelance eBay entrepreneur and his ironic sense of humor. But don't even try an essay like this if you're not funny. David, who is now at Washington and Lee, had a way with words and the moxie to pull it off.

David's Humorous Essay

ADVENTURES IN EBAY

My penchant for Ty Beanie Babies subsided by age eleven, after my peers deemed it "immature" to have such a collection. Ergo, I was left with a couple of hundred furry creatures stuffed into a trunk. About then, the subject of money infiltrated my young brain. But though I hoarded every cent, mowed lawns, sold lemonade, and scoured couches, the result was mere "chump change." I faced a situation I didn't understand how to resolve.

Then a thought struck me: Though I had jumped off the Beanie Baby bandwagon, many still collected them. The answer to my financial crisis seemed simple: sell my collection. But while my supply was large, the demand at school had diminished. I failed to sell a single Beanie Baby to another student. Next, I ran an advertisement in the local newspaper, only to be disappointed again.

Then my father mentioned an infant company, eBay, which enabled anyone to buy or sell over the Internet. Within hours I logged onto eBay's Web site, created a username and password, and set the starting bid at $20. The auction closed five days later without a single bid.

After several failed attempts, I inserted a picture of Magic the Beanie Baby and lowered the reserve price to $15. Five days later, the auction closed for $15.78. I promptly emailed the winner, informed her of my $5 shipping charge, and gave her my name and address. After the check arrived, my mother was in a state of shock. Though she was convinced I had done something illegal, I soon convinced her otherwise and asked for a ride to the post office to mail off Magic.

Mastery of eBay ensued. I sold every Beanie Baby, repaid my mother's initial costs, and ended with a net profit of several hundred dollars and a flawless eBay feedback rating. A trusted eBay seller by the time I was twelve, I sold everything I could find in the house and then began to sell items for other people at a 10 percent commission. Whether it was a mint 1961 Topps set of baseball cards for $3750, or a set of Titleist golf clubs for $800, I always obtained top dollar.

The amount I've earned, while sizeable, in no way compares to the lessons I've learned, including the resolve that I'll never turn away from a potential opportunity just because I don't understand it at first.

—*David Blake, Washington and Lee, Class of 2010*

Although the personal essay is the optimum place to promote your Hook, you may discover a more compelling story you'd like to tell in the five hundred words or less required for this essay. If so, then be absolutely sure that you write about your Hook somewhere else—either in a supplemental essay, or in the Common Application's short answer question, sometimes expressed on other applications as the "most meaningful activity" essay.

MAKE YOUR HOOK MEANINGFUL

The Common Application's short answer question asks: *Please briefly elaborate (150 words or fewer) on one of your activities (extracurricular, personal activities, or work experience).*

This brief essay can be a very effective tool for communicating your Hook. Because it's meant to be short and sweet, the short answer gives you a chance to summarize your Hook—and explain *why* the activity is meaningful. The "why" can be especially important, as you'll see in the last paragraph of an essay for New York University written by David Fell, whose Hook was music. (See David's main essay in Appendix A.)

David's Short Answer Essay

In November of my junior year, I started a band when a local Jewish youth group, "Downtown Kehilah," sponsored a Battle of the Bands event. I had been playing music for over twelve years, including piano for eight years and also drums and guitar. But even though I had always had a love for music and an affinity for learning new instruments, I had never considered playing as part of a group—and apparently neither had the other members of the band that I hastily assembled.

Despite our initial nervousness, our first performance was a success; as a result, we became determined to improve our skills, both instrumentally and compositionally. Now, a year later, our group, Robbin' Spectre, is on its way up. We have already had professional gigs in the East Village and West Village, and we have been coached in musical technique by an opera singer from the Metropolitan Opera.

Although we often get offers to do performances at new venues and are drawing bigger and bigger crowds, the greatest benefit for me is the community the band has created. Through composing and performing with Robbin' Spectre, we have created special, unique relationships within the band and have also made firm, supportive friends on the outside. Performing with the band has enriched my high school experiences to an indescribable degree and is, without question, the most meaningful activity in my life.

—*David Fell, NYU, Class of 2010*

Nicole Dubowitz, the op-ed writer who was profiled in Chapter Eleven, focused on her writing Hook for her short answer essay. She made sure to include a subtle reference to her first op-ed article in the *Baltimore Sun*.

How Nicole Found Meaning in Writing

The most fulfilling of all my extracurricular activities is, and always has been, writing. I write to express myself as a thoughtful teenager, a reflective artist, and an active citizen. Since I could pick up a pencil, writing has been my outlet of choice. Beginning in the fourth grade, I've kept a journal to record everything from daily events to questions I've been musing over. All of my struggles, triumphs, and hopes reside in my journals, and when I look back on them later, I am often amused, grateful for the passing of time and my newfound perspectives. If my house caught on fire, my journals would be the first possession I would save.

I'm also drawn to creative writing and have written short stories, poems and prose. Always looking to improve my writing, I try to emulate the styles of writers like Sylvia Plath, Edith Wharton, and Billy Collins. I love writing about ordinary things in a way that makes them appear beautiful and interesting.

Lately, I've also taken up writing about societal issues that are important to me. After having an article published in the *Baltimore Sun*, I was thrilled to discover that other people enjoy reading what I have to say and sensed my passion. I like to think that writing about the world is the first step in doing some good in it.

—Nicole Dubowitz, Trinity College, Class of 2010

The Common Application suggests a 150-word maximum for the short answer question. But if you have something important to say, don't be afraid to run a little longer as Nicole and David did. But keep it short: No more than three-quarters of a page or a page double-spaced. (Caution: If a college you're applying to insists on a precise word or character count, be sure to abide by the rules! Also, if you're using an on-line application other than the Common Application, stick to the maximum word or character count, or you might just find that part of your essay has been cut off.)

If you're using the Common Application on-line, be sure to do a "Print Preview" that will enable you to see exactly what the colleges will see. Double-check to make sure that your entire essay prints out exactly as you wrote it.

Keep in mind that you can use the Common Application's short answer essay for other colleges, such as Notre Dame's Section 8, "A Final Note," which invites applicants to submit additional information in 150 words or less: *Have we missed anything? A special interest in your intended major or research you have conducted? A talent or interest you have not had the opportunity to describe? Let us know.*

Don't be concerned if you're still in a quandary at this point about finding the right essay topics. This part of the application process has most students sweating bullets. One student procrastinated for so many weeks that his mother grounded him on weekends until he got his essays finished. Another holed up in his dad's office for two days straight, knocking off essays one after the other.

"Writing essays was the most difficult part of the process for me," confessed Kaitlin Connell, the Johns Hopkins student whose political Hook was profiled in Chapter Seven. "It's not something you can sit down and write right away. Pick something you're passionate about, and put some thought into it," she advised.

According to Dr. Kevin McCarthy, a popular professor emeritus at the University of Florida, there's a simple way to overcome essay phobia: "Start brainstorming."

BRAINSTORM WITH DR. KEVIN McCARTHY

Sit down right now by yourself or with your parents and ask a few provocative questions Dr. McCarthy has developed during his more than thirty-six years as a professional writer and English professor.

Dr. Kevin McCarthy's Essay Topic Triggers

- Have you ever overcome grief over the loss of someone/something? What did you learn from the experience that you can now use?
- Did some experience overseas or in another state have an important/dramatic effect on you? Sometimes the mundane can be more important than visiting a great museum, e.g., trying to order a hamburger in another language, trying to communicate with a taxi-cab driver who does not speak English, looking for a bathroom in a hurry, avoiding the weird-looking food your hosts presented you without offending them.
- Did a bad experience (getting robbed or rear-ended in your car or getting cut from an athletic team) teach you something worthwhile?
- Can you find some other intriguing topic that will help you avoid themes like "God is the center of my life," and "Everything I learned, I learned from sports"?

Dr. McCarthy is especially wary about these last two essay topic no-no's: preaching about your religion—any religion—and using sports as a metaphor for life. Unless you're applying to a school with a religious orientation, spirituality can sink your ship. When it comes to sports, an athletic experience, such as your incredible gumption overcoming an injury or your life sitting on the bench on the varsity basketball team, can offer an opportunity to showcase your inner qualities—*if* you write about what's inside your head. But unless you can add a fresh twist to these topics, follow Dr. McCarthy's advice and steer clear of them. (See Appendix A for samples of two sports essays that worked.)

Once you have a topic that you can run with for your main essay, then it's time to do a first draft. And a *first* draft is what you should write, with the expectation that you will rewrite and edit until you produce a final draft.

"Never, ever send in the first draft," says Dr. McCarthy. Emphasizing the importance of proofreading, Dr. McCarthy suggests that you get a second set of eyes—from either a teacher, guidance counselor, or parent—to be sure that you don't have any typos, grammatical errors, or redundancies.

GOT WRITER'S BLOCK? JUST GET STARTED

There's no such thing as writer's block. There are only writers who won't get started. So sit down at your computer—and go for it!

The key to writing good essays is to begin with a punchy "lead" that communicates your theme clearly, continue with several points or anecdotes that support your theme, and end with a conclusion that echoes the lead.

What's critical in college essays it to communicate who you are—and the lessons you've learned from experiences and individuals. Colleges want to know how you think and *feel*, especially when it comes to overcoming obstacles. This is your chance to let it all hang out, to let your passions and your voice speak more loudly than you might face-to-face. If you want your college essays to "sing," follow these fundamental writing rules:

Writing Rule 1: Start with a punchy lead. Your lead should draw in the reader and make the person want to keep reading. You might begin with a lively line or two that establishes your theme, or an anecdotal lead that summarizes your topic. But in either case, make your theme crystal-clear from the outset. Admissions readers don't have time to guess what the essay is all about. It's up to you to tell them—and tell them fast.

Writing Rule 2: Let your story unfold. Think in terms of telling a story—*your* story—and you might just find that the essay rolls out effortlessly in two or three paragraphs.

Writing Rule 3: Use the "I" word. Throw out everything you've been taught about writing academic essays for school, and write in the first person, using the "I" word liberally. Get into your own head and heart as you write, and let it rip.

Writing Rule 4: Be specific. Details bring an essay to life, so don't hesitate to expand on the particulars. Give examples that illustrate your points, and feel free to use dialogue for dramatic effect.

Writing Rule 5: Show how you've grown. An analysis of the lessons you've learned, particularly the ways you've grown or changed, is critical in college essays. Such self-reflection will help admissions readers understand who you are and why they should admit you.

Writing Rule 6: Echo your lead in the conclusion. It's important to leave the reader with a take-away that sends a message. That's especially important if you're writing about your Hook. By echoing your lead with just a word or two in the final paragraph, you can reiterate your theme *and* give the impression that your essay is brilliantly organized. Of course, you shouldn't just restate your lead but should use it as a springboard to state a broader generalization or insight about your theme.

To see how these five rules work in practice, analyze the following essays by three crackerjack writers who hit pay dirt with their college essays. Note that each of these students used a different lead format to grab the reader right from the start.

David Blake, whom we met on page 127, used an anecdotal lead to set the stage for this "obstacle" essay on overcoming a fear of public speaking. As his story unfolds, we can feel his pain and triumph—and so did the admissions committee at Washington and Lee, which admitted him Early Decision.

David Blake: Leading with an Anecdote

My hands shook uncontrollably. My heart pounded out of my chest. Breathing became difficult. But before I got cold feet, my name was called. Somehow, I managed to stand. I walked across the stage, feeling naked until I found security behind the podium. I had rehearsed countless times, but I still felt unprepared as 800 pairs of eyes burned into me.

Ironically, I had always been the talkative one. I loved being the center of attention. But when it came to public speaking, I was petrified. If someone took the initiative away from me and designated me as the cynosure, my face turned bright red and tremors rippled through my body.

But everything changed during my freshman year after I wrote that speech. Using touches of satire, I offered my own "five point plan" to eliminate stereotypes. I practiced the speech ad nauseam and managed to present it to my English class without breaking down. But I made a terrible mistake: I did too well. I was one of three people chosen from 90 freshmen to speak to the entire school.

When I looked over the assembly, I saw my mother and father in the back of the theater and the senior class preparing to judge my every word. As I began, a strange calm came over me. Note cards became unnecessary. When I paused at one point, everyone roared with laughter. I was euphoric, feeling I had tapped into some ultimate source of power. I teased the audience by pausing before punch lines and watching as they hung on my every word. I even left the refuge of the podium and ventured out into the audience, raising my voice to compensate for the lack of a microphone. As soon as the speech had started, it abruptly ended, followed by a standing ovation. I had won the ninth-grade speech competition.

My self-confidence shot through the roof, as teachers, seniors, parents, and peers showered me with praise. To this day, whenever the term "stereotype" pops up, someone will exclaim, "Stereotypes are the thorn on the rose of America!"—a catchphrase from my speech. Since conquering this obstacle, I can't get enough of public speaking. I have also learned the broader lesson not to allow feelings of inadequacy to suppress my potential for success. Now, when an opportunity to speak arises, I don't give in to fear; instead, I think "carpe diem!"

—*David Blake, Washington and Lee, Class of 2010*

David wrapped up his essay with a feel-good inspirational ending that echoed his theme. In the next essay, Courtney Moore's take-charge personality and ambitious goals infused her writing from beginning to end. Using a straightforward lead that clearly identified her as a future businesswoman, Courtney left no doubt with the admissions officers at Wellesley, Vanderbilt, and Boston College that she would be a mover and shaker. Vanderbilt got her.

Courtney Moore: Playing It Straight from Start to Finish

I found my future in a Lilly Pulitzer shop in Vero Beach, Florida. Although Lilly Pulitzer began by selling vibrant dresses for a few dollars at a lemonade stand in West Palm Beach, her stores are now a multimillion-dollar nationwide operation. Her example and my experiences as retail sales associate at The Lazy Daisy in Vero Beach, the nation's number one Lilly Pulitzer shop, have inspired me to establish my own business.

Over four years I've seen it all, from shoplifters, to women squeezing into children's clothing (in an attempt to pay half price), to haggling customers: "If I buy one, may I get the second for free?" To this day I can remember my first day at work, dreading five o'clock because the day had been so much fun. I couldn't fall asleep because I was so excited to get to work the next day.

Even today, nothing pleases me more than helping a customer choose the "perfect" dress for a wedding, dance, or graduation. But perhaps the most exciting thing is using my imagination to develop powerful selling techniques, such as wearing a vibrant, knee-length halter dress as part of a sales approach. With this saleswoman-as-model strategy, we sold out the item in only one day.

The retail business involves a curious combination of making the customer happy and the business a success. To this end, I warmly greet customers and ask if I can be of assistance, but then I allow them to browse undisturbed. Only after the shopper emerges from the dressing room do I begin my carefully selected sales pitch. Most of the time, customers viewing themselves in the mirrors ask my opinion of the apparel: "Does this look right?" "Am I too fat in this?" An ongoing challenge is to be honest so that they don't leave with the wrong purchase, but also to urge them to buy just the right sweater, shoes, or handbag.

For me The Lazy Daisy is not only a clothing shop but a delightful departure from the IB homework, school leadership, public service work, babysitting, and coaching that make up my hectic life. More than anything, working at The Lazy Daisy has revealed what I would like to do when I "grow up": be a Lilly Pulitzer and own an extremely successful, people-serving business.

—*Courtney Moore, Vanderbilt, Class of 2009*

Sometimes all it takes to set a mood is a teaser that sums up the theme in one sentence, as James Pangilinan, the Wesleyan student profiled in Chapter Nine, discovered in this essay. His catchy opening gave a flavor of his offbeat topic and dreamy mood from the get-go. His artful conclusion left the reader yearning for a taste of James's favorite pastime.

James Pangilinan: Winning with a One-Line Lead

While many go to parties and the movies for pleasure, I find bliss in tea.

I dislike neither the party's conviviality nor the movie's excitement, but both confine me to a set time, place, and company. Tea emancipates me from these limitations. In the individual sense, it arouses the senses: the fragrance clears my mind, the taste clears my palate, and the warmth fills my soul from within. In the communal sense, tea parties bring with them good discourse and dear friendships. And similar to movie genres and themes, tea has its various, wide selection.

But what is it that gives tea its emancipating qualities?

When I go to my local teahouse and drink a fine cup of tea, my being is transported throughout the world. When I pick a type of tea to drink, my decision spans three different continents and many more subcontinents. Steeping the tea, I contemplate the issues and news of the day. I smell the tea and finally sip the divine nectar. The warmth fills my body and releases my soul, gradually working me into sweat.

In taking a simple sip, I am released from the moment's confines, as I visit the tea fields of Assam or smile over the political outcry of poorly disguised Revolutionary War Bostonians. After another gentle sip, I witness in my mind's eye the delicate tea ceremonies of Japan or have my fortune told to me in China. I remember my first time drinking tea in Cambridge at the Orchard, where Ted Hughes and Sylvia Plath fell in love, and where Watson and Crick took time off from their DNA work. Yet again, with another sip, on the foothills of majestic Kilimanjaro, I am drinking *chai* with my fellow teachers at the Mwereni Primary School.

With my final sip, I debate with dear friends back in our humble teashop where next in the world to go.

—James Pangilinan, Wesleyan University, Class of 2009

These three essays share more than strong leads, clear organization, and memorable conclusions. They also avoid typos, misspellings, or egregious grammatical mistakes that might divert the reader's attention from the main messages that David, Courtney, and James tried to communicate. As a result, their essays were easy to read—and easy to remember.

In fact, James Pangilinan's essay was so memorable that when he introduced himself to an admissions officer prior to an interview at one Boston-area university, the man exclaimed, "Oh, you're the guy who wrote about tea!"

But no matter how good your résumé and essays may be, they could have limited impact if you lack the "numbers" to go with them. And that means the highest standardized test scores and grades you can achieve.

CHAPTER EIGHTEEN

Scoring Bigger with Test Scores

HOOK TIP

Contrary to the hype from many colleges, your standardized test scores do count—and they count a lot. At a time when more than 40 percent of all high schools either do not rank or refuse to report rankings, many colleges are forced to focus on test scores to separate the best students from the merely good ones.[21] But don't despair. You can put the power back in your own hands by prepping for the PSAT, SAT, SAT Subject Tests, and ACT.

The hew and cry around the country over the "mean old SAT" has created lots of news, from the controversial writing section introduced in 2005, to the egregious scoring errors discovered in March 2006. That's when the College Board notified colleges that the scores of 4,000 students who had taken the test the previous October had been misreported. In sixteen cases, the scores should have been more than 200 points higher, according to the College Board.[22] The culprit was later identified as a technical snafu in the score scanning process, due to "abnormally high moisture" in the answer sheets.[23]

But regardless of the controversies surrounding the test, the bottom line for you is that for the foreseeable future, the SAT is here to stay. And so, your best approach is to close your ears to the whining and deal with it.

Here's how Tom Parker, Dean of Admissions at Amherst, summed up the current testing realities in a letter to guidance counselors on Amherst's Web site not long ago: ". . . Average SAT and ACT scores, rightly or wrongly, tend to be the *lingua franca* of academic quality, or the closest thing we have to a common standard or means of comparison. . . ."[24]

Clearly, until colleges come up with a new means of evaluating worthy candidates, you're stuck with the tests. That's the bad news.

The good news is that the tests are actually *under your control*. Like everything else on your college application, your standardized test scores can be packaged by you to help you put your best foot forward. Here are five basic strategies for packaging your scores:

1. Prep for the tests.
2. Take both the SAT and the ACT *with* writing.
3. Play off the ACT against the SAT.
4. Take the SAT Subject Tests soon after you've taken the course.
5. Apply to colleges with flexible test reporting policies.

Now, let's take a closer look at each of these packaging strategies.

STRATEGY 1: PREP FOR THE TESTS

There is absolutely no reason why you shouldn't prep for your standardized tests, and that includes the PSAT. Start prepping for the PSAT in the summer before junior year and continue prepping for the SAT and ACT through the fall of senior year. Prepping with a competent tutor *can* make a difference. You can do it on your own, using books with real tests published by the College Board, which administers the PSAT, SAT, and SAT Subject Tests. Or you can prepare for the ACT, using books with real ACT tests. You can also get ready by using programs on-line or specialized software available at local office supply stores. Or you can take a group class. Or, perhaps best of all, you can hire a *competent* tutor, one who has a reputation in your area for helping students increase their scores.

But whatever you do, please prep. Perceptive students all over the country have learned that all of these tests are coach-able. Why not give yourself a leg up by learning the techniques—along with the math, vocabulary, and grammar—that will enable you to take your scores as high as they can go?

Prep for the PSAT: The PSAT administered in the fall of your *junior year* serves as the National Merit Scholarship Qualifying Test (NMSQT). Earning high scores on the PSAT will send a loud signal to colleges about your capabilities and could set you up for scholarships. To catch the eye of admissions officers, you should at least aim to make the first cut as a Commended Student. Keep in mind that the cutoff for Commended Student has been going up year by year (it was 203 for students who took the test in October 2005, and 202 the previous year) and so a point here or there gained by a little prepping could just push you over the top.

Even better, your scores could be high enough to win you a place as a National Merit Semifinalist, an honor that carries great weight at colleges and can be listed under "honors and awards" on your college applications. The cutoff for this category differs from state to state and from year to year. To get a ballpark idea of what you need to shoot for, check with your guidance counselor to determine the score for your state in the previous year, or check the NMQST Web site.

Semifinalists have a shot at becoming National Merit Finalists on the basis of an application, SAT exams, an essay, and recommendations. But since the final results aren't announced until February of senior year, your ticket to admission to schools with Early Action or Early Decision could be your status as a Semifinalist.

But don't stop prepping after the PSAT. Keep hitting the books to be ready for the SAT and ACT.

Prep for the SAT and ACT. Plan to commit at least a half-hour a day to studying for the SAT and ACT, starting in the fall of junior year. Don't stop prepping until after you get scores that satisfy you. That means you may keep testing through January of your senior year—or later, if necessary. Some scholarship programs (such as Florida Bright Futures) and colleges (such as Baylor) peg scholarship levels to SAT or ACT scores, and an increase in your scores as late as spring of senior year could in some cases put extra money in your pocket.

Although there is some overlap in content, because the SAT and ACT are different tests, it's important to pay attention to the differences. The SAT has three basic sections: 1.) Critical Reading, which is driven by vocabulary tested in a sentence completion part and a reading skills part; 2.) Math; and 3.) Writing, which includes a multiple choice segment (grammar/usage/rhetoric) and an essay.

The ACT has four basic sections: 1.) English, a grammar/usage/rhetoric portion that is very punctuation oriented; 2.) Reading, which puts a premium on speed; 3.) Math; and 4.) Science Reasoning, which tests your ability to read and analyze data and graphs. The ACT also offers an optional writing test, but you should regard it as mandatory. So, every time you sign up for the ACT, sign up for the ACT *with* writing.

When you are prepping for either test, don't ignore prepping for the essays. For both the SAT and ACT, it's critical that you practice answering the question types posed by the test-makers. That may seem obvious, but many students lose points on the essay score because they don't answer the question. SAT questions tend to be more philosophical or theoretical, such as, "The world is getting better and better. Agree or disagree." ACT questions tend to be more practical, such as "Should uniforms be required in high school?"

These essays are not the time for you to get creative or tricky. Speed is at a premium for SAT and ACT graders, so you need to move fast to establish a point of view that's clear and organized. Start with a clear lead that states your theme, build on the theme with three or four specific examples, and end with a strong conclusion that sums up your theme.

Writing "long" will get you points so long as you don't become redundant; so will providing detailed examples. If you practice writing a few essays ahead of time, you'll learn to expand on your ideas and develop several strong anecdotes or examples, which you will probably be able to weave into many other essay topics that may come your way on test day.

Once you've prepped in short spurts, sit down at your dining room table before the actual tests and give yourself timed practice tests, taken from the real ACT and SAT test books. (Actual tests prepared by the official SAT and ACT test-makers are better than those designed by unofficial test-prep services.) This practice may cost you a few mornings at the ball field or mall, but it could gain you precious extra points on the exams.

STRATEGY 2: TAKE BOTH THE SAT AND ACT

If you want to reduce your stress levels, take both the SAT and ACT. You may be stronger at one than the other, but you'll never know which test is best for you until you take both.

A good rule of thumb with the SAT is to take the test two or three times: once in the spring of junior year, and once or twice in the fall of senior year. The SAT reports that the average student who takes a test more than once can increase the combined Critical Reading and Math score by approximately 30 points.[25] Since most colleges claim that they'll mix-and-match your top SAT scores from all sittings, you'll be able to give yourself room to improve with the fall scores. (Note that schools in the University of California system require your best SAT from one sitting.)

But keep in mind that once you have your SAT scores sent to colleges from the College Board, the admissions committees will see *all* of your previous SAT test results, no matter how high or low they were. You can't pick and choose which SAT scores to report because the SAT reports all of them. That's why it may be best to put a cap on the number of SATs you take, so that your perennial weakness in math, let's say, doesn't stick out like a sore thumb.

When it comes to the ACT, on the other hand, you should take the ACT *with* writing as often as you can. Typically, colleges like to see your top composite score from one test date for the ACT, though this practice may be changing. Because the ACT sends colleges *only* the test scores that you choose to report, you can take the test numerous times without fear that a strong composite score will be compromised by a weaker one.

STRATEGY 3: PLAY OFF THE ACT AGAINST THE SAT

The optimum way to package your test scores is to send colleges your best, and only your best, scores. In order to do that, you need to get out of the SAT-only mind-set.

The idea that the SAT is the be-all and end-all for admission is passé. Most colleges these days say that they will accept either the SAT or the ACT, and you need to take their pronouncements at face value. In fact, the ACT is becoming so popular that many leading colleges and universities, including Amherst, Wesleyan, Penn, and Yale, accept the ACT in lieu of the SAT and SAT Subject Tests. Put another way, you don't even need SATs to apply to these schools.

What this means is that you should feel perfectly free *not* to report your SAT scores to most colleges if your ACT scores are better. The ACT could be your ace in the hole, so start thinking like a winner and be selective about which test and which scores to report.

To sum up: If your SATs are better than any of your ACT composites, send the colleges your SATs. If one or two of your ACT composites are better than your top SAT scores, send only the ACT.

Finally, what's the exact procedure for submitting your scores? Remember that most colleges require that you have test scores sent directly from the testing agency. For the SAT, it's the College Board. For the ACT it's the American College Test.

For maximum control over your scores, check to see if your high school routinely attaches SAT or ACT scores to your transcript. If it does, ask your guidance counselor to remove the scores from your transcript, so that the colleges see only the scores you choose to send from the appropriate testing agency. The scores are *yours,* and your goal should be to report only those tests that put you in the best light.

STRATEGY 4: TAKE SAT SUBJECT TESTS SOON AFTER A COURSE

If you're applying to a highly selective college that requires SAT Subject Tests, then be sure to take two to three tests while the subject is fresh in your mind.

For example, some students choose to take the American History Subject

Test in May of the year in which they are taking AP U.S. History, so that they can study for both tests simultaneously. Others opt to take the Subject Tests in June, when school is over or nearly over. Still others like to wait until the fall, so they can bone up over the summer.

But if you possibly can, take the tests when you're coming off a related course: at that point you're more likely to be up to speed. As you may know, you can take up to three Subject Tests at one sitting. You can even change or drop a choice on the day of the exam.

When it comes to SAT Subject Test requirements, colleges are all over the lot. A few highly selective colleges, such as Harvard, Princeton, and MIT, require three SAT Subject Tests, regardless of whether you submit the SAT or ACT. Dartmouth, Columbia, Williams, and the flagship colleges of the University of California system (UCLA, UC Berkeley, UC–San Diego, for example) are among those that require two. Then there are such schools as Penn, Brown, Swarthmore, Amherst, and Boston College, which are very student friendly: they require two SAT Subject Tests if you submit the SAT, but none if you submit the ACT with writing.

In the final category are colleges such as Georgetown, Northwestern, and the University of Virginia, which *strongly recommend* but don't require SAT Subject Tests. But be warned: If a college gives a recommendation, you should consider it a requirement. Although students have been admitted to colleges like these without SAT Subject Tests, in this competitive admissions climate, you need every advantage. Why take a chance? As the Nike ad says, "Just do it!"

In any case, check the specific SAT Subject Test requirements of each school carefully so that you don't get caught short. Colleges can change their policies overnight, as Boston University did in 2005, when it instituted a requirement for two SAT Subject Tests for students submitting the SAT. (The ACT with writing will work in lieu of all SAT tests.) Other schools are very specific about which SAT Subject Tests you should take and the deadline for taking them. (In the University of California system, for example, if you submit math, it must be Math 2. If you're applying for Northwestern's Honors Program in Medical Education, you'll need Math 2 plus chemistry. If you're applying to Columbia's Fu Foundation School of Engineering and Applied Science, you must submit a math and either physics or chemistry.)

If you neglected to take SAT Subject Tests in the spring of junior year or earlier, you can still take them in the fall—as late as November for some Early Action and Early Decision programs, and as late as December for most regular decision programs. You may have to select "Rush" so that the scores meet application deadlines. To find out your options, check with the admissions office of each school.

One word of warning on SAT Subject Tests: As with the SAT, you cannot pick and choose which tests to report. Once you give the go-ahead for the College Board to send your Subject Test results to colleges, every SAT you've ever taken—whether it was the Biology Subject Test you took in ninth grade when you sleep-walked through the exam, or the SAT you took in January when you had a 102-degree fever—will show up on the report.

That's why you should report your SAT Subject Tests and SATs judiciously as part of your packaging program. If your scores are great, you have no problem. If they are so-so and your ACTs are considerably better, you might consider applying only to those schools that accept the ACT in lieu of the SAT and SAT Subject Tests.

STRATEGY 5: APPLY TO COLLEGES WITH FLEXIBLE TEST REPORTING POLICIES

There's a movement afoot to give students greater flexibility in choosing which scores to report. Middlebury and Hamilton are among the colleges that put the choice in your hands. At some of these colleges, your Advanced Placement or International Baccalaureate exams by themselves can get you in the door while at others, a demonstrated competency in verbal and quantitative skills from a variety of tests can be a ticket to admission.

Middlebury College, for example, has had a three-part flexible reporting policy for years. Students can submit scores from either 1.) the SAT; 2.) three tests mixed or matched from among AP tests, IB exams, and SAT Subject Tests; or 3.) the ACT with writing.

At Hamilton, you can report your scores in a variety of ways. The school will accept the SAT or ACT (composite only), or a combination of three tests of your choice that show your verbal and math proficiency. These range from the AP English Language exam to the SAT Subject Test in chemistry. If you're confused about which tests to report, Hamilton gives you another alternative: Report *all* your test scores and the admissions committee will choose the tests that are in your "best interest."

Since requirements differ from school to school, be sure to check with the admissions office of each college for specifics.

THE "SCORE OPTIONAL" OPTION

One way to circumvent SAT and ACT scores altogether is to apply to schools that are score or test "optional." Some of the country's most selective schools, including Bowdoin, Bates, and Mount Holyoke, have

continued

eliminated their standardized test requirements, giving students the choice of whether or not to report scores. In recent years, College of the Holy Cross, Providence College, Dickinson College, Gettysburg College, Union College, and Drew University have jumped on the bandwagon.

A study of the effects of the score-optional policy at Mount Holyoke determined that there were "no meaningful differences in academic performance between students who did not submit scores and those who did," according to the college's president, Joanne Creighton, writing in an op-ed piece in the Los Angeles Times.[26]

So if your scores are fair to middling yet you have a strong academic record and a compelling Hook, why not consider including some "score-optional" schools in your list of colleges? Some schools, such as Mount Holyoke, Union, and Drew, require a graded paper in lieu of standardized exams. Others require nothing extra at all.

Of course, these "score-optional" schools will accept scores, if you choose to report them. But the option is yours.

What this all comes down to is that your scores do not control you. Whether you take the SAT, SAT Subject Tests, or ACT, you can package your scores on your application to show yourself to best advantage. The choice of how you report your scores is up to you.

But your test scores aren't the only numbers you can package for your applications. You also have considerable control over your transcript through the all-important admission factor known as the grade point average (GPA).

Chapter Nineteen

Making the Grade

Hook Tip

Even your GPA can be packaged to increase your odds of admission to one of your favorite schools. This is one area of your application over which you have almost total control. Therefore, it's up to you—and only you—to max out on your grades, especially in junior and senior year. Get your teachers invested in your success. And remember: Absolutely no Cs!

These days, terrific grades are merely a starting point. Valedictorians and salutatorians alike are getting wait-listed or rejected right and left at Penn, Yale, and Harvard, while those not much further down the pecking order are getting the ax at hot schools such as Boston College, Tufts, and Vanderbilt.

There are still open doors at hundreds of excellent colleges across the country for B and even C students. But no matter what your college goals, in order to put yourself in a position to have significant choices, you've simply got to make the grade—and that means shooting for As.

"But I'm a B student!" you may protest. "No matter what I do, I can't do any better."

An honest look at your study habits may tell you differently. Perhaps you are studying "long" but not "smart," such as by failing to make outlines of the material in a given subject or by cramming for tests rather than studying every day. Maybe you hold back from jumping into the debate in class. Or maybe you've typecast yourself as a B student and, with your confidence level at a low ebb, you have simply stopped trying.

Now is the time to change. It's never too late to pull out all the stops academically and strive for the best grades you can. Make the assumption that you can get As, and you just might do it. Not only will you increase the odds for admission to a school you love, but you'll also be setting yourself up nicely for success in college, just as Josh the photographer did in Chapter One.

To help you get focused, here are some grade-packaging dos and don'ts that could help you get a leg up in admissions. These tips aren't new. You've heard most of them before from your parents, your teachers, and your guidance counselors. But if you want choices at admissions time, you can't afford to ignore them any longer.

PACKAGING DOS AND DON'TS FOR YOUR GPA

DO Nail Your Grades Junior Year and First Semester Senior Year

No matter how well you did freshman and sophomore year, it's critical that you max out on your grades in junior year and first semester senior year. Colleges want students who will be successful at their institutions, and if you are not pulling your academic weight at this stage of your high school career, you will send a questionable signal about your staying power.

At some colleges, grades are such an important factor in the admissions equation that there's a minimum GPA for admission. One popular university in the South, for example, shows no mercy: If you're under a 3.0—even with a 2.9999 and strong scores—you'll be shown the door.

If you've bombed out freshman or sophomore year, don't be deterred from pulling out the stops junior and senior year. You still have time to come on strong and look like a "late bloomer," something your guidance counselor can attest to in his or her letter of recommendation. Many schools, including the College of Charleston, offer an opportunity on the application for you to include a mea culpa and any extenuating circumstances that might have affected your grades. If an application doesn't invite such comments, a letter from you explaining your newfound focus will go a long way toward helping your cause with admissions.

DON'T Get Any Cs

Cs are an absolute no-no, especially in junior year or the beginning of senior year. One C on an otherwise sterling transcript might be overlooked—if you or your guidance counselor can offer a compelling explanation. Especially for highly selective schools, two Cs simply won't cut it, no matter how high your standardized test scores. There are simply too many other students out there without "two big bull's-eyes on the transcript," as one counselor put it, for colleges to overlook major lapses in your record.

DO Choose AP and IB Courses if You Can

The more selective the college, the more challenging your high school courses must be. Course selection is so important that there's even a place on the Common Application's School Report form for your guidance counselor to rate the difficulty of your courses compared to those of your peers. The question reads like this:

In comparison to other college preparatory students at our school, the applicant's course selection is:

❏ most demanding ❏ very demanding ❏ demanding
❏ average ❏ less than demanding

It doesn't take a brain surgeon to see that your chances for admission will be greater if your guidance counselor checks the box that says "most demanding." This should serve as a reality check if you have opted for easy courses in order to get top grades. Colleges can see through this game, and you will inevitably pay the price, particularly with your "reach" schools, or those where your chances of admission are slim.

If you have the option, push yourself to get on an honors track that includes either Advanced Placement (AP) courses or an International Baccalaureate (IB) program. In both cases, the courses will not only weigh in on your application as "most demanding" but could also boost your GPA with extra points on your transcript.

The IB program is a standardized international curriculum offered by more than 479 schools around the country and another 872 around the world. According to surveys by IB North America, IB students have a significantly greater chance of admission to many selective colleges than non-IB students.[27]

Since the IB curriculum focuses on coursework in junior and senior year, you might still have a shot at getting into your school's IB program even if you're a sophomore. Consider the experience of a boy who had been coasting along in honors courses getting straight As freshman and sophomore year at a large public high school:

"My parents said high school was a time to have fun," he said.

But toward the end of sophomore year, he had an epiphany. "I realized I was wasting my time," he said. "I wanted to do something with my life."

With his sights set on becoming an aeronautical engineer, he talked his way into the IB program and ended up graduating in the top ten in his class. His class rank—and his participation in the IB program—helped him follow his dreams to Georgia Tech.

As for Advanced Placement courses, if your school offers AP courses, take them. "As the admissions race has hit warp speed, Advanced Placement has taken on new importance," reported the *New York Times*.[28]

"We don't expect students to take every AP that's offered," Richard Nesbitt, Dean of Admissions at Williams College told the *Times*, "but if their school has 15 APs and they've avoided them all, that would certainly say something."[29]

Although there seems to be no hard-and-fast rule about the number of APs you should take, six is often considered a minimum to be competitive at some Ivies and other selective colleges. To see what you're up against, consider the fact that in 2005, "3,000 students took seven or more AP exams," according to the *Times*.[30]

To avoid burnout, try to spread out your APs over the course of four years, rather than loading up senior year. A strong senior year program will certainly give you brownie points with colleges, but you need to give yourself enough breathing room to earn As or, at the very least, high Bs in your AP courses.

Beyond strengthening your curriculum or adding extra points to your GPA, APs have another important packaging value that is often overlooked: They can serve as an "honor" in the honors and awards section of your application. As savvy students know, if you've taken three or more AP courses and have earned a 3 or better on all of them, you could be designated as an AP Scholar, or more, by the College Board, which administers the program. (See the College Board Web site for a complete rundown of AP award levels.)

Since the College Board doesn't announce the AP awards until the summer before senior year, be sure to make yourself eligible for the AP Scholar designation by taking at least three or four AP courses and tests by the end of junior year. If you don't want to overload your school curriculum, you could always take an AP course or two on-line at a virtual school and then take the test.

Alternatively, if you're a super test-taker, you might avoid a course altogether and simply take the test, a practice that is permitted by the College Board. For example, one precocious math student from the Northeast who is now at Duke scored a 5 on the AP tests in Statistics and Macroeconomics, even though he had never taken the courses. Added to the four other courses he had under his belt—all with test scores of 4 or 5—his APs earned him the title AP Scholar with Distinction, a high honor reserved for students who average 3.5 on all AP tests and 3 or better on 5 or more. On his application, he packaged his AP achievement twice: first as an honor, and second in an essay about his relentless quest for knowledge.

But if your school doesn't have AP or IB, don't fret. When evaluating your application, colleges will take into account the profile of your particular school and the options you had available.

DO Ratchet Up Your Rank

Although many public and private schools these days are doing away with rankings or are ranking by "deciles" or tenths, if your school is one of those that still ranks, use the rankings as a packaging tool.

Some colleges use rankings as a way to identify the top students, not merely for admissions purposes but also for scholarships. Notre Dame's admission reps make no bones about its selectivity in the Early Action round: In order to be competitive, you should be in the top 1 to 3 percent of your class academically with scores to match. At Georgia Tech, three-quarters of the recipients of the prestigious President's Scholarship routinely rank in the top five students in their class.

Take a lesson from a student in an IB program at a large public high school in Colorado who was ranked in the top 10 percent of his class at the end of sophomore year. A visit to Penn that summer so fired him up that he came back to school ready to hit the books. By the time he applied to Penn Early Decision, he had pushed his rank into the top ten students in his class, leaving his smart but less focused friends in the dust. Penn gave him the nod.

The same principle applies if your school ranks in deciles. If your school has seventy students and you are languishing somewhere in the third decile (top twenty-one students), try to push yourself into the next highest decile by the time your class rankings are announced (typically at the end of junior year). It stands to reason that students in the top 20 percent will look a lot better than those in the top 30 percent—no matter how competitive your school.

DO Go for Dual Enrollment or College Courses

A surefire way to up your rank at some high schools is to take a dual-enrollment course or a summer course at a local college or junior college. Taking college courses is also a good way to bolster a Hook in a particular area, such as architecture, computer graphics, fashion design, or environmental science, which might not be available at your high school.

What's more, college courses, particularly at a school you are interested in attending, can be a way to package your academic abilities by demonstrating that you can do high-level work. Nihar Shah, for example, who had his eye on Northwestern, spent a summer in Evanston taking two 200-level courses, including one where he ended up being the top student in the class. A recommendation from his professor testifying to his achievement was one of many reasons he got a thumbs-up from Northwestern at admission time.

If you do take college courses, be sure to have transcripts sent directly from the registrar's office to all the colleges on your list, according to standard admissions requirements.

DON'T Count Out Freshman Year

"The idea that freshman year doesn't matter is a big myth," moaned one recent prep school graduate who applied to thirteen schools and was rejected or wait-listed at all but four of them, including some he regarded as sure bets. Although he's happily ensconced at the University of Miami, he says, "I had a 4.1 average for senior year and ended up with a 3.5 weighted average, but I did poorly my freshman and sophomore year. If I had it to do over again, I'd have started earlier."

If you're a freshman or the parent of a freshman reading this book, be warned: The grades in every class you take, from your shop class first thing in the morning to the AP history class you take at 2 p.m., count for college.

One New Jersey junior, who had earned a D in shop freshman year for failing to turn in a woodworking project, was chagrined to discover that the grade factored into his GPA, pulling it down below 4.0 in a transcript heavy with As and Bs in AP and honors courses. By lodging a protest he had his shop grade changed, but you shouldn't count on such concessions. Get it right from the start.

DO Get Your Teachers Invested in Your Success

Most teachers want you to succeed academically. They also want to know that you truly *care* about doing well in their particular courses. One way to show that you care is by participating in class. If you know the answer to a question but are holding back from putting up your hand out of fear of making a mistake or just plain shyness, get over it—now! Start raising your hand with answers, and also start asking questions.

Before each class, make a list of three or four questions you may have about the material, and when the timing seems appropriate, bring them up. As good journalists know, there is no such thing as a stupid question. Inevitably you'll find yourself raising issues that are on the minds of your friends as well. One question will lead to another, and before you know it, you may be the one driving the class discussion forward—something that colleges love to hear about in teacher recommendations.

Another way to show your teachers that you care is by communicating to them that you want to improve. If you're getting a B in a particular class, don't just settle for second best. Stop by and see your teacher after school and tell him or her that you want to make an A. Then ask what you need to do to achieve it.

Most teachers will be delighted by your desire to learn and by your new effort—inside and outside the classroom. You'll reap the rewards on your transcript.

By now, you should be well on the road to creating a complete and appealing application package that clearly communicates your Hook. In the preceding chapters you've learned how to find your Hook and bolster it with supplementary portfolios, CDs, contests, or internship experiences. You've acquired skills to communicate your Hook in a résumé and activities list. You've had an inside look at how to Hook your essays. And you've gained insights into packaging your standardized test scores and grades for maximum impact.

The next step involves sitting down and pulling all these pieces of your package together in your application. To get started, fill out the Common Application on-line, following a few Hook guidelines in the next chapter.

CHAPTER TWENTY

Pulling Your Package Together

HOOK TIP

As you sit down to fill out your applications, keep your Hook uppermost in your mind. When you're under the gun at deadline time, it's easy to lose sight of your Hook and simply throw things down at random.

Review your application to make sure you've communicated your Hook clearly at every opportunity, from the top of your activities list, honors, and/ or work experience to one of your essays. Also, don't forget to send every college on your list a résumé that's angled to your Hook, along with any Hook-bolstering supplementary material.

By filling out the Common Application on-line, you'll have an application ready to send to more than three hundred private and public colleges, including Harvard, Northwestern, the College of William and Mary, Caltech, Amherst, Colorado College, Binghamton, and Southern Methodist University. You'll also have a handy template to follow when you're filling out applications for colleges that require their own applications, whether it's a state university such as Michigan or the University of North Carolina at Chapel Hill, or a private college such as Brown, Wheaton in Illinois, or Georgetown. New schools are joining the Common Application every year, so check the Common Application Web site to see if your favorites are included.

Application Checklist

Using the Common Application as a guideline, you'll need the following to complete the application process at most colleges:

❑ The Common Application On-Line
❑ Common Application Supplements
❑ Application Fee
❑ Résumé
❑ Arts, Athletic, or Scientific Supplements
❑ ACT, SAT, or SAT Subject Test Scores
❑ High School Transcripts
❑ College Transcripts
❑ Teacher Recommendations
❑ Guidance Counselor Recommendations
❑ Cover Letter
❑ Alumni/College Interview
❑ Mid-Year Senior Grades

THE COLLEGE HOOK APPLICATION CHECKLIST

Here's a brief rundown of Hook packaging pointers to consider when you're filling out your Common Application:

The Common Application On-Line

As you fill in your application, ask yourself these questions:

- Did I call attention to my multicultural roots by specifying my ethnic background in the optional question?
- Did I underscore my Hook by indicating a related major?
- Did I list all colleges where I have received credit, along with a separate sheet listing my courses (including those in a field related to my Hook)?
- Did I write down scores for *either* the ACT *or* the SAT, whichever shows me to best advantage (or for both tests if my scores were equally fabulous)?
- Did I lead off the activities list with my Hook and similar activities, and follow with my secondary Hook?
- Did I emphasize my Hook under work experience?
- Did I highlight my Hook in the academic honors section?
- Did I write about my Hook in one of my essays?

Common Application Supplements

Many colleges require a supplement to the Common Application. Like the application itself, the supplements are available at the Common Application Web site or on the college's Web site.

Some supplements merely require additional information, while others will request an extra essay or essays.

Typically one of the essays will be a "why" essay: "Why do you want to attend . . . ?" This is a good place to wax eloquent about your visits or contacts with the school and to emphasize your interest in special programs that might dovetail with your Hook. If you haven't visited the school, look on the college's Web site to see what piques your interest. Such programs as leadership institutes, unusual speakers' series, research internships, and study-abroad opportunities would be important to enumerate in a "why" essay, along with specific courses and professors that appeal to you in your intended major.

If the supplement includes an open-ended essay question and you haven't already focused on your Hook in one of your other essays, *do it now!*

Application Fee

Don't forget to pay the application fee by check or on-line with a credit card. Some schools will waive the fee if you apply on-line. Others will waive the fee for low-income students who qualify (check with your guidance counselor).

But if a fee is required, double-check to make sure you've paid the right amount. One student didn't find out until April that she had underpaid, using the previous year's application fee, to a college in the South. Even though the amount she paid was only $5 short of the new fee, she was denied admission.

In another case, a student paid his fee by credit card in time for Early Action at one popular college, only to discover belatedly that the school had no record of his payment. Because of the snafu, his application was denied consideration for Early Action and thrown into the Regular Decision pile. He was later wait-listed.

To cover yourself, call the college a few days after you apply to make sure that they've received your application fee and that your application is complete.

Résumé

Send a résumé to every college on your list, unless the college specifically indicates otherwise. Some schools, such as USC's School of Cinema-TV, require a very specific résumé format that you *must* follow. Most schools, however, leave the door open for your own creativity. In those cases, your best packaging bet is to lead with your Hook, following the résumé suggestions in Chapter Sixteen.

But be sure to send a résumé, even if it is optional, in order to promote your Hook to best advantage. If there's no space to include one with an on-line application, then send it separately by mail. And if you're sending a paper application, attach a résumé to the page that lists your activities. But note that the résumé *doesn't* take the place of filling out an activities list, which most colleges require.

Arts, Athletic, or Scientific Supplements

Supplementary material in the arts and sciences can help bolster your Hook and validate your credentials, as you discovered in Chapter Sixteen. Many schools have separate arts supplements forms, with specific instructions on the number of photos or slides to include in an artistic portfolio, or the way to present drama credentials. Some schools accept the Common Application's art supplement form. For athletes, the Common Application offers an athletic supplement form accepted by many schools. (See Chapter Twenty-Four for more information on "courting coaches.")

If the schools to which you're applying have such forms, be sure to follow the instructions precisely. But even if the application doesn't have a special form, send the supplementary material yourself. For example, one student with over a decade of expertise as a concert clarinetist sent a CD to a school in Pennsylvania in response to a particular talent question on its supplement. The school came back with an offer of a $7,500 merit scholarship in music.

"Obviously the admissions department sent the CD to the music department," said the boy, who unfortunately hadn't thought to send the CD anyplace else. He even omitted his top-choice school, where he was wait-listed. He added wistfully, "I wish I had sent that CD to every school on my list."

Although not every school will evaluate CDs or DVDs, many will. And certainly most schools will welcome "anything that fits in a file folder," as the associate admissions director of a leading state university explained.

To play it safe, call college admissions offices to see what's acceptable. If you have the option, go ahead and send portfolios, CDs, scientific abstracts, and other supplements with your application.

ACT, SAT, or SAT Subject Test Scores

Have your best SAT or ACT scores sent to colleges *directly* from the testing agency. In the case of the SAT, it's the College Board; in the case of the ACT, it's the American College Test.

Most colleges require independent validation from the testing agencies themselves, even if you've self-reported your scores in your application. Allow enough time for scores to reach the colleges (typically three to five weeks for the SAT, and four to seven weeks for the ACT). If you're in a time crunch, the SAT will send your scores "Rush" for an extra fee, while the ACT will send your scores "Priority," also for an extra fee. Some colleges, notably the University of Michigan, do not accept rush scores of any kind. So find out the requirements of individual schools and prepare accordingly.

To give yourself optimum control over your scores, it's advisable not to send scores to colleges at the time you're taking the tests. Instead, wait to see your scores, and then decide which test, the SAT or ACT, serves you best. (For more on how to play the SAT against the ACT, see Chapter Eighteen, "Scoring Bigger with Test Scores.") This approach will cost you a little more money, but it could have big payoffs at admissions time.

High School Transcripts

Your official transcripts must be sent to colleges directly from every high school you've attended. If you've attended four high schools, then typically you'll need a transcript sent from each one of them, even if the information is included on your current high school transcript.

College Transcripts

If you've taken any college courses, have transcripts sent directly from those schools to all the colleges to which you're applying. Allow time for the colleges to send out the transcripts to meet your deadlines.

Teacher Recommendations

A good rule of thumb with teacher recommendations is to ask two teachers in different academic disciplines, preferably those who have taught you in junior or senior year. Be sure they are people who absolutely love you and who have given you top grades in their courses. If you're applying to specialized programs, such as an accelerated program in medicine, you're likely to need at least three recommendations.

Think "Hook" even when you're selecting teachers. If your Hook is Spanish, then be sure the Spanish teacher who taught you for two years and led your study trip to Barcelona writes one of your recommendations. If your goal is engineering, a favorite math or physics teacher would be a likely choice. If you've been active in drama or music, ask for a recommendation from the adviser as a supplemental recommendation to reinforce your Hook. You could send that recommendation to the college's drama or music director as well as to admissions.

As for timing, ask your teachers at the end of junior year or as soon as school starts senior year so that they will have time to compose a thoughtful letter. Some teachers put a cap on the number of recommendations they will write, so the sooner you ask, the more likely you are to be among those included.

Also, whatever you do, don't wait until the last minute to ask for recommendations. Take a lesson from one straight-A student whose high school required a minimum of two weeks' notice for teacher recommendations. She routinely procrastinated asking her teachers until the day before her school's deadline.

Later, she admitted, "It put me and them under stress. Next time, I would start much earlier."

Note that for schools that use the Common Application, you'll need to give your teachers a special Teacher Recommendation form to fill out along with the letter of recommendation. Other schools have their own required forms for teachers. If you run across a school without special forms or where teacher recommendations are optional, just ask your teacher for a letter. Remember: Anything on an application that's "optional" *isn't* an option for *you*. To win with admissions, you need all the ammunition you can get, and that includes "optional" teacher recommendations.

It's best to ask your teacher to write the letter of recommendation on school stationery and enclose it in a sealed envelope with his or her signature across the seal. That will signal colleges that the letter is confidential. To make things easy on your teachers, hand them envelopes addressed to each college.

When it comes to mailing the recommendations, high school procedures are all over the lot. At some high schools, teachers return the sealed envelopes to the student to mail out. At others, teachers mail the letters directly to the colleges. At still others, the guidance department mails out teacher recommendations in a packet along with transcripts and other information from the school.

There's also an increasing trend for high schools to send teacher recommendations to colleges electronically. The Common Application has rolled out a new on-line school forms program that your school may be using.

In any event, it's best to ask your guidance counselor how teacher recommendations are handled at your school before you approach any teacher with a request.

Guidance Counselor Recommendations

Your guidance counselor can be your biggest advocate. Since most colleges require a separate recommendation from your guidance counselor (see example in Appendix B), he or she can help explain any lapses in your academic record or any unusual family circumstances that might have impacted your grades.

For example, if you've started to come on strong academically after a shaky start freshman and sophomore year, your guidance counselor can point that out. If you've tripped over pre-calculus after an otherwise stellar math career, your guidance counselor can help explain why.

But if you want your guidance counselor to get behind you, it's up to you to make him or her aware of any special circumstances in your background. Your counselor may not know, for example, that the C+ you got in Honors English was actually a huge feather in your cap, because the teacher, who was the most difficult grader in the school, had moved you up to Honors in the middle of the semester. Similarly, your counselor might not know that you've managed to maintain a straight-A average in your IB program in spite of living in a trailer for months with your five-member family and three dogs after hurricanes or mud slides displaced you from your home. Or he or she might not be aware of a learning disability or physical illness that you have wrestled with and overcome.

Make an appointment to sit down with your guidance counselor and explain what's going on in your life—especially with your Hook. And don't forget to bring your résumé. As one private school guidance counselor in New York City exclaimed after receiving a student's résumé, "I can't thank you enough for showing me this. It really helps me understand your strengths."

Also, don't forget to give your guidance counselor any special guidance forms required by the colleges on your list, including the Common Application's School Report form. Typically, your guidance counselor will send the form and recommendation letter with your transcript. Check individual college Web sites for required forms, and ask your guidance counselor about your school's procedures. Because the Common Application has launched a new on-line school forms system, school guidance counselors and teachers can submit recommendations, forms, and transcripts at the push of a button. Check to see if the school forms system is available in your high school.

Cover Letter

A cover letter, preferably typed on a letterhead with your name, address, and Social Security number, is necessary only if you have special academic issues to address that you haven't covered elsewhere in your application. You can use a cover letter to explain why you nearly failed biology freshman year, or how your recently diagnosed learning disabilities might have impacted your performance.

Be sure to call attention to any major upswing in your grades or scores that would indicate how focused you've become academically. Colleges want you to be successful, and if you let admissions committees know that you are genuinely ready—and able—to take on the challenges ahead, you will go a long way toward improving your chances of admission.

Alumni/College Interview

Be alert to early sign-up deadlines for interviews on campus or with alumni in your area. It's up to you to take the initiative and set up interviews, so don't drop the ball. Particularly if you're a great "schmoozer," an interview could work to your advantage. (See Chapter Twenty-Two for interview dos and don'ts.) One boy with a gift for gab offset middling grades and abysmal scores by selling himself to the admissions officer at a college in the Northeast. Before the interview, he had prepared himself by researching the college on the Web.

"You really know a lot about our programs," the interviewer remarked after chatting with him in person for more than an hour. Clearly, the woman saw his potential: He received an "admit" package a few weeks later.

Mid-Year Senior Grades

Good mid-year senior grades can show colleges the stuff you're made of. Most colleges expect to receive mid-year transcripts from your high school. The Common Application even has a Mid-Year Grade Report form for that purpose.

You can embrace good mid-year grades as a packaging tool to burnish your image, or you can ignore them and deep-six your chances for admission. Especially if your application is languishing in a college's "maybe" pile, strong mid-year grades could give admissions committees a reason to go to bat for you.

The final word is this: Go all out first semester senior year to get the best grades you possibly can. Otherwise, you'll be sending a message that you don't care, and if you don't, why should a college?

Now, with your application package wrapped up and ready to go, it's time to begin making your pitch. Get ready to sell your Hook to every college you want to attend.

PART IV

Selling Your Hook

CHAPTER TWENTY-ONE

Pitching Your Package to Colleges

HOOK TIP

When it comes to choosing colleges, select a range of schools using the Big Ten formula: two "safety" schools you're sure you can get into; five where your chances are better than even; and three—or *more*—"reaches," which are very competitive.

Since there is very little predictability in admissions at selective colleges these days, it's better to opt for more applications than fewer. And even though it's likely that you won't listen to this advice, *don't get fixated on one school.* The truth is, you could be happy at any number of colleges, and if you keep an open mind in this chaotic admission climate, you won't be disappointed.

To maximize your chances for admission—and for merit scholarships—look especially for schools that *need you,* either because of your academic horsepower or your Hook.

So often, college counselors hear statements like this:

"If I don't get into Harvard [or substitute your favorite college], I'll just die!"

In your heart of hearts, you may be thinking something like that right now. Whether or not you've even stepped on a college campus in Cambridge, New York, Houston, Philadelphia, Chicago, or Palo Alto, you may have gotten an idea in your head that unless you get accepted at a particular college, your life is over.

That attitude can lead only to disappointment. This is a time when application rates at selective liberal arts colleges "have grown by one-third or more during the last five years alone," according to the *New York Times*.[31] So it's time to think more creatively about why and how to choose colleges and what strategies will work to your advantage when you are pitching your application package.

To readjust your mind-set, put yourself back in the marketing mode described at the beginning of Chapter Fourteen. You've got the product to sell: yourself. And you've got the package: your Hook, scores, GPA, résumé, essays, and recommendations. The next step is to find your target "market," the colleges that will be most likely to "buy" what you've got to sell.

Here are some points to ponder when you're selecting schools and making your pitch with your application package.

REACH FOR THE STARS — BUT KEEP YOUR FEET FIRMLY PLANTED ON THE GROUND

It's okay to go for broke and apply to as many "reach" schools as you want (i.e., those where your chances of admission are questionable at best). But if you go that route, you must do so as a hard-headed realist. For example, if you have a 3.3 GPA, a 30 ACT, and SAT Subject tests under 700, the chances are slim to none that you'll be looking over the Charles River from a dorm at MIT when September rolls around, no matter what your Hook. Similarly, if you've aced out with a 4.1 GPA and boast a Hook as "queen of community service," but you couldn't crack 1800 out of 2400 on your SAT, don't consider yourself a hot prospect for NYU.

Read the freshman class profiles on college Web sites to see how you fit in. If your numbers are clearly in the lower half of admitted students, take a step back and adjust your expectations accordingly. Instead of dreaming that some fairy godmother in the admissions office will magically put your application in the "admit" pile, find some colleges that are more likely to reward your selling points with admission. To give yourself a comfort zone, a good rule of thumb is to apply to several schools where your grades and scores put you in the top half, or, better yet, in the top 25 percent of admitted students.

CHOOSE COLLEGES THAT NEED YOU

One way to make your college admissions experience more predictive is to choose colleges where your ethnicity will add dramatically to the diversity on campus, or where your exceptional prowess in science, the arts, or technology will help enhance the academic profile of the school.

Whitney Morein, for example, made sure to emphasize her Hook as a Mexican-American when she was applying to such colleges as Vanderbilt and Lehigh, which were actively seeking minority students. In her main essay, she focused on the influence of her *chicana* grandmother, who on her deathbed had awakened in Whitney a growing sense of passion and responsibility for her heritage. (See Whitney's essay in Appendix A.)

To further underscore her ethnic roots, Whitney was also careful to pick colleges that offered programs in Latin American studies, which she could pursue along with her pre-med focus. Both Vanderbilt and Lehigh offered such courses, and Whitney cited them in her application. She also applied to Lehigh's special Diversity Achiever's Program, which required an extra essay.

Whitney's efforts paid off even before April 1. Although she had applied regular decision to Vanderbilt, she was notified in February that she had been admitted. In addition, she was invited to Vanderbilt's Mosaic Weekend, a recruiting event aimed at increasing the school's minority yield, or percentage of students accepting the offer of admission.

As for Lehigh, the college accepted her to the Diversity Achiever's Program and paid her way to campus in the fall for a weekend for multicultural students. She was admitted to the college in April. Ultimately, she opted for Vanderbilt.

In the case of Summer Niazi, the Pakistani-American cholesterol researcher who was profiled in Chapter Ten, her ethnicity and her Hook as a scientific powerhouse landed her offers of admission *and* hefty merit scholarships at a host of schools. The University of Rochester offered her $10,000, Mount Holyoke weighed in with $15,000, and RPI, where she was accepted to an accelerated seven-year B.S./M.D. program in conjunction with Albany Medical College, enticed her with a $15,000 scholarship *and* a laptop. She was also admitted to an eight-year medical program at Union College and Albany Medical College, as well as to Wellesley and Emory, and she finally chose Emory.

Likewise, Nicole Dubowitz, the op-ed writer whom you met in Chapter Eleven, struck gold at Northeastern with an $11,000 Dean's scholarship and also at Pitzer, which offered her a $5,000 Trustee Community Scholarship, the highest honor given by the college to an entering freshman. In addition, her writing talent earned her admission to the University of Maryland's Honors Program. Although she was tempted by the offers, she opted instead for Trinity College in Hartford.

FOLLOW YOUR HOOK

Although it may fly in the face of the current mania for the *U.S. News & World Report* rankings, why not let your Hook be your guide to picking colleges? If you do a little digging, you may discover that in your field of interest, one school might far outstrip another.

Mack Elder, for example, who exemplified the drama Hook in Chapter Twelve, didn't have a shred of doubt where he belonged: USC's School of Cinema-TV, "the number one film school in the country," as he concluded. He turned down another top-level institution, Davidson, to head for L.A., where he could move to the heartbeat of Hollywood. "USC has an auditorium named after Frank Sinatra, and he didn't even go there," said Mack.

GO AGAINST THE CROWD

If everyone else from your school is applying to Emory or Washington University in St. Louis, you might want to set your sights elsewhere. Unless you can say realistically that you are at the top of the heap of applicants among your peers, the "lemming effect" is likely to lead you to the wait list or rejection pile.

To see how students from your high school have fared at the colleges to which you're applying, ask your guidance counselor for a peek at a "scattergram," a graph that tracks scores and grades of past students admitted to various colleges. That will give you an objective comparison so that you can position yourself accordingly.

TAKE ADVANTAGE OF WOMEN'S COLLEGES

Don't let the fear of being stuck away somewhere without guys blind you to the advantages of a women's college. Schools such as Barnard, Bryn Mawr, Mills, Mount Holyoke, Scripps, Smith, and Wellesley pack a huge punch academically and can open doors to law schools and medical schools at rates much higher than the national average.

What's more, most women's colleges operate as part of consortia, where it's possible to take courses at nearby universities. Students at Bryn Mawr, for example, can study at the University of Pennsylvania, Swarthmore, or Haverford, while those at Smith and Mount Holyoke can take courses at Amherst, Hampshire, or U Mass. If a course isn't offered at Mills, you can sign up for one at UC Berkeley; and at Wellesley, there is reciprocity with MIT, Olin, Babson, and Brandeis. At Scripps, you can take classes and share libraries with Pomona, Claremont McKenna, Harvey Mudd, and Pitzer. Barnard may be the most reciprocal of all, offering unlimited cross-registration with Columbia University. A women's college worked for Hillary Rodham Clinton. Why not for you?

START EARLY

"Be one of the early birds in the door."

That's the advice of Ryan Allik, the "techie" whose rise to computer heaven at Purdue is profiled in Chapter Eight.

"I worked on my applications over the summer before senior year and finished them by late August," said Ryan. "I remember going into school and thinking, 'I'm done,' while everyone else was scrambling."

Most of the schools to which Ryan applied offered rolling admission, a system whereby applications are evaluated as they are received, rather than at a set deadline. As a result, Ryan got news of his admission decisions quickly. He heard from Purdue by mid-October. Because the school's computer engineering department was one of his top choices, he was able to settle back confidently for the remainder of senior year, secure in the knowledge that whatever acceptances came his way, he was "in" at a school that offered exactly what he wanted.

Applying early has another advantage, said Ryan. "As colleges start getting filled up with applications, they become more strict as they get a sense of the competition. They can adjust their standards accordingly."

Following Ryan's lead, make sure that you apply early to several schools with rolling admission so that you get a few speedy returns. Good news in October or November can do wonders for your psyche at a time when fear is the dominant feeling for seniors.

Also, it wouldn't hurt to send your applications far in advance to schools with specific deadlines. If you wait until the actual deadline, the college will be inundated with applications, and you may not get as careful a reading.

APPLY EARLY DECISION

If you're dead-set on one college and one college only, then applying Early Decision may be the way to go. However, Early Decision is a binding, contractual agreement. By applying Early Decision, you agree that if you are accepted, you will attend. Think long and hard before taking the ED plunge, especially if you need significant financial aid. You may want to compare financial aid packages, and if you've locked yourself into one school ED, you may not have that luxury.

Still, Early Decision may give you an edge, since some colleges have been known to admit more than half of the class early.

David Fell, the New York musician whose résumé was highlighted in Chapter Sixteen, believed that there was only one school that could satisfy his longings for a city, top-notch jazz music, and a liberal arts curriculum: New

York University. He applied Early Decision in November, and by the holidays he was sitting pretty as one of the nearly 30 percent of the class admitted at that time.

These days, some colleges are making the ED issue even more confusing—or helpful, depending on your point of view—by offering two rounds of Early Decision: Early Decision I, which is typically in the fall, and EDII, which often coincides with the regular decision application deadline.

EDII can work to your advantage if you:

- Have been deferred or rejected EDI or Early Action at another school
- Need to shore up your scores or first-semester grades
- Want more time to decide among colleges

One New Yorker who was deferred from Wake Forest University in mid-December after applying under its Early Decision program quickly switched gears and sent her application to Vanderbilt Early Decision II, which was due at the beginning of January. In the interim, she revamped her résumé and added to her application an extra essay that her English teacher had deemed her "best work ever." Vanderbilt's admissions committee liked what they saw and admitted her to the class of 2009.

"I'm glad I was deferred at Wake Forest," she said. "I couldn't be happier."

But ED II didn't work out as well for another girl, who had been deferred EDI from one of the Little Ivies, despite stellar scores. Thinking that her scientific credentials would give her a leg up at Tufts, one of her other favorites, she applied EDII. This time, she was flat-out rejected. Though she steeled herself for rejection in the regular decision round, she was ultimately vindicated by admission to one of the country's leading liberal arts colleges.

In these tempestuous times, although you may be well served by taking your chances on EDI or EDII at a school you love, try not to bank on admission. However, if you are one of the lucky ones accepted EDI or EDII, you're expected to withdraw your applications from other colleges to allow other students to have a shot at admission.

APPLY EARLY ACTION

As part of your application strategy, choose a few schools with Early Action deadlines. Under Early Action, you apply early and get a response early—sometimes as soon as December—but you don't have to make a commitment to the school until May 1.

At a time when colleges are struggling to figure out which students have a genuine interest in their institutions, Early Action is a way to signal your enthusiasm. However, applying Early Action won't always give you an advantage in admissions. At the University of North Carolina at Chapel Hill, for example, Early Action and Regular Decision candidates are judged equally by the same high standards, according to admission reps. Other schools, such as Notre Dame, have a reputation for evaluating Early Action candidates by an even higher standard than the regular admissions pool.

As a result, when you're applying Early Action, it behooves you to know the policies of the institution to which you're applying. If you have any doubts, pick up the phone, call the school, and ask to speak to an admissions counselor. Ask straight out what scores and grades the college is looking for in the Early Action round and whether you'll get any special breaks for applying early.

One obvious advantage of Early Action is that you will get the results sooner than if you applied regular decision. This could relieve stress and also help you gauge where you might stand at other colleges to which you've applied. Wellesley, for example, has its own version of Early Action called "Early Evaluation." Girls who apply under this system by January 1 receive a letter a month or so later indicating whether their chances of admission are good, fair, or unlikely. They can adjust their plans—and their expectations—accordingly.

One potential disadvantage of Early Action is that some schools, notably Stanford and Yale, have laid down a strict exclusivity rule: If you apply to one of these schools under what they call "Single Choice Early Action," you do not have to attend that school, but you are honor-bound not to apply Early Action or Early Decision to any private university or to an early or binding program at a public university. What this means in practical terms is that you can't hedge your bets by applying EA simultaneously to Notre Dame, University of Chicago, or Boston College, for example. Nor can you apply Early Decision to Columbia, Dartmouth, or Swarthmore. You can, however, apply to public universities such as those in the University of California system, which have early regular deadlines or rolling admission.

On the upside, Single Choice Early Action could be a plus if you have a strong Hook and also fit the school's profile for grades and scores. At Stanford, for example, two-thirds of students matriculating in the class of 2010 were admitted early, according to the admissions department.

Keep in mind that most colleges offering Early Action permit you to apply early to as many schools as you want. To play it safe, check individual college Web sites or call the school directly to find out your options.

Also, because early admissions policies are changing rapidly, don't rely on rumor: go straight to the source to find out the policies of your favorite colleges. Harvard, for example, announced in September 2006 that it was completely abandoning a decades-long early admission policy beginning with the 2007–2008 admission cycle.[32] Now, prospective Harvard students have only one choice of deadline: regular decision. Princeton followed suit the following week.[33] Stay tuned for other schools to fall in line.

———

At this point, you've identified a list of colleges, you've decided on an application timing strategy, and you've completed and sent your Hook-centered application package. That means your job is finished, right?

Wrong. These are only the first steps in a much bigger sales strategy for getting into college. The next step involves selling yourself and your Hook personally through direct contacts with the college, starting with an on-campus or alumni interview.

CHAPTER TWENTY-TWO

Acing the Interview

HOOK TIP

To prepare for your interview, develop two or three "talking points," including your Hook, which you can weave into the conversation with admissions interviewers on campus or with alumni in your area. Although you don't want to come across as "canned," you do want to prepare well enough to sell yourself, and that means highlighting your key interests and passions. Also, come ready to ask a few questions about programs at the college that pique your interest. Above all, go into the interview expecting to have a *conversation*. The more you can engage in a genuine give-and-take, the more relaxed you—and your interviewer—will be.

B elieve it or not, one of the biggest mistakes students make in interviews is failing to set them up at all.

"If the student doesn't bother to set up an interview, I don't go chasing after him," said "Dave," an alumni interviewer for one of America's most sought-after universities. "In the six years I've been interviewing, only two students who applied from my area failed to contact me. The first time it happened, I called the admissions office and asked, 'What should I do?'

" 'Do nothing,' the office told me. 'That tells us something about a kid.' "

Needless to say, the laggard students didn't get good news when admissions decisions rolled around. And you may not, either, if you fail to take advantage of opportunities to sell yourself face-to-face. Although many colleges are doing away with interviews altogether, there are plenty of others that still keep the door open on and off campus for personal contact with prospective students.

At some schools, such as Dartmouth, Rice, and Johns Hopkins, you're likely to be interviewed by students, typically seniors who have been hand-picked for the job. At other schools, including Carnegie Mellon, Wellesley, and the University of Chicago, you'll be able to talk with admissions staffers themselves. And if you can't make it to campus for an interview, then you may have a chance to meet with an alumnus like Dave, who sends back a recommendation for each student. In Dave's case, the recommendation includes a ranking that conforms to strict guidelines set up by the highly selective university he represents.

"We rank students on a scale from 1 to 5, with 5 being the highest," says Dave. "The form we fill out has four qualities that we rank: passion, personal qualities, potential to be a good match for the school, and an overall average of the other three."

Passion, said Dave, is the most important quality of all. "I'm looking for a passion to *be* something, to contribute to society, to be a great writer or a great scientist," he said. "Whatever your Hook may be, you have to have something that lights your fire—something that adds dimension to the school.

"Some kids come in and they are so flat that they don't have any enthusiasm about anything. It's hard to get excited about a kid like that."

Dave made it clear that you don't have to have a cheerleader's personality in order to show enthusiasm. He cited one young woman who was quiet and self-possessed but who nevertheless communicated clearly her passion for writing, as well as her love for economics and volunteering.

"What set her apart wasn't only her brilliance, but also her multidimensional profile," said Dave. "She actively pursued her writing, but she also had great music and math skills.

"I gave her a 5," said Dave. "I told the school, 'She is clearly the best I have seen this year.'" The university thought so, too: It admitted her regular decision.

POINTERS FROM AN ALUMNI INTERVIEWER

If you want to score a 5 on your college interview, follow some pointed advice that Dave has gleaned from his years as a management consultant and corporate recruiter at such schools as Harvard Business School and Wharton. You just might want to keep his tips in your back pocket: they'll serve you well not only when you're applying to college, but also when you're applying for summer internships and future jobs. Here's what Dave has to say in his own words:

• *Bring a Résumé*

The well-prepared kids walk in with a short, two-page résumé that highlights their achievements. That's helpful, because it lets me put their activities in context with their academics. It's best if they lead the résumé with their GPA and test scores, so that I don't have to waste time in the interview drawing out that information.

• *Try to Relax*

Sometimes students come in with sweaty palms. I can see that they're under real tension. I had one student show up with his father. The dad's palms were sweatier than his son's. I had to excuse the dad so that I could get to know the kid without interference. "Thanks for coming, but would you mind coming back in an hour?" I said. He sat in the car, and after the interview, I invited him back for fifteen minutes.

• *Be Personable*

I look for interpersonal skills. I like a kid to look me in the eye, and then, after the initial five or ten minutes, I like to see a student settle back and carry on a conversation. The demeanor is very important.

• *Show Some Humility*

If a student is too arrogant, he or she won't come across well. Back when I was interviewing job candidates at Harvard Business School, nine out of ten candidates were so arrogant I wouldn't even think of inviting them to our home office for the next round of interviews. The same goes for college interviews. Don't assume that you're the smartest person on earth. One boy actually had an e-mail address that read genethegenius@. . . . He was very bright, but I didn't need an e-mail to tell me.

• *Be Sincere*

Some kids sound staged or too rehearsed. A good interviewer can pick that up in a minute. It's certainly okay to talk about your special achievements, but don't try to impress by being someone you're not. The more natural you can be, the better. Again, an interview is a conversation, not an interrogation.

• *Share Your Family Circumstances*

Don't be afraid to explain what your daily life is like at home, including such things as family dynamics and personal responsibilities that might not be apparent from your application. One girl had spent the past twelve years helping her mother take care of a disabled younger brother. This was important information that I passed along to the school. I rated the girl a 5.

• *Communicate Passion*

Colleges do have a noble cause: They want to make it a better world. They're looking for kids who want to make a difference in the world and do something for others. That's why I want to see your passion: passion for your Hook, passion for your major, and passion for where you want to go in life. If you just want to come to a university because it's a good school but you don't really know what you want to study, then you won't make a good impression.

• *Indicate Your Interest*

I try to pick up as many clues as I can from the candidates about the probability of their accepting an offer of admission. It's not important to me, but it is important to the school. If the admissions office is trying to decide between two kids who are equal, they're likely to look more favorably on the one who shows the greatest commitment.

• *Be Neat*

Some boys come in khakis and a sport shirt, while others come in a blue blazer and tie. Girls wear everything from skirts to slacks with a modest sweater or blouse. As long as they're neat, that's all I care about.

• *Don't Miss the Interview Deadline*

Students shouldn't wait to be called for an interview. Some schools have deadlines long before Christmas, even for regular admission. Call or e-mail the admissions office to sign up for an interview as soon as you can.

• *Don't Assume the Interview Doesn't Count*

I interview half a dozen students a year, and every year one or two are accepted. If the school's evaluation of a student is similar to the alumni interviewer's, then the admission office feels comfortable. If the school is high on a kid and the interviewer is not, it raises a red flag. In such cases, the admissions office has to go back to the drawing board to find out why there's a disconnect.

TWENTY QUESTIONS

If you follow Dave's advice, you'll be relaxed, enthusiastic, and confident during your interview. But if you want to be even more prepared, you might consider role-playing with a friend, teacher, or family member. Here are twenty questions admissions interviewers might throw at you:

1. How do you like to spend your free time?
2. What are you doing this summer?
3. Who is your hero?
4. What's your favorite book? Movie?
5. What brings you to (name of school)?
6. What specifically appeals to you about (name of school)?
7. What excites you about (school politics, science, volunteering, writing, or whatever your Hook might be)?
8. Where does (this university) stand on your list? Why?
9. Have you thought about a major?
10. What drives you academically?
11. What academic experience has given you the most satisfaction?
12. What are your goals after college?
13. What do you think (name of school) will contribute to your future life?
14. What do you think you might contribute to the school and student body?
15. What do you consider your greatest strength? Explain.
16. What's your biggest weakness? Explain.
17. Can you tell me a little bit about your family?
18. What was your most satisfying summer experience?
19. What's your biggest passion?
20. Do you have any questions?

FOLLOWING UP

Once the interview is over, it's time to write a follow-up note to Dave or whoever interviewed you, indicating how much you enjoyed the interview and how eager you are to attend the school.

In order to write a note, you have to know the name and contact information of the person who interviewed you, so before you leave the interview, get a business card so that you can keep in touch. More often than not, students are so focused on themselves and their performance in the interview that they fail to find out pertinent information about their interviewer at the time they meet. That means they have to play catch-up afterwards.

Also, some students fail to follow up because they think a thank-you note is phony. "I don't want to look like I'm 'kissing up,'" one student said.

But what may seem like apple-polishing to you is merely good etiquette. In polite society, a thank-you note is expected; just as you would in a job interview, you need to respond graciously to an alumnus or alumna you've met. A letter and an e-mail to an admissions officer would be equally fitting, especially since most schools keep close tabs on student contacts.

When you write your note, don't forget to make reference to your Hook in a casual way. If you're a politico, you might say something like, "I'm really looking forward to trying out for the leadership program." If you're a musician, you could say, "I can't wait to play my tuba in the band." If you're a community service specialist, you could mention, "I can easily see myself working in (name of school's) elementary school tutoring program." Here's a sample:

SAMPLE THANK-YOU LETTER

STEVE STUDENT

(Your street address)

(City, State, Zip Code)

Date

Mr. or Ms. _____
(Title: e.g., Associate Director of Admissions)
College
Address
City, State, Zip

Dear Mr. or Ms. _____:

I just wanted to let you know how much I enjoyed meeting you on (date) and getting to learn more about (name of college). I was especially excited to discover (the opportunities available for African-American students, or your new program in Latin American studies, or your new center for marine biology—or whatever).

Since my visit, I'm more convinced than ever that (name of college) is where I want to be next September. I'll look forward to sending in my application and hope to be part of the (name of college) community.

Sincerely,

(Your signature)

(Your name)

As important as it may be, an interview is only one of the ways that you can make a personal impact on colleges. Another critical tool is personal contacts with admissions staffers who deal with your school or area of the country.

CHAPTER TWENTY-THREE

Romancing Admissions

HOOK TIP

Make a personal connection with the admissions rep who handles your school, state, or region, and then keep in touch regularly by e-mail, phone, or mail. If you're a minority student, contact the college's multicultural admissions coordinator.

Names and e-mail addresses of admissions staffers and their bailiwicks are often posted on college Web sites. Since many schools have elaborate electronic tracking systems to keep tabs on student contact, your "demonstrated interest," as it's called, could give you an edge. Don't be a nudge, but also don't be afraid to ask questions about what the school is looking for and how you can increase your chances for admission. If you bond with an admissions rep, you might very well gain an advocate who lobbies for you at decision time.

Unlike Elle Woods, Reese Witherspoon's aspiring Harvard Law School character in the hit movie *Legally Blonde*, Courtney Moore did not try to woo admissions with a video of herself emerging from a pool in a spangled pink bikini. Nor did she send a résumé on scented pink paper.

But Courtney did her own star turn as a "schmoozer" extraordinaire by making personal contacts with admissions reps at some of the colleges on her list, including Vanderbilt and Villanova. A senior class president with an interest in fashion and a top-ten ranking in an IB program at Sebastian River High School, a large public school in Florida, Courtney started working the e-mails and phones even before her applications were in the mail.

"I was worried about my scores," said Courtney, who feared that her 29 composite on the ACT, including a 34 out of a maximum 36 in English, might be her "downfall" at such schools as Wellesley, Vanderbilt, Georgetown, George Washington, Boston College, and Villanova.

"I figured that I needed to take the initiative to defuse any questions," she said.

Her first phone calls were to Villanova, where she had applied Early Action.

"I talked to an admissions rep at Villanova early senior year, around October or November," said Courtney. "I confessed my anxiety about my scores, but she was reassuring."

Over the course of the next few weeks, Courtney called the woman several more times to raise questions about the curriculum or to give an update on the senior class projects she was leading. Just days before she expected to hear about Early Action decisions, Courtney again called the rep. The woman's tone of voice and encouraging words gave every indication that the news would be good.

"You have nothing to worry about," she assured Courtney. "Check the decisions on-line tomorrow."

Courtney breathed a sigh of relief, but the next day, when she logged on to villanova.edu to check her admission status, she was shocked to discover that she had been deferred.

Immediately, Courtney fired off an e-mail to the admissions rep, asking about her chances of being accepted in the regular decision round. Once again, said Courtney, the woman oozed optimism.

"She told me the Early Action applicant pool was stronger than usual and that they had taken kids with higher scores than the normal cutoff," said Courtney. "But she seemed confident that I would get in."

But unwilling to bank on yet another disappointment from Villanova, Courtney turned her attention to Vanderbilt, which was one of the schools that was highest on her list.

"Although I had never seen the school, I decided to apply Early Decision II," said Courtney. To get an idea of her chances, she said, "I called the Florida admissions rep, who turned out to be the adviser who would actually read the applications from my town. She had just graduated from Vanderbilt the year before, and we ended up clicking."

Courtney confided in the young woman her concerns over her scores and the application process in general.

"She knew how nervous I was about the whole thing," said Courtney. "She calmed me down by describing her own college application experience, and we ended up talking a lot."

Sensing a soul mate, Courtney started calling the young woman regularly for advice. On one call, she mentioned that she was torn between two schools within Vanderbilt, the College of Arts and Sciences and Peabody College, and she wondered which way to go. On another call, which she made after sending in her application, she brought attention to her essays by asking for feedback.

"She liked the fact that the essays showed different sides of my personality," said Courtney, who had written her main essay about a crisis with her dad and another about her job at a Lilly Pulitzer boutique (see Chapter Seventeen, "Hooking Your Essay"). "Specifically, she mentioned that the essay about my father demonstrated that I had endured a lot, while the other showed my dedication and passion for fashion."

As it turned out, Courtney's essays weren't the only parts of her sales pitch to hit the mark with admissions. Her personal networking skills left such a powerful impression that when she visited Vanderbilt's Nashville campus for the first time in mid-February, the first thing the admissions rep told her was, "I know you so well that I recognize your phone number from the area code on the caller ID!"

Courtney's meeting with the rep was especially sweet because just hours earlier, her grandmother had called with the news that the mail had brought with it a letter of admission to Vanderbilt.

"I got lucky," said Courtney of her contacts with the admissions rep. "I was lucky that this girl was a recent graduate who liked the same things I did. But even if the rep had been a sixty-year-old man, I would have tried to establish contact. I'm convinced that taking the initiative and showing interest made a difference."

You may not think you have Courtney's people skills, but if you take the first step toward making a connection with admissions officers, you're likely to discover that they will welcome your interest. After all, admissions staffers are in a people-oriented business, and as such, they are eager to find out who you are and what makes you tick. What's more, part of their job is to ascertain how much you really care about their particular school. The more they know about you and your goals, the better able they'll be to evaluate your potential for admission and get behind your application. Since demonstrating interest in a college is vitally important to your admission strategy, here are some simple guidelines for selling yourself one-on-one to admissions:

MEET THE ADMISSIONS REPS ASSIGNED TO YOUR AREA

Most colleges have admissions reps assigned to a particular high school, city, state, or region. Others assign reps alphabetically, according to your last name. These reps are often the very same person who will be the first reader on your application. That's why it's imperative that you sign up to see college reps when they visit your high school or are hosting a meeting at a hotel or other venue in your area.

It's up to you to be assertive and chat with the rep personally. Stick around after the crowd leaves and ask a question or two about the school. If it seems appropriate, mention something about your Hook and find out how the college's programs might fit your interests. Above all, be sure to get the rep's business card and follow up with an e-mail.

If no reps are coming to your school or area, call the college and get the name and e-mail address of the admissions person who covers your school. Then send an e-mail explaining who you are, where you go to school, and why you are interested in attending. Get a dialogue going, and follow up with information or questions as they arise.

Check with your guidance counselor for a schedule of visits.

GET CONNECTED WITH MULTICULTURAL ADMISSIONS COORDINATORS

Multiculturalism is such a buzzword on campuses that many colleges have a diversity coordinator in the admissions department who acts as a point person for minority recruitment. Sometimes diversity is interpreted broadly to include low-income students regardless of minority status. If you consider yourself a multicultural person by virtue of your ethnicity, nationality, or income, don't hesitate to get on the radar screen of the diversity coordinator. Get e-mail addresses and phone numbers from the college, and be aggressive about asking questions and indicating your interest in what the school has to offer multicultural students.

VISIT THE CAMPUS

An on-campus visit can be a helpful way for you to demonstrate interest in a college. If you go, be sure to arrange in advance to take a tour and sit in on an information session, where you'll get lots of statistics on the school and its requirements. Also, make an advance appointment for an on-campus interview (see Chapter Twenty-Two, "Acing the Interview").

Regardless of who interviews you, don't forget to stop at the desk and ask if you can meet the admissions rep who handles your area. If he or she is not around, get a business card. Also get a business card of the rep who presents your info session.

While you're on campus, try to contact a professor in an academic department that interests you, or stop by to see the band director or coach. (For more on athletics, see Chapter Twenty-Four, "Courting Coaches.")

When you get back home, immediately send a thank-you e-mail to every person you met, indicating how much you enjoyed your visit and how much you want to attend.

Along with giving you personal connections, campus visits can also help you decide if a college is right for you. One student who was scheduled for a tour at a college in Maine, for example, took one step out of his car and promptly jumped back in.

"Let's go!" he told his mom. "Too many trees!"

Although a campus visit may be the ideal way to size up a school and make connections, if you can't take a road trip, either because of finances or time constraints, don't despair: just work harder at e-mail and phone contact with admissions.

ATTEND SPECIAL OPEN-HOUSE PROGRAMS

If your time is limited, pay attention to special open-house weekends at the colleges that interest you most. Typically, these programs, which are often held in early summer or fall, will pull out all the stops to show off the campus. The admissions staff will be out in force, along with a select group of current students and professors.

These open houses can be a good time to get more personally connected with staff members at the school, so be sure to sign up early. For starters, check out the following programs, some of which are earmarked for multicultural students or those with special interests:

Vanderbilt University: Several *PreVU* days, held in the summer and fall, offer students a chance to spend a day on campus rubbing shoulders with faculty, admissions reps, and current students. *PreVU* is specifically for seniors or rising seniors. For juniors and sophomores, there are several Black & Gold Days held each spring to give students beginning their college search an opportunity to explore Vanderbilt's academic offerings and experience a typical day on a college campus.

Carnegie Mellon University: During one of the university's Sleeping Bag Weekends, students have the opportunity to stay overnight with a current student in a residence hall, attend classes, and tour the campus. Fall weekends are open to prospective students, while spring weekends are reserved for students who have already applied.

Mount Holyoke College: This highly selective women's college offers fall open houses for seniors with special interests, including Focus on the Arts, Focus on Athletics, Focus on Diversity, Focus on Science and Math, and Focus on Riding for equestrians. The programs give students a slice of campus life, including panel discussions, workshops, and a chance to sit in on classes.

Amherst College: Two fall Diversity Open House Weekends running Saturday through Monday offer an opportunity for students of color *and* low-income students of all backgrounds to visit the campus, talk with students and faculty, attend classes, and spend time in a residence hall. Up to 200 students are selected for the weekends, based on an application, essay, and transcript. Typically 100 percent of costs are covered, including travel. Amherst prioritizes students from under-represented cultural groups such as African-American, Hispanic/Latino American, Native American, and Asian-American backgrounds. Application deadline: early August.

Bates College: It's no accident that diversity is important at this renowned liberal arts college in Maine, which was founded by Abolitionists in 1855. The school invites students of all ethnic backgrounds to apply to Prologue to Bates, a multicultural program held at the college's Lewiston campus during two weekends in the fall. Students chosen for the program live with student hosts and get a taste of academic and social life on campus. The application, which is due in the early fall, requires an essay, counselor recommendation, and transcript. Although room and board are covered for all students, travel scholarships are available based on demonstrated need.

Lehigh University: A fully paid, two-day Diversity Achievers Program in the fall of senior year is open to academically qualified students from diverse ethnic backgrounds at this popular university in Bethlehem, Pennsylvania. Selected students spend the night with undergraduate hosts, attend classes, meet the faculty, and tour the campus. Applications are available the summer before senior year. Requirements include an unofficial transcript, SAT or ACT scores, a letter of recommendation, and an essay.

SEND UPDATES WITH NEW INFORMATION AND AWARDS

As you are keeping in touch with admissions staffers, make a special point of sending new information about your accomplishments. Keep in mind that it's not too late to send supplementary information *after* you've applied. In fact, new accolades, particularly those relevant to your Hook, could help to tip the admissions scales in your favor.

The fashion columns you wrote in January for your hometown paper would be a good bet as an update. So would your award in December as Best Delegate at the Model UN conference at Brown University. Also, don't forget to send along a copy of your senior thesis and the euphoric letter you received from a school administrator who was blown away by your oral presentation.

Although you can send a letter with updates whenever you have something to report, focusing on a few strategic times may be especially helpful: 1.) in mid- to late January, when your Mid-Year transcript is sent out to colleges; 2.) as soon as possible after you've been deferred or wait-listed (see Chapter Twenty-Five,

"Working the Wait List"); or 3.) when you're bargaining to increase a scholarship award.

Consider the case of one Colorado senior who had been admitted to a noted midwestern technology school with a financial aid package that covered three-quarters of his tuition. After his admission, he learned that he had won a major architecture award. He sent that information along with a sample of his winning design to the college's financial aid office. The school rewarded him with a full-tuition scholarship *and* half the money he needed for room and board. He's planning to earn the remaining $4,000 by holding down a campus job.

The personal touch, which is important in wooing admissions and financial aid officers, is even more critical when it comes to selling yourself to coaches. If you're an athlete capable of playing a Division I, II, or III sport, you should approach making the team as you would getting a job—and that starts with initiating the first contact.

CHAPTER TWENTY-FOUR

Courting Coaches

HOOK TIP

Don't wait to be "discovered" by a college coach. Instead, break the ice by contacting the coach yourself.

Although some athletes are identified as prospects by Division I coaches as early as ninth grade, others, particularly those with potential to play at Division III colleges, are likely to remain in obscurity.

To get on a coach's radar screen, send a letter along with your stats, and don't be afraid to follow up with a phone call or e-mail. Ask the coach if he or she needs a videotape or DVD to evaluate your potential, and if so, find out exactly what should be on it.

Check the college's Web site to review the stats of team members and to identify which players are graduating. You may find that the coach needs a tight end, a small forward, a discus thrower, or a specialist in the 100-meter butterfly. If there's a hole in the team, you could be just the one to fill it.

Coaches do have some pull," said Chelo Canino, the Princeton pole-vaulter who was profiled in Chapter Four. "On the record, the Ivy League schools may say admission is all based on academics. But then they want to know: Are you a legacy? Are you a big athlete? Did you win some big award?

"Everyone at Princeton had something special," she said. The level of achievement at Princeton was so high, said Chelo, that on the first day of orientation, a joke spread around campus: "You spend your first couple of days in awe, saying to yourself, 'I can't believe I got in.' Then you spend the next few weeks saying, 'How the heck did he get in?'"

"For me," said Chelo, "athletics opened a lot of doors."

Athletics might be the Hook for you, too. The secret is not to sit back and wait, but to be proactive, positioning yourself to get recruited. In Chelo's case, though coaches from schools such as Kansas, Georgia, and Cornell started seeking her out, it was she who made the first overtures to Stanford and Princeton. (See Chelo's tips for student athletes at the end of Chapter Four.)

Another Division I athlete, Rosemary Sherry, who was captain of Lehigh's Women's Lacrosse Team, spent a post-graduate year working for the athletic department as a recruiter. Like Chelo, she has some practical advice for student athletes in all sports:

MARKETING TIPS FROM RECRUITER ROSEMARY SHERRY

- **Go to camps.** That's the number one way to showcase your talent and get recruited. Some camps are run at a university by the college coach; others are by invitation only. Attending a camp at a college that is high on your list is a great way for you to be seen by the coach and start a personal relationship. Coaches receive letters from hundreds of would-be recruits, and if they can connect your name to a face and playing style, you'll have a big advantage over other players.

     When it comes to invitational or elite camps, college coaches routinely scout camps for hot prospects. So try your best to attend one of these camps and light up the playing field with your abilities. An added bonus of these high-powered camps is that you'll pick up new skills and strategies that will improve your game. You'll also be able to size up your out-of-state competition.
- **Strengthen your academics.** The better your grades and scores, the more marketable you are to a coach. You'll have a better chance of gaining admission if you are strong academically. Coaches want to make sure you can handle playing a sport in college. If you have a hard time managing your time in high school, you may in college, too. Coaches look at the whole package.
- **Send in any special athletic forms on the application or fill them out online.** This will get you in the coach's database. Alternatively, send a picture and résumé that includes the camps you've attended, your statistics, your coach's phone number, and your school activities. (See Appendix B for a sample stats sheet.)
- **Send a DVD or videotape.** Don't send a highlight tape, because highlights can make anyone look good. Instead, send half a game or ten-minute

clips. Also, be sure to have clips that show you when you have the ball and also when you're off the ball. Coaches want an overall view of how you play. They want to know, "Are you just standing there doing nothing when someone is setting up a play, or are you creating something?" In lacrosse, for example, are you a "cherry-picker," simply waiting for someone to pass to you and score, or are you cutting to get the ball and setting picks?

- **Stay in contact.** It's good to be aggressive but not too aggressive. If you haven't heard from the coach after sending a tape, follow up with an e-mail. Then continue to keep in touch no more than once a month. Getting recruited is almost like applying for a job: you want to make sure the coach knows you're out there, but you don't want to appear too needy.

- **Request a meeting.** If you don't get offered a recruiting trip, make an appointment to meet the coach on campus anyway, and don't forget to bring a tape. You want to see if you can gel with the coach and team, since you'll be spending a lot of time with them. Team chemistry is very important. (See Appendix B for a sample letter.)

- **Ask the coach about playing time.** Be straight up and ask, "What are my odds of playing freshman year?" At some schools, you might not get to play until junior year. If it's important to you to play as a freshman, then find out your options.

- **Talk to the team.** If you're on a recruiting trip, ask the athletes on the team what they think about the college and the coach. Do they like playing for the coach? How demanding is it to play on the team? What's the training regime? Do they like their classes?

- **Ask where you stand on the recruiting list.** Chances are the coach will give you honest feedback. But even if you're on the coach's list, don't get complacent. You might be one of two goalies on the list, and if one with better stats gets admitted, you may be out of luck.

Although these tips are directed to students aiming at Division I or Division II schools, many of the same principles apply in Division III. At these typically small liberal arts colleges, the level of athletic competition may seem slightly less intense, but don't be fooled. These days, because of the stiff competition for admission to highly selective colleges, athletes who might once have looked only at Division I schools or the Ivy League are now vying for spots on Division III teams. As a result, in recent years Division III coaches have been deluged with videotapes and DVDs from prospective athletes around the country, a phenomenon that is intensifying year by year.

"We used to look for kids to develop into good college athletes," Haverford College's former athletic director, Greg Kannerstein, told the *New York Times*. "Now we pick among the polished athletes."[34]

Nonetheless, although your skill level at basketball, for example, may not be up to the standards of a Georgetown or Indiana, you may still have a shot at playing ball at a Division III school such as Williams, Amherst, Bates, Franklin

& Marshall, Trinity, or Haverford, if you work the system. At Haverford, according to a report by Bill Pennington in the *New York Times,* nearly 21 percent of the 315 students expected in the class of 2011 were recruited athletes. For another 50 students, athletics "played some role," the dean of admissions told the *Times.*[35]

But the pressure for spaces is intense. In recent years some liberal arts colleges have reduced the number of admissions slots for recruited athletes under pressure from the faculty, causing havoc with the recruiting system for coaches and students. One baseball prospect visiting a top college in the Northeast, for example, learned that he had been axed from the recruiting list just moments after the coach picked him up at the airport.

"I just found out that instead of six slots, I have two," the coach told the boy on the ride to campus. "You were my sixth pick. I'm sorry." Although the news made the visit somewhat awkward, the coach made up for it by sharing some tips on how the boy could increase his chances of admission elsewhere.

"Coaches at many top Division III schools have recruiting slots for students with high SAT scores," the coach told the boy confidentially. "So I suggest you really prepare for those SATs."

The boy took the coach's advice to heart. He prepped for his SAT and scored a 1450 on the verbal and math sections and over 700 on the writing. He was later recruited for a different sport at one of the Little Ivies.

As this student discovered, an athletic Hook can still play a significant role in admission at the Division III level—especially if you have the academics to back it up.

HEIGHT AND HAIKU AT DIVISION III

When it came to college admissions, Chas Woodward sensed he had a lot going for him. A student of Chinese, he had impressed his teacher by unabashedly bursting out in the language wherever he went on his high school campus and cajoling his friends to answer back. To further his Asian interests, he had spent two weeks one summer in a selective Asian cultural immersion program at Sewanee, the University of the South. And he had even penned some haiku for a Teen Writers Workshop he attended regularly. The haiku was published in a "chapbook," or small book of poetry, and sold on consignment at City Lights Bookstore, the famed home of the Beat Generation in San Francisco.

Despite such multicultural interests and credentials, Chas had "one thing" that held promise as an even stronger Hook: his height. At six-foot-eight, he towered over his teammates as the center on his school's varsity basketball team.

Coming from a small prep school, Chas knew he probably wouldn't have a shot at playing at the Division I level. If he wanted to play ball in college, he would have to focus his efforts on Division III. As a result, when senior year began, he put together his top choices: small liberal arts colleges, mostly in the Northeast, where academics were paramount. Among them were Sewanee, Williams, Colby, Bates, and Bowdoin, all schools where he could feed his passion for things Chinese and play ball at the same time.

Since basketball season didn't begin until November his senior year, Chas felt somewhat cowed by the process of courting coaches. He had contacted a few of them by e-mail, and he knew that in order to sell himself, he would need a videotape and some strong stats. Yet his team's season had been somewhat lackluster junior year, and none of the game tapes showed him to advantage.

Instead of giving up, Chas threw his energies into writing his essays and getting out his applications. By the time he dropped them in the mail in December, basketball season was in full swing. As the season progressed, Chas could feel himself growing as a player. Night after night, despite being double- or triple-teamed, he put up double digits.

Before long, he had the tape he needed: one explosive game where he was all over the court, blocking shots, elbowing opponents, and dunking.

Immediately he made copies of the tape for all the coaches on his list. To be sure they would stand out from all the other videotapes stacked up on coaches' desks, he wrote in bold black lettering on the spine: 6'8" CENTER; SAT SCORE 1380. With his SAT scores for Critical Reading and Math squarely in the mid–50 percent range of admitted students for most of the Division III colleges to which he was applying, he was signaling that he had the right stuff academically and athletically.

After sending out his videotapes, he began to step up his personal contacts with coaches, first through a guidance counselor, and then through e-mails of his own. Some coaches showed interest; others failed to respond at all. With those who showed interest, he continued to keep in touch by e-mail and phone.

His personal campaign to get recruited culminated one weekend in late February, when he flew to Maine on his own nickel to meet the coaches and basketball teams at several colleges. At Colby, the coach rolled out the red carpet, making sure Chas stayed overnight with team members and even setting him up to eat lunch at the Chinese language table.

Chas was duly impressed: "I loved the coach and team at Colby," said Chas. "I knew I could fit in."

Back home, encouraged by the Colby coach's overtures during his visit to Maine, he relaxed, waiting for the admissions decisions to arrive.

The good news from Sewanee, where he had participated in the Asian culture program, came several weeks early. He was "in," even though the coach hadn't recruited him for the team. The coach later told him he could try to join the team as a "walk-on."

When the admissions decision from Colby arrived around April 1, the news devastated him: wait-listed.

Despite all Chas's efforts—and the good feelings his college visit seemed to have generated—his hoop dreams hadn't materialized.

What should he do? At first, he decided to go with one of his top choices, Sewanee, where he knew many professors and loved the campus. But the more he thought about it, the more he wanted to keep his options open. And so in early May he began to work the wait list at Colby, the school where the coach, the team, and the academics best fit his style. He e-mailed the coach and the admissions office, indicating his desire to attend. Phone calls back and forth to Colby came next, and before long, the coach was telling Chas, "I want you. I need your height for the team."

But there was no word from admissions, and so little by little, Chas started to give up.

"One weekend, my mom asked me to clean up my room for a party," he said. "I came across all the Colby memorabilia I had collected on my visit, things like stickers for the car and some brochures. I looked at them for a minute or two, debating whether or not I should throw them away. Then I tossed them in the garbage."

Two days later, Chas got a call from an admissions official.

"We're *not* going to our wait list this year," he told Chas. "But we *are* offering you a place in the class. The coach has been in here every day asking for you."

"I'm coming!" Chas replied.

So the next time you're on the Colby campus in Waterville, Maine, if you happen to see a six-foot-eight student dribbling a basketball and babbling in Chinese, say hi to Chas. He's likely to respond, *Ni hao.*

By courting the coach until the very end of the admissions process, Chas learned a lesson in persistence that will last him a lifetime. But you don't have to be an athlete to keep up the pressure on admissions, even after the first round of decisions has been handed down. No matter what your Hook, you can "work the wait list" by following some simple principles in the next chapter that have led countless students to a successful outcome.

Chapter Twenty-Five

Working the Wait List

Hook Tip

If you've been deferred or wait-listed, *do not* roll over and play dead. Instead, get aggressive and "work the wait list" by hitting the admissions committees with everything you've got.

As quickly as possible, fire off a letter by mail or e-mail to the admissions office indicating how much you want to attend. If the school is your first choice, then say it. Send an update with new achievements, particularly those related to your Hook. If possible, try to set up an interview on campus. Even more important, keep your name on the wait list until the very end of the summer. As Yogi Berra said, "It ain't over till it's over."

You have four choices if you've been put on the wait list at a school or schools you really love: 1.) feel sorry for yourself and give up; 2.) feel good about the schools that have accepted you and make the most of those opportunities; 3.) work the wait list as far as it will take you; or, the best choice of all: 4.) move forward with a combination of 2. and 3.

Although it may be a major blow to your ego to be put on a wait list, don't consider it a failure. Popular wisdom dictates that if you are good enough to be wait-listed, you are good enough to be admitted. It's just that forces beyond your control—and enrollment pressures beyond the college's control—have conspired to keep you from getting that magical envelope that says "Welcome to the Class of ——."

As the admissions officer of one New England college told Phil, an anxious student who had dropped by to press the flesh two weeks after being wait-listed,

"There is absolutely nothing wrong with your credentials. You did everything right. It's just a matter of finding a place for you. Call me after May 1 and I'll see what I can do."

This may seem cold comfort, but it's the real world, and like other disappointments in life, how you respond could shape your character for years to come. It might even provide a good essay topic for grad school.

Consider Phil's reaction. Although he had been devastated to learn that he had been wait-listed, he didn't give up. Soon after getting his wait-list letter, he sucked in his pride and quickly headed for New England, where he managed to talk his way into a face-to-face meeting with the admissions rep for his area. Buoyed by the man's remarks, he left the campus feeling that he might have a chance.

As it turned out, not long afterward Phil spent a day at another college, one that had accepted him Early Action. He was so bowled over by the energy and creativity on campus that by the time the visit was over, he had made up his mind:

"This is exactly where I want to be!" he announced unequivocally. "I absolutely love it!"

He dropped off the New England school's wait list and never looked back.

But no matter how happy Phil was in the end, he didn't start out that way—and that's normal. It's okay to feel sorry for yourself if you've been deferred from Early Decision or Early Action or wait-listed in the regular round. After all, you have devoted years of hard work to this moment in your life, and your expectations have been completely dashed. If you're like most students, you've hoped against hope that you would be one of the select few admitted to the University of Pennsylvania, let's say, when instead you were one of 1400 sent to that no-man's-land known as the wait list.[36]

But there is a ray of hope—albeit a slim one. Students do get admitted off the wait list, and you could be one of them. Swarthmore, for example, took eighteen students from its wait list in 2005. In 2006 it took even more.[37]

No matter what the odds of success, why not work the wait list? Give yourself two or three days for a pity-party, and then pull yourself up by your bootstraps and do everything in your power to communicate to the top college or colleges on your list how much you want to attend. As the Marines say, "When the going gets tough, the tough get going."

Although working the wait list can't be equated to the life-and-death struggle of a military skirmish, it does involve strong inner fortitude and some strategic action that involves an element of risk. After all, there's a chance that no matter how much you wheel and deal with admissions offices, the wait list won't budge; or if it does, you won't be among those admitted.

But don't let that deter you. Instead, follow the lead of two students who took a risk to work the wait list and ultimately reaped the reward. Their pluck and persistence demonstrate an inner strength of character that is bound to lead to success throughout their lives.

OVERCOMING THOSE WAIT-LIST WOES: A TALE OF TWO STUDENTS

Case Study 1

"There's a kid here who says he's been wait-listed!"

James Pangilinan couldn't believe what he was hearing. He had come all the way to Georgetown from Florida hoping for an interview to boost his wait-list chances, only to have the student receptionist broadcast his request unceremoniously down the hall.

"It *was* awkward," admitted James, who was understandably put off by the student's less-than-gracious welcome. "It put a face on the impersonal nature of the admissions process."

Fortunately, James wasn't about to let the remarks of an insensitive student stop him from pursuing his goals. Although he quickly lost interest in Georgetown, he immediately headed north to Middletown, Connecticut, where Wesleyan University, one of the Little Ivies, had also put him on its wait list.

"I got there on a special weekend for admitted students," said James. "I felt a little displaced as the only student who had not been accepted, but I had no intention of giving up."

After sitting in on a few classes and meeting some students, James was convinced that the school was a perfect fit.

This would be a great place to go, he thought to himself.

Determined to get off the wait list, he walked boldly into the admissions office and asked to speak to an admissions officer. This time he got a warm welcome, and while he settled back in a chair waiting to be called for the interview, he flipped through some brochures to get a clearer picture of the college and how he might fit in.

"I could see that it was pretty much a regional school," said James. "More than 60 percent of the students came from New England and the Middle Atlantic states. Coming from the South, I thought I might have a chance."

Emboldened by the information, James walked into the interview confident that he had something to offer. The interview started with some broad questions about James's interests and background. But soon James turned the interview around, by asking direct questions about what qualities the admissions office would be looking for when it dipped into the wait list.

Pressing the interviewer for details, he learned that the school was striving for a balance in the class. Diversity was a big plus.

I'm okay there, thought James, pleased that his Asian-American background might be an asset.

And yes, geographic distribution could be important.

Check that off, too, he thought.

By the time the interview was over, James felt he had a deeper insight into the school and some ammunition for future e-mails.

"Although the interviewer was pretty neutral about my chances, I came away feeling that I had a good way of approaching the college," said James.

As soon as he got home, James immediately sought out Wesleyan's multi-cultural adviser and initiated a discourse by e-mail. "With each e-mail, I would add a new piece of information, such as the fact that I came from Florida, or my summer experience in Africa," he said.

Just before graduation, James was on a boat cruising off the coast of Fort Lauderdale when his cell phone rang with a call from his dad.

"Wesleyan's dean of admissions called to ask if you would accept an offer of admission," his dad told him. "I told the dean, 'Sure.'"

Added James, "I had a good evening that night."

Case Study 2

Margaret Fuller couldn't help but give a wry smile the day a student on a campus tour she was leading at Bowdoin College asked about her own admissions experience.

"I was wait-listed," she said matter-of-factly. "Believe it or not, I was wait-listed until June 21, the longest day of the year. For me it was symbolic of the longest application process ever."

As the students and parents in her tour group stood shaking their heads in dismay, Margaret went on to explain how she had learned the news of her acceptance.

"The school called and said, 'We have a spot. Would you like to accept an offer of admission?'"

By then, Margaret told her audience, she was sick and tired of the whole process, but nevertheless, she said "Fine."

"How excited could I be at that point?" she asked rhetorically. "I thought 'Enough already.'"

Enough, indeed. Margaret had set her heart on Bowdoin, but when the mail arrived a few days after April 1, there was nothing but a thin envelope bearing the words she dreaded to hear: Wait list!

Margaret thought she had done everything right. An A- student at a prestigious public school in suburban New York, she had scored a 1330 on the math and verbal sections of the "old" SAT. Although Bowdoin is "score optional" and as such didn't require submission of SATs, Margaret had submitted hers and had also clocked in with a perfect 800 on the Writing Subject Test. Her other SAT Subject Tests were stellar: 750 in French and 700 in U.S. History. Her AP tests were equally as strong, with three scores of 5 and one of 4. As a dual citizen (France and the U.S.), the world was her stomping ground: she boasted regular travels to her family in Paris and the French Alps, along with side trips to Morocco, Italy, Cambodia, and England with her parents and three older brothers.

What's more, she was a go-getter. She excelled in music (as a pianist and member of the all-state choir), sports (as a varsity soccer and tennis player), and service (as a weekly tutor in Harlem through the East Harlem Tutorial Program). On top of that, she had a solid Hook as a writer, with frequent articles in her local newspaper and a summer internship as the only teenager working at the *International Herald Tribune* in Paris. She wrote about the experience in her main essay.

With such a background, Margaret had no reason to think she wouldn't be admitted.

"You'll get in," her guidance counselor had assured her.

Confident of her chances, she applied Early Decision to Amherst and regular decision to only four other schools: Bowdoin, Harvard, Dartmouth, and the American University in Paris.

When the admissions letters started to arrive, the only good news came from the American University in Paris, where her brother had graduated. Although she liked what she had heard about the school, what she most yearned for was an all-American college experience, filled with athletic teams, a capella groups, and dorm life. Bowdoin seemed to have it all.

"I loved the campus when I visited," she said, "and I had heard great things about the English department. Also, the fact that it was closer to home was a plus. It seemed a little much to be in Paris for four years."

Although she was disappointed at being put on the wait list, Margaret moved quickly to keep her options alive. Two days after receiving the letter, she and her parents drove six hours to Bowdoin's Brunswick, Maine, campus to do what they could to work the wait list.

"I met with an admissions officer I had e-mailed," said Margaret. "Nothing immediate came of that interview, but it felt good to make contact. All she said to me was, 'Wait.'"

As it happened, while Margaret was having her interview, her dad was sitting in the waiting room reading *Bowdoin* magazine, where he spotted a photo of the admissions director. A few minutes later, he looked up to see the same man walking down the stairs. Being a gregarious guy, Margaret's dad walked up to the man and introduced himself by name.

The admissions director didn't skip a beat. "Oh, you're Margaret Fuller's dad," he responded. "I'll give her application a hard look."

"He knew my name," Margaret said. "That was one of those coincidences I'll never be able to explain."

Having done what she could to get her name around at Bowdoin, Margaret also relied on a full-court press by a string of supporters back home. Among them was her principal, who picked up the phone and lobbied for her with the admissions office.

"You're making a terrible mistake," he insisted.

Next came a local alumna, who seemed miffed because the college hadn't accepted anyone from Margaret's high school for several years.

"I'm going to call and complain," she told Margaret's dad.

"I don't know which one pushed the most," said Margaret, "but I think all these things helped."

As for Margaret, she kept up her own lobbying campaign by contacting Bowdoin's admissions office in May to see where she stood on the wait list.

"I learned there were two wait lists," said Margaret. "There was one in May, for students who might be admitted after the school determined how many spots were available from regular decision, and one in the summer. I was put on the summer wait list."

Although Margaret began to gear herself up for Paris, on the first day of summer she got the call she thought might never come. When fall rolled around, she was happily situated in a dorm at Bowdoin, living the American college dream: varsity squash team, a capella singing group, chamber choir.

In one of the greatest ironies of all, Margaret was one of a handful of freshmen chosen to work at the Bowdoin admissions office leading campus tours.

"The selection process was more competitive than getting admitted to college," Margaret said with a laugh. "But it was fun to show people around. I think it helped for students to realize that I had been in their shoes not too long ago."

As for advice, Margaret knows exactly what she would do if she had to do it over again.

"I'd apply to more schools and ones that are easier to get into," she said unequivocally. "And I would have applied to Bowdoin Early Decision or Early Decision II, which had a January deadline. Most likely, I would have gotten in then, because colleges like the yield. They like to know you are definitely committing. In talking to other members of my class, I found that a fair number got in early."

As it turned out, said Margaret, the application process toughened her up and taught her some lasting lessons. And she shared those lessons routinely with tour groups of prospective students when they asked, "What's the key to getting in?"

"It's not a key," Margaret liked to respond, borrowing a concept from an admissions officer she had once heard at a Harvard information session. "It's a combination lock, and you have to fit certain areas."

Speaking with wisdom born of experience, Margaret counseled, "Colleges aren't rating you as a person. You're just a piece of paper. Some people take it too personally. They forget that the process is really about what the college needs. It's about numbers, rather than actual people. Does the college need more scientists? Does it need more students in the liberal arts? The college is doing what it has to do in order to fill a class."

As for Margaret, she did what she had to do to make sure that when Bowdoin filled its class, she was among those admitted.

"I think I pulled out all the stops," she said. "It paid off, not only for me, but also for other students who came after me. In the past couple of years, Bowdoin has admitted four other students from my school."

QUICK TIPS FOR WORKING THE WAIT LIST

1. **Send in the colleges' wait-list response cards immediately.** Even if you're equivocating, buy yourself some time by keeping the wait list in play. With the pressures of prom, IB and AP exams, finals, and graduation bearing down on you, don't close down your future options just because you're overwhelmed today.

2. **Indicate that you want to stay on the wait list until September 1.** Many students assume that they need to get off the wait list by May 1, the date when colleges require deposits. But if you are dead-set on going to the school that wait-listed you, make a deposit at another school and keep your name on the wait list at your first choice as long as necessary. Please note, however, that you should make a deposit at *only one* school. It's considered bad form to double-deposit.

3. **Send an e-mail to the admissions rep in charge of the wait list.** At some schools, one admissions rep is designated to handle the wait list. That person may be different from the rep who handles your area of the country or section of the alphabet. Call the admissions office and get the name and e-mail address of the staffer in charge, and then send an e-mail making clear your desire to remain on the wait list.

4. **Write a letter requesting to stay on the wait list.** A formal letter that can be added to your file is always a good idea. Be sure to mention any new accomplishments or awards, especially those related to your Hook. Also include any supplemental material, such as newly published articles or even an extra essay that shows another dimension of your personality.

5. **Keep in touch every week to ten days.** When and if the wait list does move, you want it to move in your direction. A simple note that asks a question, indicates your continued interest, or adds a new piece of information, will help keep you on the college's radar screen. The same goes for a phone call. Surprisingly enough, many admissions reps are more than happy to talk to you personally. But don't be buggy. "And don't tell them everything at once," recommends James Pangilinan. "Spread out your attributes over a couple of e-mails or phone calls so that you have something to say."

6. **Visit the school immediately and see if you can meet with an admissions rep.** If you can't get an appointment in advance, show up anyway and see if you can meet with an admissions counselor. You have nothing to lose and everything to gain. Be sure to follow up your visit with an enthusiastic e-mail or letter.

7. **Don't give up until the first day of college.** Colleges have been known to admit students from the wait list up until the very end of summer. By then, you might be packing up your car and happily heading for another college. But if you're prepared to change your plans on a dime, go for it.

If you need any further encouragement to work the wait list, consider the following letter, written by a father whose son held out for a school he loved, despite the pressures to give up when deposits were due on May 1:

Pam—

Our recent experience with the "wait list game" generated a very successful result—closing almost 50% of the distance between our son's May 1st choice and the top of the US News Liberal Arts College Rankings. That's a dramatic result and one that our son is thrilled about.

What surprised me was the degree to which this part of the college application process seemed unnatural and uncomfortable. It was somewhat hard to follow your advice and stay in the wait list groove.

For almost a year and a half leading up to the college application deadlines we have been very focused and oriented to just that: deadlines. PSAT dates, SAT and ACT testing dates, special activities in anticipation of the resume, more than enough hosted college nights, myriad deadlines for applications and financial aid requests at 19 colleges, etc.

On the flip side, the deadlines for the colleges to notify our son were more organized. Most operated on an April 1 notification deadline and expected a response by May 1. The closer we got to May 1st, the more questions (pressure) we fielded from friends, relatives and other parents going through the college application process. The collective sense of relief about a final decision was targeted for May 1st. And we participated as our son accepted his optimum offer on May 1st—the deadline.

As you know, our son also was wait listed at two schools. He chose to pursue the one that was his favorite and near the very top of his list of 19. Some of his friends were in the same boat—accepting the best school offered and hoping for an upgrade by saying "yes" to the wait list for their favorites. Turns out you can do this for a while without too much stress. But the pressure and stress builds as his high school had senior t-shirt day (display your accepted school), all of the cars and trucks sprouted college decals, and everyone talked about their experiences with relief.

Displaying one allegiance while working the wait list at another college—calls and emails *every* three days—is tough. I can see why many parents and students give up early and drop off the wait lists. With your urging, our son stuck at it and succeeded, but I must tell you that he was feeling sort of "out-on-a-limb" just before he received that call from the Dean of Admissions saying he was off the wait list and could enroll (decision due within 24 hours).

My point is that our son, his mother and I really had to shelve our desire to "stop the madness/deadlines" and say we were done. You kept us going. Thanks for encouraging all of us to stick with the wait list process. The result is awesome.

As this student and his parents discovered, working the wait list can be a crucial strategy in selling your Hook to colleges. The results for you may be awesome, too, if you're willing to stick it out.

But at some point in the process—and that point is up to you—it will be time to take the long view and embrace the final result. Chances are, by the end of your freshman year in college, you will look back on the whole admissions experience and remember not what you might have lost, but what you've gained: life skills, personal fortitude, insights, and a sense of confidence that will carry you forward through the rest of your college experience to the job market and beyond.

Conclusion: From College to Self-Confidence

In the end, applying to college is all about empowerment. It's about discovering who you are through your Hook, and then learning how to promote yourself on paper and in person at every stage of the application process.

Many students start out overwhelmed, not merely by the application process itself, but by the prospect of leaving home and beginning the first phase of their adult lives. You may swear up and down that you can't wait to be on your own, or you might protest that you're living for the day when mom and dad aren't breathing down your neck. But the fact is, most students on the cusp of college are fighting to hold it all together emotionally. For most of them, going off to college is a daunting transition, and filling out applications is a reminder of what lies ahead.

Some students fight the process. Some procrastinate. And some grab hold of the experience, take command, and run with it all the way through the gates of Northwestern, Davidson, Rollins, Colby, Penn, USC, or Georgia Tech.

For those of you who are ready to grab hold of your own destiny, this book can serve as a guidebook not just for college, but for later life. Through these pages, you've learned how to find your Hook, you've gained insights into how to bolster that Hook through significant activities, and you've discovered how to present yourself in a résumé that communicates your strengths powerfully.

You've learned to write essays that dig deep into your personal psyche and experiences to reveal how you've overcome difficulties, faced challenges, gained insights from individuals, been inspired by works of art, or wrestled with provocative issues. These essays may have given you a window into yourself and your own amazing abilities.

What's more, in this book you've discovered how to sell yourself personally through interviews, e-mails, phone calls, and personal contacts with admissions officers and coaches.

And, last but not least, you've learned how to stick with it until the very end of the wait-list process, reaching forward even when everyone else has given up, to capture a prize that could very well be yours: admission to the college of your choice.

But no matter what college you ultimately choose, if you've followed the marketing principles of *The College Hook* each step of the way and taken its lessons to heart, you will have hooked an even bigger prize at the end of the process: a sense of who you are and what you can do. With this knowledge, you can begin the next chapter of your life with confidence—confidence that you can step onto any college campus or into any job and be successful.

Many recent college graduates are using these same principles to shape their lives after college, by hiring consultants who teach them to "brand and sell themselves," according to the *New York Times,* as they look to careers that will fit their interests and give them meaning.[38] But you have a head start. You know the secret to packaging yourself, and it starts with your Hook, which is just the beginning of a lifetime of self-assured achievement. There's an old saying that goes, "Hitch your wagon to a star."

I say, forget the wagon. Follow your Hook, and you'll *be* a star.

Sample Essays

Although there is no surefire formula for finding the right subject matter, essays typically fall into categories that bear replicating. Take a lesson from students whose essays earned them big payoffs in admissions. For examples of other successful essays that worked at other schools, see Chapter Seventeen, Hooking Your Essay.

THE CONFESSIONAL ESSAY

David Fell wrote his way into New York University Early Decision with his ruthless honesty about his mistakes as an exchange student in Costa Rica. He used his "most meaningful activity" essay (see page 128) to describe his music Hook.

As I was growing up Jewish in the 1990s, comedy became a large part of my personality. In school I tried to win friends with humor, sometimes even reaching "class clown" status. However, as I got older and altered my sense of humor to fit my age, I slowly transitioned from benign jokes to sarcastic comments, which usually guaranteed some laughter, but also one or two insulted faces.

Finally, my evolving sense of humor plunged me into a personal crisis during the summer before tenth grade. I was faced with a difficult decision: returning to the B'nai Brith Perlman camp, or spending five weeks in Costa Rica. When I learned that I could live with a local Costa Rican family and construct a community center for a poor, rural community, there was no question which program was for me.

Upon arriving in Costa Rica, we were warned about cultural misunderstandings and the importance of being extremely sensitive with our families. Though in hindsight these seem wise words, my arrogance at the time told me that my charm would easily overwhelm my family. I was wrong.

After a one-week orientation, I headed with fellow students Dan and Alex to La Florida, our home for the next few weeks—and I was immediately impressed by the beauty of our magnificent, turquoise-stone residence. When we knocked, a short, stout woman with a tremendous smile enveloping her face opened the door. She immediately exclaimed, "Bienvenidos!" which means welcome in Spanish. Then she introduced us to her family and sat us down at their dining table.

Dan commented on the beauty of their home, and Alex nodded shyly. Then it was my turn. I looked around, smiled pompously, and said, in the most sarcastic tone I could conjure, "What are you guys talking about? This place is disgusting!"

With head down, I awaited my applause. Then I glanced up at my friends, who had not said a word since my comment. They were frozen, unable to look me or our host family in the face. Slowly, realizing what I had done, I looked at my hostess. Her eyes had sunk beneath the table, and then, in a montage of humiliation and mortification, she looked wordlessly toward her husband and children.

It took me the entire first week to explain the concept of sarcasm to her, but she never understood completely. In the end, she settled for a strong apology. She was very forgiving. Soon, it began to dawn on me that sarcasm isn't clever, it isn't interesting, and it certainly isn't funny. Sarcasm is simply a way of masking your own personality problems behind crude comments, which might be funny to some, but are consistently hurtful to the person who is the target.

Since that encounter, I have made it a high priority to avoid sarcasm. When I returned home, I found I had become more attuned to the motives and feelings of others. When my friends were sarcastic, I tried explaining to them the potential harm, but they brushed me off. Barriers arose when I refused to laugh at their "jokes." They seemed subtly to resent me.

Finally, I took drastic action. The next time a friend sarcastically insulted me, I acted as though I were extremely hurt. I separated myself from him for a week and watched him try to apologize as I rejected all of his advances. At the end of the week I approached him, told him that I was not really offended, and related my Costa Rican story. Since then, I have noticed a significant change. My friends avoid sarcasm, at least around me. It seems that by leaving sarcasm behind, I have developed healthier relationships—and have actually started to become funny again.

—*David Fell, New York University, Class of 2010*

THE NONCONFORMIST ESSAY

Sometimes your Hook is simply your personality. Lenny Strom got hers across in an essay that left no mistake about who she was.

I am a girl named Leonard.

Although I have always been known as "Lenny," my real name has given me a life of countless questions and disgusted looks that follow my answer to the question, "Lenny? Is that short for something?" Throughout elementary and middle school, my more masculine and peculiar name brought me shame and caused me to stand out, a situation that for a girl of ten or twelve is the worst thing imaginable.

The first day of school brought with it my ongoing fear of red-faced roll calls. Although my classmates knew me by my more easily accepted nickname, attendance lists never failed to reveal the truth. Teachers' double-takes when the little girl in the front raised *her* hand following the unquestionably *male* name that had just been called led me to wish time and time again that my name was something more normal, such as Sally or Katie, or any of the other names of my girl classmates. *They* didn't have to explain as I did, "No, my parents weren't hoping for a boy," or, "No, it isn't a misprint." I got tired of giving the same response: "Believe it or not, my parents thought it would be a *good* idea to name their only daughter after her grandfather, who had died just two years before her birth."

Once people realized that my name was legitimate, the laughter and questions about my parents' sanity followed. Although my parents weren't cruel people playing a joke on their child, as many of my peers and even adults had jeered, the common speculation that they were rather unusual actually wasn't too far-fetched.

"What kind of people would name their daughter Leonard?" people asked repeatedly.

The truth behind this question lies in my parents' utter disregard for the comments and biases of others, as well as in their close identity and pride in family. Those who spend time with my family soon see that the concept of a girl named Leonard doesn't seem quite so odd. For one thing, we're a family of radical individualists. When I was in seventh grade, for example, my parents abruptly moved us to Paris, where for a year my dad studied painting and my mother took cooking classes at the Ritz Escoffier. My brother and I attended an international school, where we were surrounded by students from every faith and culture on the globe. As a result of such experiences, by the time I reached high school, I began to understand that my unique name had the advantage of immediate recognition, and not just the burden of standing out.

In fact, as I've prayed through the embarrassment and discomfort over the years, I've discovered that I am a perfect Leonard. I am the only female Leonard that most people have ever met, and I'm also the only young woman that many people have encountered who is quite like me. My family's offbeat streak has set the stage for me to be a girl with a difference in more ways than a name. Whether I'm risking my neck doing full-out scaling up a mountain in the Tetons, or riding the Metro alone in the middle of Paris during a period of anti-American demonstrations, or watching patiently at midnight as endangered Leatherback turtles come ashore to lay their eggs on the beaches that were the playground of my childhood, I am always ready for the unusual.

—*Leonard Marie Strom, Appalachian State University, Class of 2008*

THE SPORTS ESSAY

Although many counselors urge students not to write about sports, the subject can work if you focus on what's happening inside you rather than on your victories on the playing field. That approach worked for Greg Daniels, whose passion for golf—and his ability to write about it—became his Hook.

The personal experience that has given me the greatest feeling of satisfaction in recent years is the challenge of playing competitive golf. After a slice into the woods, a duff into the water, a failed escape from the sand trap, and a dreadful three putt, I often find myself wondering, what exactly is it that keeps me coming back for more? The uncompromising frustration associated with the game is consistently unbearable—so why do I put up with such torture?

The beginning of an answer came after I survived round after round and found my mind filled with great moments highlighted by unbelievable shots. These memories have caused me to continue to strive for perfection, concentration, self-control, respect, and competition—and to develop an unconditional love for the game.

I, for one, am addicted to golf because it forces the mind and body to strive for perfection. Golf can never be conquered. It is impossible to be content with my performance because there is always room for improvement. No matter how well I shoot, someone else out there shoots just as well or better. So, in order to make an impact, I must never stop improving, or I'll fall behind the pack.

Golf also demands my utmost concentration. If I am not completely focused on my next shot, there is no way I'll be able to execute it properly. I find it most advantageous to forget everything that has happened earlier in the round and concern myself only with the upcoming shot. Also, I have learned not to get discouraged while in the middle of a round because, no matter what, I have to finish. I must remain confident in my ability to make it to the end or I will never be able to execute under pressure. This pressure is something else that I live for because it forces me to keep my concentration.

Finally, golf encourages self-control, which prevents my emotions from getting the better of me. Even as I respect the rules of the game, the difficulty of the course, and my opponents, I understand that golf is a game where I compete primarily against myself. Because I cannot control the actions of my opponents, I become my ultimate opponent. To me, the game of golf epitomizes the ultimate challenges of life, and that is why I look forward to taking it on every day of my life.

—*Gregory Daniels, Georgia Tech, Class of 2010*

THE FAVORITE FILM/BOOK ESSAY

Many colleges ask you to write about the impact of a favorite book or creative work. Mack Elder's insights into the film Blade Runner *provide a window into the thought processes that shaped his future goals.*

I saw Ridley Scott's *Blade Runner: The Director's Cut* at a special screening at Radio City Music Hall. From the opening shot of the flying cars and huge pyramid skyscraper that dominated Scott's landscape, I was transfixed.

The film became my instant favorite, with a regular ritual of viewing between the new releases I rented from the local Blockbuster. Each time I watched the movie, I saw something new. I studied the performances of Scott's actors and analyzed how their movements and expressions were linked to the dialogue, the scene and the setting. I even read the book the movie was based on, *Do Robots Dream of Electric Sheep?,* and compared author Philip K. Dick's darker vision with the world that Scott created in his film.

As I read and compared, I began to appreciate that a director's task is not simply to translate a book or script into a visual medium, but to create a world within his film that is fully realized in itself, yet also envelopes the audience. Once I had this epiphany, I was no longer hooked just on *Blade Runner;* I was hooked on film. Film in all its aspects became a passion to read about, study, relax with, write about, and review. Writing and directing film became my ultimate goal, though it seemed unattainable for a teenager with no training or connections.

Then last summer, I worked as an intern at the American Museum of the Moving Image. My first day on the job, as I was walking through the special effects exhibit, I could hardly believe my eyes. There in front of me was the model used to create the skyscraper pyramid in the opening shot of *Blade Runner*. But now, instead of a hulking building projected on a huge screen, I was looking at tiny windows, ceiling fans, and lights in a foot-high pyramid. The great art of directors, cinematographers and others had transformed these Lilliputian objects into a scene that was larger than life. Now I understood that with the right tools and training, my goal was attainable after all.

—Michael MacCook Elder, USC's School of Cinema–TV, Class of 2006

THE INFLUENTIAL PERSON ESSAY

The Common Application's question "Indicate a person who has had a significant impact on you, and describe that influence" may seem like a fairly prosaic topic, until you read Anum Niazi's essay about her encounter with a woman in Pakistan.

I never truly grasped the concept of "community service" until I met the woman with the gloves. She lived in a dilapidated village outside Lahore, Pakistan, where I met her last summer. I was writing case studies for a group called Development Action for Mobilization and Emancipation (DAMEN), which gives small loans to women to start businesses in their homes.

With two social workers from DAMEN, I walked cautiously through a narrow alley toward the woman's house, avoiding the open sewage flowing on both sides and skirting the puddles that had been left in the dirt from the previous night's rain. On either side of me, houses with dirt walls cemented by cow dung pressed close.

Halfway down the alley, the social workers turned up a crooked dirt stairway, which led to the rooftop of a house overlooking green and yellow fields. Off to the side, a toddler with a tattered dress stood staring, ignoring the flies that swarmed around her half-eaten biscuit. Moments later, a dark-skinned woman came out of a doorway and smiled. I could see the happiness in her dark brown eyes, but there was another, more troubled expression, which was hard to ignore.

At the social worker's urging, I introduced myself, explaining in

Urdu that I was a student working with DAMEN. The woman's gratitude for the financial assistance the organization was providing became obvious, as she quickly hugged me and the social workers. She introduced herself as Gullam Fatima and then led us into a dark room.

In the darkness, I could barely make out the form of a young boy, scissors in hand, sitting cross-legged on the dirt floor surrounded by fabric. My shock at seeing the little boy hard at work in the dark was tempered by Gullam Fatima's glowing pride, as she presented her oldest child and began to explain her glove-making business. The words flowed from her mouth onto my notepad as I jotted down her general history. Every now and then, I peered at the young boy, who was working rapidly, cutting a pair of gloves from the fabric. His fingers appeared swollen and rough, while his face, in contrast, betrayed his innocence and intense concentration.

The woman's statements about her business seemed fairly routine, until I heard words that made my blood rush cold, despite the sweltering heat. Gullam Fatima was supporting her entire family of six on a profit of ten cents per glove! Based on the value of the rupee, this was barely enough in Pakistan to support one person.

As the enormity of Gullam Fatima's situation settled on me, the room seemed to grow silent, except for the snipping of the little boy's scissors. Jumbled thoughts of my life in Florida flooded my mind. I remembered the service projects I had been involved in through the Boys & Girls Club, the tutoring I had done, and the leadership conferences I had attended. Suddenly, I knew that I needed to do something to help Gullam Fatima. All the community service I had ever done up to that moment had been preparation, but for what? What could I do as a high school student in Florida?

I asked Gullam Fatima to show me one of her best gloves, and as my fingers explored the neatness of the edges and the meticulous needlework, an idea began to form in my mind. Perhaps I could bring her work gloves back to America and make a business deal for her with a store like Home Depot. Excited by the possibilities, I told her my idea. Her face lit up in a state of happiness beyond anything I had ever seen. As her joy became my joy, I could feel my motivation increase. To me, she was no longer just a glove-maker, but a woman I now understood emotionally at a deep level.

I may not be able to help everyone in the world, but perhaps I can help Gullam Fatima. Whether or not I succeed in helping her with her business, my service to a woman who makes gloves in Pakistan has helped me by increasing my desire to serve and assist others.

—*Anum Niazi, Vanderbilt, Class of 2008*

THE CREATIVE ESSAY

What could be more creative than taking a standard topic and giving it an unusual twist? For this essay for Dartmouth, Amanda used the "influential person" theme, but discussed it in a surprising way.

> **". . . As water reflects a face, so a man's heart reflects the man."**
> **—Proverbs 27:19 (NIV)**

Most New Yorkers will remember the Blizzard of '96 as the time Potamkin dealerships promised leases with "no money down" if the snow reached twenty-four inches in Central Park (it reached twenty-three). But I remember it as the time I met the girl from North Carolina.

I was on a crowded commuter train, headed for New York City's Grand Central Station. It was the first day of rehearsal for a new play I had been cast in a week before. Feeling the long dormant cocoons in my stomach hatch into large butterflies, I decided to strike up a conversation with the girl sitting near me.

She had a twangy southern accent that spoke of broken fences, hardscrabble farms, and green hills. The whole time we talked she faced directly forward. Never once did she turn her head toward me. I thought maybe she had a neck cramp of some sort, so I didn't ask questions, and instead listened to her hard r's and tried to copy them in silence.

It wasn't until we got off the train that I realized there was a specific reason for her not letting me see her whole face. She had a scar that ran clear across her cheek. It was so dramatic it seemed to slice her left cheek in two and then make sort of a half-moon by her lip.

I was so startled by the sight, I let out a little gasp. She noticed my immediate revulsion and gave me a particularly nasty look. Of course, I felt terrible and tried to apologize. But before I could say a word, she was lost in the crowd of whole faces leaving Grand Central Station.

Coincidentally, over the next few months, I found myself on many train rides with the girl from North Carolina. It seemed we both took the 10:07 A.M. to the city and the 10:35 P.M. home—both on-peak. I did eventually get to apologize, and she, in turn accepted.

I loved those train rides. We would always try to get one of the two-seaters that faced forward in car four. That way we were always sure to meet up.

At first, I thought of myself as better than she. She had a poor education, and it showed. She dressed shabbily and was ignorant of pop-culture, which made me feel like the most cosmopolitan teenager around. But she was quick-witted, and ended up proving me wrong.

Over the weeks of commuting, I discovered how intelligent she truly was. Her discernment of people was enough to knock me off my seat. Sometimes she would watch one person on the train very closely, and by the time we got to his stop, she would be able to predict exactly how this man would get off the train—would he clear his throat or straighten his tie? She always knew. She also taught me a lot about Christianity. She was a devout Protestant, and I, being Jewish, never really did see eye to eye with her about matters of a higher power. However, I did learn to understand why her faith provided such a wonderful motivating force in her life.

As we grew closer, we became more and more like one and the same person. Her ability to look deep into my heart and see my problems like a crystal clear well nearly brought me to tears. I found, too, that she had deeper scars on the inside than on the outside. Her mother had died during childbirth, her father was a poor farmer, and she was an only child. She lived on top of a hill, miles away from any neighbors. She wasn't lonely, though. She said New York, with its eight-million inhabitants, was a "hell of a lot lonelier than the foothills of North Carolina." I believe her.

In reality, the girl from North Carolina was just a character I played in a show entitled "Violet." This is the story of how I came to know her and embody her as a real person. The lessons she taught me remain the same, even if our interactions took place only in my mind.

The most important thing I learned from her was to look inside myself—to see what I was really feeling, and express it in a productive way. Because of her, as the Proverb says, I know the "water" I look into every day reflects a smile.

—*Amanda, Dartmouth College, Class of 2003*

THE OFFBEAT ESSAY

Mack Elder's essay for USC'S School of Cinema-TV positioned him as a creative guy who knew his stuff and wasn't afraid to take a risk. He used a screenplay format to muse on his struggles to write the perfect college essay.

1. Int. A bathroom. Day.

A frustrated applicant to USC's School of Critical Studies, named MACK, sits in an empty bathtub with a laptop, staring at the blank page of a word processor program and rolling Clementine oranges back and forth on the edge of the bathtub with the palm of his hand. MACK is dressed very casually. He begins to speak in voice-over.

MACK (V.O.)

How do you boil down everything you have done and want to do into one page of expository writing? How do you talk about your love of film and your aspiration to be part of the film-making process any way you can? Do you simply list your credentials as they appear on your resume? Do you use some sort of cliché phrase? Do you talk about how you're writing in the bathroom because your room was too distracting, and move on from there? Do you employ some sort of gimmick?

He opens the CD tray of the computer and inserts a disc.

MACK (V.O.)

Sure, I could sit here and describe to you how I've spent the last three summers on the campus of the University of Virginia, living in the dorms, writing plays and drinking soda. I could pontificate for hours about the advantages and hardships of going to a selective high school, or about my various theater experiences and how I've grown from what I've experienced while acting or directing or working on a crew.

CUT TO a close shot of the computer screen. The page is still blank. A CD program blinks, putters, and displays the track listing. Punk rock wheezes out of the tiny speakers of the laptop. CUT TO MACK, still staring at the screen, hands still motionless over the keyboard.

MACK (V.O.)

Of course, I could always talk about when I first decided that I would be involved in film, that day that Star Trek: The Next Generation premiered. But then you'd be wondering for the rest of the statement why I decided at the age of three what I wanted to do with my life. I could describe the day I saw The Rocketeer for the first time, and how I came out of the theater wondering who actually writes the movies that I see. Or, I could talk about that old Microsoft CD-ROM, the one with all the inane movie synopses and film clips and filmographies, and how I would sit there for hours and look through those movies, some that I had seen, some that I hadn't, and remember almost everything I learned about them.

DISSOLVE TO

2. Int. A bathroom. Night.

MACK continues to sit in front of the computer screen. He has shifted in the tub a bit from the last time we saw him. The dissected rinds of the Clementines lie scattered near his feet. The music has changed to a fast rockabilly tune.

MACK (V.O.)

> I could always go for the kicker and say that one cannot do until one knows how, and that the School of Critical Studies would provide me with the knowledge of how a film is crafted, so that I can make a film of my own someday.

MACK leans forward a bit. He pauses, then begins to type.

MACK (V.O.)

> Of course, once you have eliminated what you could do, what you are going to do presents itself.

FADE OUT to the sound of exaggerated keystrokes.

—*Michael MacCook Elder, USC's School of Cinema-TV, Class of 2006*

THE DIVERSITY ESSAY #1

Diversity is so important to colleges these days that if you've got a multicultural connection, turn it into a Hook through an essay. Aezad Aftab did just that and was accepted Early Action to Binghamton University, the premier school in the State University of New York system.

As the first day of my first year of high school commenced and the daily announcements began, I heard a young woman's voice say something that sounded like "hola." Assuming she was saying the word "hello" in some unknown language, I listened vaguely as she went on to introduce herself as President of Williamsville North's Cultural Awareness Club. Soon, along with most of the students around me, I tuned her out and began looking around to see who else would be sharing first period with me.

Then, the "hola" announcer said words that were sure to get my attention: "free food this Wednesday in room A-242." That is how it began—my four-year passion to change views and stereotypes involving different creeds, races, and religions of those I encountered.

I can still recall quite vividly that first meeting and those that followed during the next three years. The president of the club introduced herself and her fellow officers, then immediately greeted new members with a warmth and enthusiasm I found remarkable. After introductions, the meeting became a lively meeting spot for an eclectic group of North students as well as teachers and administrators; the club truly was a microcosm of Williamsville North High School. As I attended more meetings, I found myself not only learning about other cultures, but also getting more involved with the club and its efforts to make our high school community more accepting of those from other lands and traditions.

At the end of my sophomore year in high school, I decided to run for office and was elected president of the club. By December of my junior year in high school, a cultural awareness tornado was whirling around me at five on the Fujita scale. What had begun as something so innocent as wanting free food had become a campaign to help resolve racial and religious stereotypes not only in our school but also in our town.

The other club members and I began volunteering at refugee centers and holding numerous drives to gather books and winter apparel for the needy. This senior year is also the year when I must plan and run an assembly where all of North will be able to witness the many different cultural traditions and talents of our peers.

As my senior year began, I began thinking about how the decisions I had made freshman year had affected my life thus far, and I came to this conclusion: it may not have been a few big decisions that have made me who I am; instead, the small choices, such as joining clubs like Cultural Awareness, have been the transforming triggers. Today I possess many different skills, thought processes, and leadership qualities that I am sure I could not have gained anywhere else and certainly not in a textbook, but only in room A-242 every Wednesday.

—*Aezad Aftab, Binghamton University, Class of 2008*

THE DIVERSITY ESSAY #2

Whitney Morein revealed her awakening to her Mexican roots in an essay that clearly established her identity. She was accepted to a host of colleges, including Vanderbilt University, her first choice.

I am Hispanic, but most people would never guess it. I have light skin, blonde hair and blue eyes. Also, I never focused on my true ethnic identity until just a few months ago when my grandmother became very ill.

When I was little, she was always buying me books with a Mexican theme. It was fun to visit her in the summer because she and her Mexican cook, Trini, made the greatest Mexican cuisine. Trini and Grandma introduced me to the Mexican way of cooking tamales, enchiladas, chorizo, and my favorite, Trini's lemonade. As she worked, Grandma, a full-blooded Mexican, regularly referred to my own Mexican background. But at the time, I was more interested in smelling and tasting her food than in listening to her stories.

My awareness of my Hispanic roots deepened this past summer when my grandmother's longstanding breast cancer got worse. When I arrived at her home for a one-week visit, my heart sank. She was so weak and frail. Toward the end of the week, as I was sitting at the kitchen table, Grandma got out of bed, pulled me in front of the refrigerator, and took out two avocados, which she placed in my hand. She then sat in the seat next to the counter and taught me how to make her special guacamole. Finally, she looked me in the eye and said, "Whitney, I want you to promise me something: Always remember our family's past and never forget our people."

A month later my whole family flew out to be with Grandma. The hospice nurse had told my grandfather that she had only a few more days to live. Grandpa told us she might not talk or recognize us. When we saw her, it was hard not to cry. Seeing Grandma lying there, a shell of her old self, was more than my heart could bear. But the next day she rallied, and the following week, other details of my Hispanic heritage emerged.

At one evening meal, for instance, I was wearing my mom's gold Mexican Peso necklace. My uncle asked me if it was one of the coins that my great-grandma—Grandma's mother—had when she left Mexico for the United States. I took off the necklace and saw that the date on the coin was 1918. Then my uncle told this great story about how the President of Mexico had given my great-grandmother a bag of gold coins to help her get to the United States. She hid the coins in her undergarments, and when she came across the border into California, she was robbed. But the thieves overlooked the gold coins.

My uncle then told about my great-grandmother's struggles to survive in her new land and about how she wanted her children to be born in the United States so they could have a better life. He described the troubles growing up in the barrio on the north side of Los Angeles with other immigrant workers. As he spoke, I glanced at my grandma, whose face was radiant as she nodded her head in agreement. Though my grandmother was dying, it was clear that she was proud for us to hear of our family's struggles and triumphs as Hispanic immigrants.

My grandmother lost her battle with cancer on August 17, 2004. At her memorial service the minister spoke of her pride at being Hispanic. He told how she had helped immigrant workers deal with their landlords and bosses while she lived in Sedona. She had also worked at the library as a bilingual librarian and volunteered at the Old Towne Mission as a translator. Her life had demonstrated her commitment to giving back to her community and affirming her heritage. After my experiences with her this past summer, I have made a firm promise: "Grandma, I won't forget."

—*Whitney Morein, Vanderbilt University, Class of 2010*

THE DIVERSITY ESSAY #3

Josh, the photographer who was highlighted in Chapter One, had another selling point for his college applications: his newly discovered biracial heritage. Here's how he revealed the secret of his grandfather's hidden ethnicity.

As I lay on my hard old futon mattress, supported by piles of books, I attempted to comprehend the idea that my father was only half Jewish. After hours of tedious mental labor, I slowly began to understand how my father, a true Zionist, was coping with discovering his South American and Asian roots.

To me, it was not such a surprise. I have vague memories of people commenting on the almond shape of my brother's eyes, and someone once even asked me, "Who is that 'China man' in all of the pictures on your wall?" I always knew that my father's complexion would never be categorized as "Caucasian," but I never even hypothesized that his father was anything other than Jewish.

But four years ago, after sixty years of not knowing anything about his biological father, my dad found out that his father was an ethnic Chinese from Colombia. After a few phone calls and emails, my father learned that his grandfather was Chinese, his grandmother was a native islander from the Caribbean, and his own birthplace was Panama. Within hours he was speaking to his half-sister on Providencia Island, a tiny Colombian island off the coast of Nicaragua. Within days he was speaking to newfound cousins all throughout America. And within weeks he was standing in front of his father's tombstone on Providencia Island.

Since then my parents and I have traveled to China, Panama, Colombia, and the two small Caribbean islands, San Andres and Providencia, where my father's family lives, to research our heritage.

Although this radical change in our lives is still somewhat confusing, what intrigues me most is watching my father attempt to understand his ethnicity. Throughout this process, which is by no means finished, I have slowly begun to understand myself. I have come to realize that ethnicity, although superficially important, does not necessarily determine one's identity. It serves no other purpose than to categorize certain people by the color of their skin.

My father's discovery at age sixty that he was born to a Chinese-Colombian father has not taken anything away from the identity that he believes is his: an American Jew. Even after sleeping in the same house as his Colombian half-sister, who speaks broken English and practices Seventh Day Adventism, my father has not lost any of his faith in himself as an ardent member of the Jewish people.

The impact of this experience on my outlook on life has been incalculable. With all the complexities of my ethnicity and the ambiguities of my feelings, the events that have occurred over the past four years have served to reinforce my commitment to cultural diversity, which, without knowing why, I have been drawn to since childhood. As a result, I've been motivated to set up a cultural awareness program at my school as student council president, and I've found myself approaching everything I do with newfound intensity.

For now, I'm content to identify myself as a true New Yorker—a melange culturally, ethnically, and racially. Now I lie here, still on the same old hard futon mattress, supported by piles of books, pondering not only who I am, but also who I will become.

—*Josh, Bard College, Class of 2004*

THE FAMOUS QUOTE ESSAY

Although quotes can make an essay overly stuffy and pedantic, they can often elevate an ordinary experience into something extraordinary, as they did in this supplemental essay on street basketball. The essay was chosen as one of Amherst College's "Voices of the Class" during freshman orientation for the Class of 2002.

> **I think that, as life is action and passion, it is required of a man that he should share the passion and action of his time at peril of being judged not to have lived.**
>
> **—Justice Oliver Wendell Holmes, Jr.**

This observation, made by Justice Holmes during a Memorial Day speech in 1884, sums up the way I have tried to live and the way I hope to live the rest of my life. My passion is people, and my action is communicating with those from every walk of life and every level of society.

I have hobnobbed with European diplomats and Argentine polo players during a month-long stay with a French family in Deauville. I have danced the *salsa* in Yauco, Puerto Rico, with a friend's aunts, cousins, and grandmother. I have even portaged canoes across the wilds of southern Canada with a team of survivalists, and have waited for the perfect wave with surfers off the east coast of Florida. But perhaps where I've learned the most about communication—and where I've truly shared the passion and action of my time—is on the public basketball courts of New York City.

For me, street basketball has been an extension of the episodes described in one of my favorite books, Rick Telander's *Heaven Is a Playground,* which captures the camaraderie of the inner-city game and the joy felt by those who participate. While living in New York as a middle-school student—and later on special trips back to the City— I ate, slept, and breathed basketball. Every day after school, I would go to the Stuyvesant Town playgrounds and test my skills against the best players in the neighborhood. On weekends, I might shoot hoops at West Fourth Street or in Tompkins Square Park.

But playing wasn't the most important thing I did on the hot asphalt courts of lower Manhattan; even more valuable were the friendships I made and the people I met. On those courts I played with people from all ethnic backgrounds and from every rung on the economic ladder. Prep-school kids, high-school dropouts, lawyers, accountants, bartenders and drug dealers played together with one common goal—to improve and win at the game they loved so much.

What I came to understand was that the basketball court shattered racial barriers and class distinctions. We could make real friends on the court because we all shared a common tie, a bond that bound us together as brothers. Anyone watching us run up and down the court would see the smiles on our faces and the lights in our eyes and would be compelled to conclude, as Justice Holmes might have, "they have lived."

—Michael Moore Proctor, Amherst College, Class of 2002

THE FUNKY PASTIME ESSAY

Sometimes it's the little things you do in your spare time that can create the best essay topic—and a memorable Hook. That's what happened to Peter Ford, who cashed in on his obsession with Monopoly when he was accepted to Washington and Lee Early Decision.

The best advice I ever received is, "Buy Railroads!" But I didn't hear it in quite the way you might expect.

While both my parents and peers have pushed me to be the best in school and athletics, the real roots of my peculiar competitive spirit are found in board games. The joy of this kind of intellectual combat gripped me at an early age as my family introduced me to the thrill of winning and the agony of defeat that ensues from classic board games such as Monopoly and Scrabble. Both of these pastimes have always been within arm's reach of our dinner table, and in case of a loss of game equipment, there is usually a back-up board on hand.

As the years passed, I began to experience the mood-lifting exhilaration these games could provide. No matter how bad a day it might have been, if I could somehow escape with a victory, preferably over my father, an inner peace would follow. Simply knowing that I had even the slightest chance of winning stirred my body into eruptions of goose bumps, which were soon replaced by bullets of perspiration. If the mental struggle was particularly intense, my body would be completely shot by the end of the game, but the fatigue would be balanced by my blissful grin.

It wasn't until my teenage years that I realized the true worth of a board game. When my sister began bringing home prospective boyfriends, my father was quick to challenge them to a friendly game of Scrabble. If the boy could provide some half-decent competition, he was considered acceptable.

For me, board games have also provided life lessons that have reached well beyond the thrill of head-to-head intellectual sparring. For example, when the average novice plunges into Monopoly, his first instinct is to buy out the high-ticket properties, like Boardwalk and Park Place, because they charge the highest rent. I was no exception, but I soon was informed that I was playing "stupid Monopoly." The end result was usually bankruptcy, the ultimate loss that thoroughly embarrasses any experienced player.

The key in this complex game is to purchase the properties that everyone is constantly landing on but passing up—those ubiquitous railroads. At first they may seem like a good-for-nothing investment. But as time slowly moves on, the profit will grow along with the player's confidence and the frustration of rival competitors.

Such board-game insights have taught me lessons in strategic thinking that can be applied to school, business, or the meaning of life. I have learned that like railroads in Monopoly, sure and steady may win the race. In fact, Monopoly, to me, is a metaphor for life that deals with knowing one's limits: when to push forward, and when to hold back.

—*Peter Ford, Washington and Lee, Class of 2003*

THE TRIUMPH-OVER-ADVERSITY ESSAY

Challenging life experiences, whether they arise from poverty, physical danger, or psychological trauma, can provide topics that tap into a reader's sense of compassion. Robert McGovern's description of living with his grandmother for two years after his grandfather's death gave a powerful insight into a young man's heart.

Adversity has always made me stronger, whether on the athletic field, at my desk during school, or in relationships. But one instance of adversity more than any others altered my life over a period of two years, and had a profound impact on the way I now live my life. This was the experience of living alone with my grandmother.

About five years ago after I had just turned thirteen, I was living the life of the average thirteen-year-old. But I had always had an especially good relationship with my grandfather and grandmother, and had fallen into the ritual of visiting them every weekend. My grandfather and I would walk the same route to the toy store, where he would always buy me the coolest toy. When we returned to their home, my grandmother would be waiting with her stories about what she was like when she was my age.

It wasn't until my grandfather passed away that I realized how much I really loved those times and how I had taken them for granted. My grandfather was a very kind man, but he was very sick. He had to constantly go through dialysis due to a malfunction in his kidneys.

After awhile, when he got sick of the constant pain, he decided to go through surgery that could potentially let him live his life to its fullest. Unfortunately, things didn't work out this way. The next months were tough on the whole family as we prayed for the surgery to be successful. Day after day, the news on his health would change, causing our mood to shift back and forth, from relief to worry.

Then one day the bad news came, only a few days after my birthday. My grandfather had passed away. I was so shocked that I didn't want to believe my father's voice on the phone. It seemed unfair to have someone so kind and loving be taken away.

My grandmother is one of the strongest people I have ever met in my life. But when my grandfather died, that was one of the few times when she showed any sign of weakness. I knew she was trying to hide her full emotions, but she was vulnerable because she had lost a major part of her life. Finally, she had to move closer to us due to the fact that she never received her driver's license. When I went over to her new house one day and sensed the despair and emptiness, I realized Grandma needed someone to stay with her. That's when I asked my parents' permission to move in with her.

They agreed, but the adjustments I had to make weren't easy. For instance, Grandma would leave the air-conditioning off at night and put the fans on full blast. She complained that otherwise, she would, "freeze," but I remember sweating heavily as I lay on my bed during the summer. There were also other quirks. We never used the front door because of a bevy of wasp nests right outside. Instead, we had to go in and out through a side door, which was always locked. The only way I could get in was by giving a signature ring on an old doorbell so she would know I was the one standing outside.

Also, Grandma was never one for cable, so our television viewing was limited to twelve channels, three of which were infomercial stations. Since we had sixty stations at home, I felt pretty confined. To top it all off, Grandma liked to watch "oldie" movies, and of course she wanted me to watch them with her. You don't know what boredom is until you've seen "*Gone With the Wind*" thirty times.

These things concerned me, but not nearly as much as the fact that I had no outside social life. I missed out on ninety-nine percent of what my friends were doing. There were so many times that I wished I could leave and chill with my buddies, but I didn't have access to a car. So I stayed and watched the oldies with Grandma.

You might think that such restrictions would make any teenager resentful, but it wasn't that way with me. When the time came for my grandmother to move again, it was almost like I lost a piece of myself in the process. I helped her carry stuff out of her house, the same way that I had helped her move in years before. I watched that television, the one on which I had seen so many oldies, find its place on the truck. Then, I saw my grandmother lock the side door for the last time.

She came up to me that day right before she got into the car and said, "Thanks for everything."

As I stood there looking at the woman with whom I had spent the last few years of my life, I couldn't think of any answer except to say, "No problem."

I gave her a big hug and opened the car door and stepped back as the driver took her away and the U-Haul truck followed with all of my memories.

As I sit at home now and flip through the channels, I still sometimes stop for a split second at number twelve. Then, I continue. When I talk to my grandmother on the phone, we continue old conversations, and she re-tells stories I've heard a hundred times before. But it doesn't bother me because deep down, I know that I have a connection with her that most people don't have with anyone. I'll miss those times with her and the things she taught me.

Also, it's funny but I find my friends don't like sleeping over at my house too much. Maybe it's because I don't use air-conditioning most of the time. I just leave the fan on.

—*Robert McGovern, University of Massachusetts, Class of 2005*

MOST-MEANINGFUL-ACTIVITY ESSAYS

Even though it's meant to be short, the "activity" essay on the Common Application can give you a chance to display your Hook or show another side of your personality, as it did for these students.

If men say, "Dogs are a man's best friend," then I say, "Horses are a woman's best friend." I don't know what I would have done without a horse in my life. Within the time it takes to step out of my car, walk to the barn, and distinguish the neighing of Gallant Heart, I immediately begin to lose the day's troubles—and float away into peacefulness.

Having started riding before I could even walk, I have been actively involved with horses for as long as I can remember. My grandfather was a professional horse trainer, and so I suppose you could say the love of horses is in the genes.

People find many ways to de-stress: getting a massage, shopping, exercising like crazy, being alone, seeing a psychiatrist, or even screaming and yelling. My solution is Gallant Heart. Riding is my sanctuary, my most meaningful activity—for life.

—*Sara Gore, Villanova University, Class of 2010*

Although I work as hard as anyone on studies and community service, I make sure I take regular breaks to enjoy my most meaningful activity—salsa dancing. At a popular *discoteca* in Cadiz, Spain, last year, I quickly realized that, despite a few lessons, I knew nothing about the soul of salsa. At first, I had to overcome an innate reluctance to express myself on the dance floor in a crowd of unfamiliar people. But soon, I became absorbed in the rhythms and danced for hours, not thinking about anything except the music and the beat of my heart.

My love of salsa dancing followed me home to Florida and inspired me to found a salsa club at my school, with 60 students signing up. During a summer internship at Northwestern University, I actually found time to dance salsa to live music at the Chicago SummerDance series in Grant Park. Regardless of my mood, the Latin beat lifts me up, even when I'm feeling down.

—*Nihar Shah, Northwestern University, Class of 2010*

I grew up surrounded by scientists. I knew the periodic table of elements before I could read *The Cat in the Hat*. As I grew up, I became a full-fledged science geek. My AP Physics class even got t-shirts made that say "100% Nerd." I guess that's why the last place I expected to find fulfillment was on the football field.

It must have been the excitement of trying something new that prompted me to take the position of Varsity Football manager. Certainly, it wasn't a special affection for high school athletes. Having never been that athletic myself, I was intimidated by those who were. It was the soccer players who were popular in elementary school, and the lacrosse players who were popular in middle school. Although in high school there was no long popularity due to athleticism, I could still never truly let go of those ideals that defined our adolescent social position.

In any event, I found myself in early September gearing up for a season on the gridiron. My first days of managing were extremely trying, with seven a.m. weekend wake-up calls and mind-numbing labor that included lugging ten-gallon water coolers and carting medical kits on my back. I would try to dodge around my two-hundred-pound peers, too afraid to make eye-contact.

However, week by week, as I became more practiced at my job, I held my head up a little higher, and my smile became a little less pinched.

Slowly but surely, these hulking teenagers in maroon-and-white jerseys became not just my friends, but my team. I began to feel an ownership of them, like a mother lioness to her cubs. From the running back with a broken arm who sits with me on the sidelines, to the tight end who told me with tears in his eyes how his girlfriend cheated on him, the players are my "pride." These days, doling out pills of Excedrin, while single handedly taking down rushing and passing statistics, or soothing the coaches after a bad game, has become not only my specialty, but my pleasure. Now, I can't imagine a better way to spend a Saturday afternoon than standing on the sidelines screaming, "Run Raiders, Run!"

Next year, when I go to college, I don't know if I'll walk down this same avenue. But wherever I end up, I'll be sure to be in the stands at the football games with my memories and a bottle of Excedrin.

—*Amanda, Dartmouth College, Class of 2003*

For me, music communicates a message as nothing else can. That's why my most meaningful activity is leading worship at my church's Sunday morning "Celebrate" service and also at school twice a week, when middle and upper school students gather for a group called FOCUS (Fellowship of Christians in Universities and Schools).

My emotion and expression when I sing a song are completely different from how I communicate in conversation. When I lead worship, I have a sense of freedom to pour out my feelings without being constrained to say the "right thing." The music says it all.

What I love most as a worship leader is looking around a room full of people and catching the eye of someone who is normally reserved, singing with all his heart. In that moment when our eyes meet, I sense that he is not only following me, but also connecting with me, in a dimension beyond words.

—*Lindsey Perkins, Furman University, Class of 2005*

Exotic rhapsodies hinting of faraway lands drifted from the portable stereo. "This music is from the Cirque du Soleil," commented Graciela Binaghi, my mime teacher, in a soothing Argentinean accent. Five years later, I was no longer studying mime and had forgotten the name of the music Graciela used. Yet the mysterious melodies frequently resurfaced in my memory. I was an eighth-grader fascinated by the dot-com boom and the emergence of a world of new Internet technology when my aunt, vacationing from Detroit, announced she was taking me to see the Cirque du Soleil's production of *La Nouba* in Orlando, Florida.

At the mention of Cirque du Soleil, the company responsible for the music that illuminated my childhood, my heart leapt. I searched the Internet for more information, but to no avail. There was no Web site for *La Nouba* and not even a reference to it on Cirque's home page. Before long, however, my disappointment turned into determination as I set out to create the first fan site dedicated exclusively to *La Nouba*.

Being a twelve-year-old suddenly immersed in the corporate world is not easy. At first, the people involved with *La Nouba* doubted my capabilities and didn't take me seriously. But over the next few years, I persevered, devoting more than 2,500 hours to the project. The Web site, now approaching its fourth anniversary, has been truly a fascinating intellectual journey. I've learned the latest technologies, both in programming and graphic design; conducted interviews; and dealt with copyright laws. I've developed time management skills, interviewed artists, and worked with the show's publicist.

I'm proud to say that what began as a quest for information resulted not only in the creation of *La Nouba*'s number one fan Internet site, but also in one of the most intellectually stimulating—and meaningful—experiences of my life.

—*Erika Pagano, Georgetown University, Class of 2008*

Sample Supplements and Letters

A GUIDANCE COUNSELOR'S RECOMMENDATION

High school guidance counselor Valerie Brant-Wilson has been working with the best and the brightest at Vero Beach High School for more than twenty years. Here's how she helped sell Jeff Daniels, the "Music Man" profiled in Chapter Six, to Boston College.

Dear Admission Officer:

It is an honor and a privilege to recommend Jeffrey R. Daniels to you, and I do so without any reservation. I have known this talented young man, who is known by his peers as Mr. Music Man, for three years. I have enjoyed every aspect of our counselor-counselee relationship. He has never entered my office without a plan of action for implementation in achieving his goals. Since serving as an altar server as a young boy, Jeffrey has been making plans to enter Boston College. His desire to have the opportunity to matriculate at Boston College has been his primary goal. The first day I met him, he was declaring Boston College is the place for me.

Scholastically, Jeffrey has a 3.9318 un-weighted cumulative grade point average and a 4.5227 weighted cumulative grade point average. Jeffrey is ranked in the top 2% of his class. He has taken at least eleven advanced placement courses giving him the distinction of graduating as an Advanced Placement Honor Scholar. Because of Jeffrey's academic success, he will also graduate as a Florida Medallion Scholar. Whatever chosen career path he takes he will do exceptionally well.

I would be remiss if I did not point out to you that this gifted and industrious leader has been a vital contributor in all areas from academic to extra curricular activities, especially with our highly acclaimed marching band that has won numerous district, state, and national awards. His impressive resume gives credence to his work ethic, time management and organizational skills. The opportunity to enter Boston College will be the highlight of his academic accomplishment. Academically he should be able to compete within the application pool your university attracts.

Combining all of his attributes and personal persona, I do not think you could find a better rounded student for admission. This energetic and unselfish young man will add much sparkle to the freshman class. I am confident that his academic promise and competitive spirit will enable him to hold his own at your university. It is for these reasons I support his application whole-heartedly. He is that rare gem that shines so brightly in the midst of other stones. Michael J. McCarthy so succinctly states: "You are in charge. You have the ability to master your destiny." Certainly, Mr. Jeffrey R. Daniels is that individual. Will you carefully consider him for admission? I know he will be ecstatic to hear the good news welcoming him to Boston College.

Sincerely,

Valerie Brant-Wilson
Guidance Counselor

SUPPLEMENTS TO A SCIENCE HOOK

To emphasize her Hook as a Third-World researcher, Summer Niazi (profiled in Chapter Ten) included with all her college applications copies of the scientific abstracts of the two cholesterol research projects she had conducted in Pakistan. To add to the mystique, she included photos of herself doing cholesterol testing while wearing a *shalwar kameez*, the traditional Pakistani garb.

ABSTRACT YEAR I:
EVALUATING LIPID PROFILE IN YOUNG HEALTHY MALES OF A
DEVELOPING COUNTRY
Anum A. Niazi
Vanderbilt University, Tennessee, USA
Summer A. Niazi
Chattahoochee High School, Alpharetta, Georgia, USA

Cardiovascular and cerebrovascular diseases are leading causes of mortality in the western world associated with dyslipidemias, reflected predominately as high total and LDL cholesterol with low HDL. Lipid profiles have not been well evaluated in many of the developing countries. The purpose of this study was to analyze lipid profiles of young healthy males from a developing country.

The study population comprised of young healthy male factory workers in Pakistan. 107 subjects were tested, on no cholesterol lowering medication. Lipid results of 103 subjects were obtained. Four subjects did not have the reaction occur to calculate the lipid profile. Mean age was 23 (17–45) years, mean weight 60 (±8) kg., and seven smokers (6.8%). Diabetes and major diseases were absent. Lipid profile was measured using the enzymatic methodology (Cholestech L.D.X Lipid Profile II, from Cholestech corporation, Hayward, California), and calibrated using the controls provided by the manufacturer. Informed consent was obtained prior to 12 hour fast. Blood was placed onto the lipid profile cassette. Lipid profile, heart rate, and blood pressure were measured.

Average heart rate 76 (±11) bpm, average blood pressure 112/70 mmHg., average total cholesterol 125(±21) mg/dL., average HDL 33(±6) mg/dL., average LDL 71 (±19) mg/dL., and average triglyceride 92(±35) mg/dL.

In conclusion, the tested group does not have elevated total, LDL cholesterol or triglyceride levels. HDL cholesterol is significantly abnormal. Heart rate and blood pressure were normal. The precursor of increased vascular diseases in developing countries may be low HDL values treatment of which may be helpful.

ABSTRACT YEAR 2:
EVALUATING LIPID PROFILE IN YOUNG HEALTHY FEMALES OF A DEVELOPING COUNTRY: Year 2
Summer A. Niazi and Faraze A. Niazi
Chattahoochee High School, Alpharetta, Georgia, USA
Anum A. Niazi
Vanderbilt University, Tennessee, USA
Zehra Aftab
University of Buffalo, New York, USA

Cardiovascular and cerebrovascular diseases are leading causes of mortality in the western world associated with dyslipidemias, reflected predominately as high total and LDL cholesterol with low HDL. Lipid profiles have not been well evaluated in many of the developing countries. The purpose of this study was to analyze lipid profiles of young healthy females from a developing country, and compare to young men of the first year study.

The study population comprised of young healthy female factory workers in Pakistan. 82 subjects were tested, neither on any cholesterol lowering medication nor any smokers. Lipid results of 78 subjects were obtained. Four subjects did not have reaction occur to calculate lipid profile. Mean age was 22 (18–35) years, and mean weight 48 (±7) kg. Diabetes and major diseases were absent. Lipid profile was measured using the enzymatic methodology (Cholestech L.D.X Lipid Profile II, from Cholestech corporation, Hayward, California), and calibrated using the controls provided by the manufacturer. Informed consent was obtained prior to 12 hour fast. Blood was placed onto the lipid profile cassette. Lipid profile, heart rate, and blood pressure were measured.

Average heart rate 85(±13) bpm, average blood pressure 117/76 mmHg, average total cholesterol 146(±27) mg/dL, average HDL 44(±9) mg/dL, average LDL 87(±25) mg/dL, average triglyceride 88(±41) mg/dL, and average glucose 87(±8 mg/dL).

In conclusion, the tested group does not have elevated total, LDL cholesterol or triglyceride levels. HDL cholesterol is low. Glucose, heart rate, and blood pressure were normal. These results are consistent with the first year study results regarding young men. The precursor of increased vascular diseases in developing countries may be related to low HDL values treatment of which may be helpful.

SUPPLEMENT TO A WRITING HOOK

Profiled in Chapter Eleven, Nicole Dubowitz's first op-ed piece in the *Baltimore Sun* generated reader response—and a regular assignment as the only teenage opinion writer for the newspaper.

STUDENT MOVED, ENCOURAGED BY ANTI-WAR RALLY

By Nicole Dubowitz

October 5, 2005
    I didn't get arrested when I went to the anti-war rally near the White House.
    My friend Gina and I, high school seniors, decked ourselves in

peace-promoting attire and carried home-made signs. Mine simply stated, "Bring 'em home." Hers read: "$13,000 a second." That's how much my teacher says the war costs. And for what? To liberate Iraqis? I was able to march Sept. 24 with 100,000 others who don't buy it.

There were the Vietnam vets, anxious mothers waiting for their children in Iraq to come home, "Grandmothers for Peace," young rebels with a cause, even scattered clusters of people who support the war. Most brought their own signs, with messages from moving to amusing, including pleas for President Bush to bring home a son or husband.

Gina and I were dumbfounded by the displays of tombstones and combat boots representing the more than 1,900 U.S. troops who have died in Iraq so far. It's one thing to see a statistic in the newspaper, but putting a name to a number and a face to a name is heart wrenching. The reminder that every boot and plywood cross in the ground stood for what I think is a death in vain was for me the most poignant part of the rally—that, and for each of the deaths, a family suffering.

I smiled at a group of college kids perched on a statue holding a sign that read, "We're not extremists!" It's difficult for a kid to have an opposing opinion without being labeled a radical or a traitor. Mr. Bush has said: If you're not with us, you're with them. I am not on the side of terrorists. But I'm also not on the side of an avoidable war—a war that was not a last resort and that has robbed America of its reputation as a humane and respectful nation.

It saddens me that Iraqi children suffered under Saddam Hussein and our war has brought more violence to their lives. What hope can they have in a world that has given them so much grief? And it hurts that we pay hundreds of billions of dollars for the war in Iraq when a fraction of that could feed starving people around the world or could have built levees in New Orleans before Hurricane Katrina.

I want so badly to have confidence in my government, but I can't seem to find the bright side of this war. The more I hear about it, the more I am convinced that the minimal progress in Iraq is severely outweighed by the massive destruction. This damage isn't only taking place overseas. America is terribly divided over such an undeniably colossal mess. When Mr. Bush went to war, he told us it would increase homeland security. I don't feel very secure.

Although I didn't agree with everyone's sign or callous accusation, I still appreciated the passion of the crowd at the United for Peace and Justice rally. High school is almost a bubble, full of many apathetic teenagers who don't believe they can make a difference. Being part of the anti-war rally gave me a renewed sense of patriotism and assurance that there are many people like me who believe in nonviolence.

As the war has continued with no end in sight, I feel distraught and betrayed by our government. Maybe the rally alone won't be enough to change the minds of those who want to continue this war, but it restored my belief in the goodness of people. If others feel the same way, then in my eyes, the rally was a great success.

Nicole Dubowitz, 17, is a senior at Bethesda-Chevy Chase High School in Bethesda.

Copyright 2005 Nicole Dubowitz

SUPPLEMENT TO AN INTERNATIONAL HOOK

Erika Pagano's "Letter from Japan," a column she filed with the *Press Journal* as a foreign correspondent during a stint as an exchange student in the city of Akita, demonstrated both her flair for writing and her eye for multicultural contrasts. Erika, who is highlighted in Chapter Five, submitted all five of her published articles, including the one that follows, in a portfolio to supplement her college applications.

July 19, 2003

Surprisingly, High School in Japan Is Fun

Editor's Note: Erika Pagano, 15, soon to be a senior at St. Edward's Upper School, has arrived in Japan for a Japan–U.S. Senate Exchange after earning a scholarship from Youth for Understanding USA. She is staying with a family in Akita, about 300 miles north of Tokyo. Erika will work on a 20-minute documentary comparing Japanese and American youth culture.

Every article I read prior to arriving in Japan emphasized the tense atmosphere and rigidity of Japanese high school.

Some articles went so far as to liken the classroom environment to a jail so, naturally, I was a bit apprehensive on my first day of Japanese high school.

The authors of the aforementioned articles desperately need to re-examine their work. What tense atmosphere? What rigidity? I have yet to experience any circumstance that resembles a jail in the slightest. In fact, I believe I'm having an unhealthy amount of fun.

It's hard to discredit my school. Akita High School is the prefecture's top high school and one of the best in the nation.

My fellow students are drawn from a 100-kilometer radius, which means one-way commutes of 40 minutes or more by bike, train or feet is the norm. These students are truly elite—they nearly ace Japan's infamous high-school entrance exams. I couldn't have asked for a more welcoming, relaxed and fun school environment.

Akita High is roughly 1,000 students divided into grades 1, 2 and 3—equivalent to our grades 10, 11 and 12, respectively. Students in each grade are then divided into Kumi, or classes, consisting of about 40 students each. Some Kumi are specialized; for instance, the 2-I and 3-I (2nd and 3rd grades, I class) are for students wishing to pursue careers in medicine. Students stay with their Kumi in one classroom all day and, unlike American schools, teachers move from class to class.

Each period is 55 minutes long, followed by a 10-minute intermission. There are six periods plus lunch each day and Japanese students usually take 8 or 9 different subjects. Each class begins by the teacher entering the classroom, followed by a designated student announcing "Kiritsu!" (Stand up!) then by "Rei!" (Bow!).

During the Rei, students say "Onegaishimasu" (Please teach us) in unison. To conclude class, the same student announces the Kiritsu, and during this Rei, students say "Arigato gozaimasu" (Thank you very much). This, along with a policy of not speaking unless spoken to, creates a great (and deserved) respect for the teacher.

Unlike most high schools in Japan, Akita High's uniform is optional. While many girls choose to wear the school uniform that does indeed resemble a Sailor Moon (a popular Japanese animated series) costume, jeans plus a shirt or the infamous "everything goes" Japanese fashion is accepted as well.

Many clubs (or as we say, sports) have unwritten specific dress and behavioral rules, so distinguishing baseball players and rugby players from other students is an easy task. For example, only rugby players flip their collars up, and only baseball players shave their heads.

Another unique feature worth mentioning is the changing of shoes. Students typically possess two pairs of shoes for school: one pair to be worn outside the building and one pair to be worn inside. Should a student forget their inside shoes, they must don a pair of brown, vinyl slippers that look as though they've been freshly delivered from a 1970s sitcom.

I've loved every day at Akita High so far. It's cause for a good laugh when a Sensei (teacher) finds out halfway through class you haven't understood a word he or she has said. Communicating with fellow students whose English skills are about as nonexistent as your Japanese skills is sometimes a daunting task, yet kindness always works, as does the universal symbol of gratitude—a smile.

SUPPLEMENT TO A TECHNOLOGY HOOK

Ryan Allik, whose story is chronicled in Chapter Eight, wrote this article about a national technology youth conference that was published in the Fort Lauderdale *Sun-Sentinel*, one of the foremost newspapers in south Florida. He attached the article to his résumé and sent it with his college applications.

Jocks Play Games while Techies Tackle Future

By Ryan Allik

OK, I'll be honest. The first thought that went through my head as I approached my flight gate in Atlanta en route to Austin, Texas, was "Ryan, remind me again why you wanted to attend this technology conference?"

I looked around, and all I saw were "nerds." A group of them huddled at the gate discussing the latest cyber-arcana. At first, I tried to distance myself from them. I chuckled as I watched, but I was also fascinated. Despite my initial reaction, something seemed to tell me I had happened upon citizens of my native country, where all spoke a familiar language. At that moment, I began to realize that these teenagers, my peers, who seemed lost in their own strange world, were actually pretty interesting, and will probably be the leaders of tomorrow's technology.

The conference I was attending for nine days this summer was known as the "Young Technology Leaders Conference (YTL)," sponsored and organized by a company called "Envision," which stages student conclaves around the country. Schools elected 1,064 students like me from around the country to hear successful business tycoons such as Michael Dell, CEO of Dell Computers, and Dr. Vinton Cerf, senior vice president of Data Architecture for MCI (WorldCom). We also had the option of attending site visits to places such as AMD Corporation in Austin, the University of Texas, and Dell's computer assembly plant.

The conference epicenter was the Renaissance Hotel in Austin, where YTL had the company Rentsys set up more than 400 PCs in the downstairs convention room, and a 40-computer Mac lab in a smaller auditorium. In these facilities, students could spend their spare time surfing a high-speed network or competing with one another in the latest multiplayer action games. Apple had also set up a pavilion showcasing its latest technology with on-site representatives from the company. It was a Nerd's Paradise. Or as Joe Tkach, a 16-year-old conference participant from Fontana, Calif., said, "It's geek summer camp."

Anyhow, against my better judgment, I was hooked. But it wasn't just the technology that attracted me. I was also tantalized by the experiences of my fellow students, who led seminars on topics ranging from "Building Car MP3 Players" to "E-mail Spam and Anti-Spam Technology." I decided to attend the Linux Introduction Seminar, even though I already have a fair knowledge of the subject, and it turned out to be more of a brainstorming session than a lecture.

Brian, another young leader attending the summit, led the seminar using his handheld Visor PDA and a projector linked to a laptop. Later that evening, I found him hovering around the cyber cafe, persuading Windows users to move to the open-source Linux. As I watched him in operation, I began to realize that teenagers like Brian are transforming the "nerd" stereotype. We teenage tech-wads need to get out front and say, "Hey, I've got brains and skills most other guys lack, and I'm ready to show them off."

I have to admit that before I attended the conference, my main hype was to hear Michael Dell because of his recent success in the computer industry. Once I was at YTL, though, I found myself moved by the bright people who surrounded me. My fellow students made me realize the opportunities I had right in front of me, opportunities that I had taken for granted. Listening to Michael Dell expound on his business strategies was inspiring, but not as motivating as hearing about the successes of my peers.

For example, Austin Agarwal, a 15-year-old student at Fairfield Prep in Fairfield, Conn., has already earned his Cisco Networking License, and has written programs that have been mentioned or published in books and magazines. He also owns a custom computer business, a Web services/networking company and a software development company. When I asked him his opinion on youth-initiated businesses, he said, "We're making it easier for future generations to earn respect in the 'adult' world."

So how do these young tech leaders cope with social pressures and sport jockeys, the main guys who dominate the high school scene? Austin claims he's earned both respect and jealousy because of his high level of success and in-depth knowledge.

"There's no question that a computer geek can make more money than an athlete," he said. "However, athletes get more attention because of popular interest. If people realized how much they relied on computer geeks, I'm sure the focus would shift."

Joe Tkach's philosophy on the big-man-on-campus matter goes like this: "It's nice to be recognized, but for me personally, I just want to code. Computers intimidate people. Most new technology does. People fear what they don't understand. Sports are something everyone can understand and participate in, so they respect that kind of skill over skill with computers."

As for the future, Joe, who hopes to teach computer science at the college level, predicts that tech types will inevitably emerge as a significant force for shaping our culture: "Some of the things we associate with geekdom will become mainstream, and so geeks will just find other, even more complicated things to become geeky about."

Young technology leaders like Joe and Austin will almost certainly define the future of technology and business. As for me, I've implemented Linux to run half our network at my high school, St. Andrew's in Boca Raton. These days I'm not reluctant to mention the work I do because I realize I am a new generation that's setting an aggressive standard that redefines the "nerd" image and vocabulary.

Because of my expertise, I've got status, position, and, even more, a vision for the future, unlike many my age. I've already started my own business doing computer consulting, and I've discovered what it takes to succeed: unwavering confidence in your ideas and a determination to work hard to bring your ideas to fruition.

OK, so maybe the time really has arrived for me to step outside my box of self-denial. I'm a nerd, and I'm proud of it!

THE EXPANDED ACTIVITIES SUPPLEMENT

In Chapter Fourteen, we met Amanda, a professional actress who elaborated on her extensive achievements by attaching separate sheets to her application to Dartmouth.

Professional Actress
GRADES 9–12 (4 HOURS/WEEK, 52 WEEKS/YEAR)

(For expanded professional bio, reviews, and recordings, see portfolio submitted with the application.)

- Off-Broadway, Grade 9: Featured role as "Young Violet" in the award-winning musical, *Violet.* Reviewers said: • "The evening's strengths are . . . the memory songs featuring Violet's younger self (Amanda . . . , who is excellent)."—Ben Brantley, *The New York Times.*

  - "As the young Violet, a major role, Amanda . . . of Westchester makes a remarkable alter-ego for (leading lady) Ward." —*Gannett Newspapers;* • "Amanda . . . is plucky, tough, and strong-voiced."—David Sheward, *Back Stage.*

- Broadway/Off-Broadway, Grades 9–12 Roles in various workshops and readings, including: • the Roundabout Theatre's *Tom Sawyer, the Musical,* a project under development with director Scott Ellis; • Manhattan Theatre Club's *Ridin' High* (High Society), under director Arthur Kopit; • MCC Theatre's *The English Teacher* and *The Mystery School;* and • Musical Theatre Works' *Theo Talis, Tailor.*

- ESL Tapes and Voice-Overs, Grades 9–12 Recorded voices for: "Tiny Tots" interactive tape; more than 30 ESL CD's for Macmillan Publishers; and 24 commercials for Della Famina. (Up to 10 hours/wk)

Vocal Music
GRADES 9–12 (5 HOURS/WEEK, 52 WEEKS/YEAR)

During the past four years, worked with several voice coaches to expand vocal range and technique beyond the Broadway genre. Professional recordings include:

- Original Cast Album, *Violet*

- *Everybody Is a Star*

- *I Am the Cute One* (with the Olsen Twins)

continued

Varsity Football Manager
GRADE 12 (20 HOURS/WEEK, 20 WEEKS/YEAR)

As manager of the football team, had responsibility for offensive and de-fensive statistics, water, and equipment at all games.

High School Drama Club
GRADES 9–12 (15 HOURS, 16 WEEKS)

While maintaining professional commitments, participated fully in the drama offerings at school, including: • How to Succeed in Business Without Really Trying *(9ᵗʰ Grade);* • Guys and Dolls *(10ᵗʰ Grade);* • Free to Be You and Me *(10ᵗʰ Grade);* • Once Upon a Mattress *(11ᵗʰ Grade);* • On the Twentieth Century *(12ᵗʰ Grade).*

Peer Counselor
GRADES 10–12 (2 HOURS/WEEK, 40 WEEKS/YEAR)

Selected after in-depth interviews by the guidance counselor and teach-ers to advise peers on problems ranging from drugs to parent relations.

Fairness Council
GRADE 12 (2 HOURS/WEEK, 40 WEEKS/YEAR)

One of four student mediators who preside over disputes between stu-dents and students; between teachers and students; or between students and administration.

Drug/Alcohol Task Force
GRADES 10–12 (1 HOUR/WEEK, 40 WEEKS/YEAR)

School representative to this Westchester community council made up of teachers, police officers, parents and students.

Orientation Retreat
Grade 12 (5 hours/week, 2 weeks/year)

Leader of three-day retreat for new students. Planned activities and led discussions.

Varsity Track
Grade 10 (10 hours/week, 16 weeks/year)

Gold medalist in 400m dash in All-County sophomore meet.

Teaching Intern, Westchester Elementary School
January, Grade 11 (35 hours/week)

Worked as assistant to 5th grade teacher. Taught science; directed students in two plays by Mark Twain.

Clinical Trials Assist., Pharmaceutical Company
January, Grade 10 (35 hours/week)

Worked in biostatistical division of this multinational drug and chemical company. Created spreadsheets to chart the accuracy of the Immuno I, the in vitro testing machine the company was using and marketing for Prostate Specific Antigen (PSA). Helped to create a database of patients to determine efficacy of PSA as a marker for other cancers.

Camp Counselor
Summer, Grade 11 (40 hours/week)

Worked as a day camp counselor for boys and girls aged 7–11. Specialized in teaching field hockey and floor hockey. Chaperoned several out-of-state trips.

MODEL LETTER TO COACH

STEVE STUDENT

(your address)

(your phone number/e-mail)

(date)

Mr./Ms. (name of coach)
Head Coach, Men's/Women's Basketball
Department of Athletics and Recreation
Address

Dear Coach (name):

I am planning to apply to (name of school) and am very interested in playing (sport) for you. As you can see from the attached sheet, I'm (captain, co-captain, high scorer, etc.) of the varsity (sport) team at (your school name), averaged (your stats—batting average, points per game basketball, etc.), and have had a serious commitment to the sport ever since I was in elementary school.

I'd like very much to meet with you personally to discuss your (sport: baseball, basketball, football, etc.) program and how I might fit in. I'll be visiting (name of college) (dates of visit), and hope you might be free to meet with me at that time.

I will call you in a few days to see when you might be available. Thanks so much.

Sincerely,

(your signature)

(your full name)

MODEL STAT SHEET

STEVE STUDENT
Address; e-mail address; phone number

Guard: 6'3" • 170 pounds

All-State Guard (Year)
Captain, Varsity Basketball Team

(name of high school, Class 4A)
(Latest Season) Basketball Statistics
16 Points Per Game
9 Rebounds Per Game
3 Assists Per Game
2 Blocks Per Game
4 Steals Per Game
Field Goal Percentage: 47%
Free Throw Percentage: 69%
Three-Point Percentage: 45%
State Semi-Finalists (Year)
Regional Champs (Year)
Starter, 10th, 11th, and 12th Grades
Three Varsity Letters
JV Captain

Other Basketball Achievements:
Camper of the Week, State Invitational, Summer (year)
Five-Star Basketball Camp, Summer (year)
Eastern Invitational Basketball Camp, Summer (year)
University of Central Florida Invitational, Fall (year)
Interscholastic Middle School Varsity Basketball, Grades 7–8
Middle School Varsity Captain, Grade 8
County Rec League, since 4th Grade

Contact: (Coach's Name)
Coach's home phone number • School phone number • Cell phone number

Selected References

Abramowicz, David. "Recruiting Practices Differ Among Extracurriculars." *The Amherst Student Online,* Issue 006.

Arenson, Karen W. "Officials Say Scoring Errors for SAT Were Understated." *The New York Times,* March 9, 2006.

Beatty, Sally. "Volunteering Because You Must." *The Wall Street Journal,* April 7, 2006.

"Best National Universities," *America's Best Colleges, 2005 Edition.* U.S. News & World Report, 2004.

"Best National Universities," *America's Best Colleges, 2006 Edition.* U.S. News & World Report, 2005.

Chaker, Anne Marie. "Colleges Admit Few Students Off the Wait List." *The Wall Street Journal,* May 16, 2006.

————. "Who Got Into College?" *The Wall Street Journal,* April 13, 2006.

————, and Hechinger, John. "In Wake of Grading Errors, Kids Counseled to Pay College Board for Hand Grading, Answer Keys." *The New York Times,* March 15, 2006.

"Class of 2010: Admit Rate of 24 Percent Sets New Benchmark at Barnard." Barnard College Office of Public Affairs, 2006.

Creighton, Joanne V. "It Doesn't Test for Success." *Los Angeles Times,* March 13, 2006.

Finder, Alan. "In New Twist on College Search, a First Choice and 20 Backups." *The New York Times,* March 21, 2006.

————. "Princeton Stops Its Early Admissions, Joining Movement to Make Process Fairer." *The New York Times,* September 19, 2006.

————. "Schools Avoid Class Ranking, Vexing Colleges." *The New York Times,* March 5, 2006.

————, and Arenson, Karen. "Harvard Ends Early Admission, Citing Barrier to Disadvantaged." *The New York Times,* September 12, 2006.

Freedman, Samuel G. "In College Entrance Frenzy, a Lesson Out of Left Field." *The New York Times,* April 26, 2006.

Gamerman, Ellen. "The Politically Incorrect Science Fair." *The Wall Street Journal,* February 18, 2006.

Goodnough, Abby. "Wanting Facts Firsthand, Teenager Makes Secret Trip to Iraq." *The New York Times,* December 31, 2005.

Goodwin, Robert, Kinkade, Thomas, and Proctor, Pam. *Points of Light: A Celebration of the American Spirit of Giving.* New York: Center Street, 2006.

Griffin, Shari Chaney. "Student a Smooth Operator with Film," *The Gazette,* April 16, 2006.

Lewin, Tamar. "Students' Path to Small Colleges Can Bypass SAT." *The New York Times,* August 31, 2006.

Lewin, Tamar. "The Two Faces of A.P." *The New York Times,* January 8, 2006.

Marklein, Mary Beth. "SAT Scores Drop: Some See Red Flag." *USA Today,* May 10, 2006.

"New UCLA Admissions Data Show High Academic Quality Maintained for Students Admitted for Fall 2006 Freshman Class." UCLA Office of Media Relations, April 19, 2006.

Parker, Tom. "A Note from the Dean on the Class of 2009." *Amherst Fifty-Ninth Annual Report to Secondary Schools,* www.amherst.edu/admission/secondaryschoolreport09.pdf. 4/19/06.

Pennington, Bill. "The Recruiting Carousel Stops." *The New York Times,* May 21, 2006.

"Princeton Offers Admission to 10.2 Percent of Applicants." Princeton University Office of Communications, April 2006.

Rodriguez, Marissa. "The Top 25 Colleges for Latinos." *Hispanic Magazine,* March 2006.

Sanoff, Alvin P. "College Applications Take Off." *USA Today,* February 13, 2006.

"2003 United States Student Survey of High School Seniors Participating in the International Baccalaureate Program," IBO North America and Caribbean, New York, 2003.

Zimmerman, Eilene. "Hoping to Get on the Fast Track, Students Turn to Career Coaches." *The New York Times,* May 21, 2006.

ENDNOTES

1. Chaker, Anne Marie, "Who Got Into College?" *The Wall Street Journal,* April 13, 2006, p. D1.

2. "Princeton offers admission to 10.2 percent of applicants," Princeton University Office of Communications, April 5, 2006. www.princeton.edu/main/news/archive.

3. "New UCLA Admissions Data Show High Academic Quality Maintained for Students Admitted for Fall 2006 Freshman Class." UCLA Office of Media Relations, April 19, 2006.

4. Sanoff, Alvin P. "College Applications Take Off." *USA Today,* February 13, 2006.

5. Finder, Alan. "In New Twist on College Search, a First Choice, and 20 Backups." *The New York Times,* March 21, 2006.

6. "Class of 2010: Admit Rate of 24 Percent Sets New Benchmark at Barnard." Barnard College Office of Public Affairs. www.barnard.edu/newnews/news033106.html.

7. Ibid.

8. Abramowicz, David. "Recruiting Practices Differ Among Extracurriculars." *The Amherst Student Online.* www.amherst.edu/~astudent/1999-2000/issue006/news/02/shtml.

9. Beatty, Sally. "Volunteering Because You Must." *The Wall Street Journal,* April 7, 2006, p. W2.

10. Gamerman, Ellen. "The Politically Incorrect Science Fair." *The Wall Street Journal,* February 18, 2006, p. W1.

11. "Best National Universities," *America's Best Colleges, 2005 Edition.* U.S. News & World Report, 2004, p. 83.

12. "Best National Universities," *America's Best Colleges, 2006 Edition.* U.S. News & World Report, 2005, p. 81.

13. Rodriguez, Marissa. "The Top 25 Colleges for Latinos." *Hispanic Magazine,* March 2006.

14. Marklein, Mary Beth. "SAT Scores Drop: Some See Red Flag." *USA Today,* May 10, 2006, p. 1.

15. Banerjee, Neela. "Muslims' Plight in Sudan Resonates With Jews in U.S." *The New York Times,* April 30, 2006, p. 19.

16. Griffin, Shari Chaney. "Student a Smooth Operator with Film," *The Gazette*, April 16, 2006, p. 1.

17. Goodwin, Robert, Kinkade, Thomas, and Proctor, Pam. *Points of Light: A Celebration of the American Spirit of Giving*. New York: Center Street, 2006.

18. Goodnough, Abby. "Wanting Facts Firsthand, Teenager Makes Secret Trip to Iraq." *The New York Times*, December 31, 2005.

19. Ibid.

20. Ibid.

21. Finder, Alan. "Schools Avoid Class Ranking, Vexing Colleges." *The New York Times*, March 5, 2006.

22. Arenson, Karen W. "Officials Say Scoring Errors for SAT Were Understated." *The New York Times*, March 9, 2006.

23. Chaker, Anne Marie, and Hechinger, John. "In Wake of Grading Errors, Kids Counseled to Pay College Board for Hand Grading, Answer Keys." *The New York Times*, March 15, 2006, p. D1.

24. Parker, Tom. "A Note from the Dean on the Class of 2009." *Amherst Fifty-Ninth Annual Report to Secondary Schools*, www.amherst.edu/admission/secondaryschoolreport09.pdf. 4/19/06.

25. Marklein, Mary Beth. "SAT Scores Drop: Some See Red Flag." *USA Today*, May 10, 2006.

26. Creighton, Joanne V. "It Doesn't Test for Success." *Los Angeles Times*, March 13, 2006.

27. "2003 United States Student Survey of High School Seniors Participating in the International Baccalaureate Program," IBO North America and Caribbean, New York, 2003.

28. Lewin, Tamar. "The Two Faces of A.P." *The New York Times*, January 8, 2006.

29. Ibid.

30. Ibid.

31. Freedman, Samuel G. "In College Entrance Frenzy, a Lesson Out of Left Field." *The New York Times*, April 26, 2006.

32. Finder, Alan, and Arenson, Karen. "Harvard Ends Early Admission, Citing Barrier to Disadvantaged." *The New York Times*, September 12, 2006.

33. Finder, Alan. "Princeton Stops Its Early Admissions, Joining Movement to Make Process Fairer." *The New York Times*, September 19, 2006.

34. Pennington, Bill. "The Recruiting Carousel Stops." *The New York Times*, May 21, 2006.

35. Ibid.

36. Chaker, Anne Marie. "Colleges Admit Few Students Off the Wait List." *The Wall Street Journal*, May 16, 2006.

37. Ibid.

38. Zimmerman, Eilene. "Hoping to Get on the Fast Track, Students Turn to Career Coaches." *The New York Times*, May 21, 2006.

INDEX

academic interest questionnaire, 20–22

acting hook, 81–86

  bright ideas for, 85–86

activities questionnaire, 15–17

ACTs, 94

  Common Application and, 154–55

  playing the SAT against, 141

  prepping for, 139–40

  sections of, 139

  significance of, 138

  taking both the SAT and, 140

admissions bloodbath, xii

admissions reps, 175–81

  meeting, 177–78

  multicultural, 178

  open-house programs, 179–80

  tip for, 175

  updates and awards, 180–81

  visiting the campus, 178–79

Advanced Placement (AP) courses, 143

  choosing, 147–48

Advanced Placement Scholar, 148

Aftab, Aezad:

  diversity essay of, 211–12

Aftab, Zehra, 68

  scientific abstracts of, 227–28

Albany College of Medicine, 69, 163

Alliance for Young Artists & Writers,
  78, 107

Allik, Ryan, 53–57, 165

  Sun-Sentinel article of, 232–34

American Cancer Society, 59

American Childhood, An, 61–62

American College Test, 141, 154

American Jewish World Service, 104

American Legion, 49, 50, 51

American Psychological Association, 75

American University in Paris, 193

Amherst College, 12, 32, 104, 106,
  137–38, 141, 142, 151, 164,
  185, 193

  essay for, 215–17

  open house at, 179–80

Appalachian State, essay for,
  203–204

Armstrong, Neil, 57

artists, bright ideas for, 107–108

  Common Application and, 154

Associated Press, 121–22

athletic hook, 29–33

  bright ideas for, 32–33

  coaches and, *see* coaches, courting

  Common Application and, 154

  essay for, 204–205

AutoCAD, 108

award updates, 180–81

Babson College, 164

Baltimore Sun, 76–77, 228–30

Bard College, 8

  essay for, 214–15

Barnard College, 11–12, 164

Bates College, 125, 143, 185, 187

  open house at, 180

Baylor University, xii, 12, 139

beauty pageants, 86

Belmont University, 104

Bentley College, 51

Big Ten formula for applying to schools, 161

Binghamton University, 151

essay for, 211–12

BioGENEius Challenge, 69

Blade Runner, 83–84

essay about, 205–206

Blake, David, 13, 132

anecdotal essay of, 133

humorous essay of, 127

bolstering your hook, 103–108

for historians, 106–107

for photographers and artists, 107–108

success stories, 104–106

Boston College, 44, 45, 133, 142, 145, 167, 176

guidance counselor's letter to, 225–26

Boston University, 142

Bowdoin College, 143, 187

wait-listed at, 192–94

Boys and Girls Club, 46

Boys State, 51

Brandeis University, 164

Brant-Wilson, Valerie, 225–26

Brown University, 142, 151

Bryn Mawr College, 164

Bucknell Book Award, 62

Buffalo, University of, 227–28

Bush, George H. W., 63

California, University of, 104, 140, 142, 164, 167

at Los Angeles (UCLA), xi, 31, 39, 142

at San Diego, 12–13

Caltech, 151

campus visits, 178–79

Canino, Chelo, 29–33, 183–84

bright ideas for athletes of, 32–33

Carnegie Mellon University, 57, 170

open-house at, 179

Carnesale, Albert, xi

Catholic Heart Work Camp, 59

Central Florida, University of (UCF), 55

Chicago, University of, 167, 170

Chips, 74

Cholestech, 66–67

Claremont McKenna, 106, 164

Clinton, Bill, 49

Clinton, Hillary Rodham, 164

coaches, courting, 183–88

height and Haiku at Division III, 186–88

marketing tips, 184–86

model letter, 238

model stat sheet, 238–39

tip for, 183

Colby College, 187–88

College Board, 70, 137, 140, 141, 148, 154

college courses, 149

College Democrats, 51

College of Charleston, 146

College of the Holy Cross, 144

Collins, Billy, 74

Colorado College, 151

Columbia University, 12, 142, 164, 167

Common Application, xii, 41, 42, 50, 62, 151–58

ACT, SAT, or SAT subject test scores, 154–55

alumni/college interview, 157
application fee, 153
artists and, 154
athletes and, 154
brainstorm with Dr. McCarthy, 130–31
checklist, 152
colleges accepting, 151
college transcripts, 155
cover letter, 157
guidance counselor recommendations, 156–57
high school transcripts, 155
mid-year senior, 158
on-line, 151, 152
personal essay topics, 123–28
résumé, 153–54
scientists and, 154
short answer essays, 128–30
supplements, 153, 154
teacher recommendations, 155–56
Concord Review, 106
confessional essay, 201–202
Connell, Kaitlin, 47–52, 130
cooking up a hook, 15–26
questionnaires and, 15–22
Cornell University, 29, 31, 51, 89, 184
Cotter, Holland, 8
cover letter, 157
creative essay, 208–209
Creighton, Joanne, 144

Daily Points of Light Award, 63
Daniels, Gregory:
sports essay of, 204–05

Daniels, Jeffrey, 41–46
teacher recommendation for, 225–26
Dartmouth College, 95, 142, 167, 170, 193
essays for, 208–209, 221–22
expanded activities supplement for, 234–37
Davidson College, 85, 164
Dell, Michael, 55
demographics, xii–xiv
Depth of Field, 85
Dick, Philip K., 83
Dickinson College, 144
diversity essays, 211–15
drama hook, 81–86, 164
bright ideas for, 85–86
Drew University, 144
dual enrollment, 149
Dubowitz, Nicole, 73–79, 163
Baltimore Sun op-ed article of, 228–30
meaningful activity essay of, 129
Duke University, 13, 148
Global Dialogues Institute, 49, 50, 51
Great Debates Institute, 51
Leadership Institute, 51
Talent Identification Program, 51, 70, 79, 86

Early Action, 38, 139, 148, 153, 190
applying, 166–68, 176
Early Decision, 33, 89, 139, 149, 190
applying, 165–66, 176, 193, 194
Elder, Michael MacCook, 81–86, 164
favorite film essay of, 205–06
offbeat essay of, 209–11

Emory University, 69, 163

Escher, M. C., 65

essays, 121–35

  brainstorming with Dr. McCarthy, 130–31

  for the Common Application, 123–30

  leading with an anecdote, 132–33

  personal, 123–28

  playing it straight from start to finish, 134

  sample, *see* sample essays

  short answer, 128–30

  start with your hook, 123–28

  winning with a one-line lead, 135

  writer's block, 131–35

ethnicity hook, 87–90

  admissions coordinators and, 178

  bright ideas for, 90

  choosing colleges that need you, 162–63

  essays for, 211–15

  Third-World researcher, 65–70

exchange students, 35–39

expanded activities supplement, 234–37

famous quote essay, 215–17

favorite film/book essay, 205–206

Fell, David, 115–120, 165–66

  activity list of, 119–20

  confessional essay of, 201–02

  meaningful activity essay of, 128–29

  résumé of, 115–18

  work experience of, 120

Florida Bright Futures, 139

Florida Today, 78

Ford, Peter:

  funky pastime essay of, 217–18

Franklin & Marshall College, 185–86

Fuller, Margaret, 192–94

funky pastime essay, 217–18

Furman University, essay for, 222

Georgetown University, 35–38, 52, 62, 125, 142, 151, 176, 185, 191

  essay for, 222–23

George Washington University, 51, 62, 63, 176

  Presidential Arts Scholarship, 81

Georgia, University of, 31, 184

Georgia Tech, 13, 55, 147

  essay for, 204–205

  President's Scholarship, 149

Geselowitz, Kira, 13, 87–90

Gettysburg College, 144

Girls State, 49, 50, 51

Gore, Sara, 112–115, 119–21

  activity list of, 119

  meaningful activity essay of, 220–221

  résumé of, 113–15

grade point average (GPA), 145–50

  choose AP and IB courses, 147–48

  dual enrollment or college courses, 149

  freshman year, 149–50

  mid-year senior, 158

  nailing your grades junior year and first semester of senior year, 146

  No "Cs," 146

  racheting up you rank, 148–49

  teacher involvement, 150

  transcript of, 155

guidance counselor recommendations, 156–57
  sample letter, 225–26
Guideposts magazine:
  Grace Award, 125
  Young Writers contest, 78

Habitat for Humanity, 59
Hamilton College, 143
Hampshire College, 8, 164
Harvard University, xi, 104, 106, 142, 145, 151, 167, 193, 194
  Business School, 170, 171
Harvey Mudd College, 164
Hassan, Farris, 121–22
Haverford College, 164, 185, 186
Hill Rag, 76
Hispanic magazine, 90
historians, birght ideas for, 106–107
Holmes, Oliver Wendell, Jr., 216
Holocaust Museum, 104
Hughes, Sarah, 29
humanitarian hook, 59–64
  bright ideas for, 63–64
Hunter College High School, 82

Indiana University, 185
influential person essay, 206–207
Intel Science Talent Search, 104
International Baccalaureate (IB) program, 12, 48, 49, 89, 143, 149
  choosing, 147–48
international hook, 35–39
  bright ideas for, 38–39
  personal essay for, 123–25
  supplement for, 230–32

International Thespian Society, 85
Internet, xii
interviews, 169–74
  alumni interviewers, 169, 170
  deadlines and, 172
  demeanor and, 171
  family circumstances and, 171
  following up, 173–74
  humility and, 171
  interest and, 172
  neatness and, 172
  passion and, 170, 172
  preparation for questions, 172–73
  relaxing and, 171
  résumés and, 170–71
  significance of, 172
  sincerity and, 171
  student interviewers, 160
  taking the initiative for, 157, 169
  thank-you letter, 174
  tip for, 169
  see also admissions reps
inventions and patents, 71
Ivy League, xii*n*, 25

Japan United States Senate Exchange (JUSSE), 35–37
Javier, Marya Delia, 60–61
Johns Hopkins University, 48, 50, 130, 170
Julliard School, 81
Junior Stateman of America Summer School, 52

Kappel, Zach, 105–06
  activity list of, 105

Kannerstein, Greg, 185
Kansas, University of, 31, 184
King's College, 62

Lawryk, Mike, 32
legacies, 25
Legally Blonde, 175
Lehigh University, 44, 163, 184
    open house at, 180
letters of acceptance, 33
letters of recommendation:
    from guidance counselor,
        156–57
    from teachers, 155–56
linguistic hook, 35–39
Little Ivies, xii*n*, 41, 62, 186, 191
Los Angeles Times, 144
Lucas, George, 82
Lucido, Dr. Jerome, xiii

McCarthy, Dr. Kevin, 130–31
McGovern, Robert:
    triumph-over-adversity essay of,
        218–20
McGuirk, Leslie, 36
Mama D's Kitchen, 60–61
marketing your college application,
    93–101
    Broadway Baby, 95–101
    Early Decision, 101
    high-performance hook, 97
    hooking the application,
        98–100
    portfolio, 97–98
    selling the hook, 101
    seven selling points, 94–95

Maryland, University of, 17, 163
Massachusetts, University of, 164
    essay for, 218–20
Masterminds, 89
medical hook, 65–71
    bright ideas for, 70–71
Medill School of Journalism, 78
Miami, University of, 12, 149
Michigan, University of, 44, 45, 55,
    151, 154
Middlebury College, 143
Million Mom March, 74
Mills College, 164
MIT, 105, 142, 162, 164
Model United Nations, 15, 35, 38
Moore, Courtney, 133, 175–77
    essay of, 134
Morein, Whitney, 163
    diversity essay of, 213–14
most-meaningful-activity essays,
    220–23
Mount Holyoke College, 69, 143, 144,
    163, 164
    open house at, 179
    Take the Lead program, 63
multicultural hook, *see* ethnicity hook
Museum of the Moving Image, 83
music hook, 41–46
    bright ideas for, 45–46
    Common Application and, 154
    short answer essay for, 128–29

Nanny, 77
National Forensics League, 52
National High School Game
    Academy, 57

National History Club, 106

National Merit Finalist, 139

National Merit Scholarship, 76,
    163
  Commended Student, 138–39
  Qualifying Test, 138–39

National Merit Semifinalist, 139

National Writing Board, 106

Nesbitt, Richard, 147

New School for Jazz and Contemporary
    Music, 46

New York Times, xii, 121–22, 147–48,
    162, 185–86, 200

New York University, 13, 104, 115, 128,
    162, 165–66
  essay for, 201–202

Niazi, Anum, 66–68
  influential person essay of, 206–07
  scientific abstracts of, 226–27

Niazi, Faraze, 68
  scientific abstract of, 227–28

Niazi, Summer, 65–71, 163
  scientific abstracts of, 226–28

nonconformist essay, 203–204

North Carolina, University of, 104,
    151, 167

Northeastern University, 77, 163

Northwestern University, 13, 52, 81, 89,
    104, 142, 149, 151
  essay for, 221
  National High School Institute in
    Acting, 85
  National High School Institute in
    Debate, 52
  National High School Institute in
    Journalism, 78

Notre Dame University, 25, 106, 130,
    148, 167
  African American Scholars at, 90
  Global Issues Seminar, 64
  Latino Community Leadership
    Seminars at, 90

Oberst, Conor, 74

offbeat essay, 209–11

Olin College, 164

100 Seconds of Solitude, 62

open-house programs, 179–80

Operation Smile, 63

Pagano, Erika, 15, 35–39
  activity essay of, 222–23
  hot-topic essay of, 124–25
  Letter from Japan of, 230–32

Pangilinan, James, 59–64, 134–35,
    191–92
  essay of, 135

Parade, 77

parent questionnaire, 17–20

Parker, Tom, 137–38

Pennington, Bill, 186

Pennsylvania, University of, 141, 142,
    145, 149, 164, 190
  Wharton, 170

Perkins, Lindsey:
  meaningful activity essay of, 222

personal essays:
  Adventures in eBay, 127–28
  Safety deposit, 125–27
  Teen prostitution in Japan, 123–25

photographers, 105–106
  bright ideas for, 107–108

pitching your package to colleges, 161–68
  applying early, 165
  applying Early Action, 166–68
  applying Early Decision, 165–66
  choosing colleges that need you, 162–63
  ethnicity hook and, 162–63
  fixating on one school, 161–62
  following your hook, 163–64
  freshman class profiles and, 162
  going against the crowd, 164
  "reach" schools, 162
  tip for, 161
  women's colleges, 164
Pitzer College, 77, 163, 164
Poet's Market, 78
Points of Light Foundation, 63, 105
political hook, 47–52
  bright ideas for, 51–52
Pomona College, 164
power of the hook, 3–10
  from college to self-confidence, 9
  a "genius" at photography, 7–9
  running with a résumé, 6–7
  something more, 4–6
Princeton University, xi, 29–33, 52, 105, 142, 167, 183–84
Proctor, Michael Moore:
  famous quote essay of, 215–17
Project Books and Blankies, 105
Providence College, 144
PSATs, 94
  prepping for, 138–39
publication of work, 70–71, 78, 79
Purdue University, 53–57, 165

quick guide to the college hook program, 9–10

Rand, Ayn, 88
"reach" schools, 162
recipe for a hook, 15–26
  academic interest questionnaire, 20–22
  activities questionnaire, 15–17
  cooking up a hook, 22–26
  parent questionnaire, 17–20
recruitment:
  for athletes, 32–33
  for musicians, 46
Red Cross, 59
Reel Expressions: Filmmaking, 86
Rensselaer Polytechnic Institute, 69, 163
résumé power play, 109–20
  Common Application and, 153–54
  dramatizing the details, 112–18
  examples of, 113–18
  hooking the activities list, 118–20
  interviews and, 170–71
  lies or half-truths, 112
  organize according to categories, 110–12
Rice University, 170
Richmond, University of, 125
Robert Wood Johnson Foundation, 70
Rochester, University of, 89, 163
Rollins College, 115
Rutgers University, Summer Acting Conservatory, 86

Salvation Army, 59
sample essays:
  confessional, 201–202
  creative, 208–209

diversity, 211–15

famous quote, 215–17

favorite film/book, 205–206

funky pastime, 217–18

influential person, 206–207

most-meaningful-activity, 220–23

nonconformist, 203–204

offbeat, 209–11

sports, 204–205

triumph-over-adversity, 218–20

Sarah Lawrence College, 8

SATs, 94

Common Application and, 154–55

playing the ACT against, 141

prepping for, 139–40

sections of, 139

significance of, 138

taking with the ACTs and, 140

SAT Subject Tests, 94

Common Application and, 154–55

taking, soon after a course, 141–43

Save Darfur Coalition, 104

scholarships, 81, 138, 149, 163, 181

athletic, 32–33

Bloomberg, 48, 50

merit, see National Merit Scholarship

music, 154

Scholastic Art & Writing Awards,
78, 107

science hook, 65–71

bright ideas for, 70–71

Common Application and, 154

supplements for, 226–28

Scripps College, 164

Sea Scouts, 88

secret life, 96–101

self-confidence, 9

Sewanee, 186–88

Young Writers' Conference, 78

Shah, Nihar, 149

essay of, 221

Sherry, Rosemary, 184–86

short answer essays, 128–30

to Dartmouth, 221–22

to Furman, 222

to Georgetown, 222–23

to Northwestern, 221

to Villanova, 220–21

Single Choice Early Action, 167

Sister Cities International, 38

Smick, Amy, 125

essay of, 126–27

Smith College, 164

Southern Methodist University,
115, 151

sports essay, 204–205

sports hook, see athletic hook

Stanford University, 29, 31, 52, 104, 105,
106, 167, 184

Strom, Leonard Marie:

nonconformist essay of, 203

summer internship, 70

supplements and letters, 225–39

expanded activities, 234–37

guidance counselor's recommendation,
225–26

international hook and, 230–32

model letter to coach, 238

model stat sheet, 238–39

science hook and, 226–28

technology hook and, 232–34

writing hook and, 228–30

Swarthmore College, 32, 142, 164, 167, 190
Syracuse University, 44

teachers, high school:
  involvement in grades, 150
  recommendations from, 155–56
technology hook, 53–57
  bright ideas for, 57
  supplement for, 232–34
Teen Court, 48–49, 50
Teen Writers Workshop, 37
test scores, 137–44
  apply to colleges with flexible test
    reporting policies, 143
  playing the ACT against the SAT, 141
  prepping for the tests, 138–40
  "score optional" option, 143–44
  taking both the SAT and ACT, 140
  taking the SAT subject tests soon after
    a course, 141–43
Third-World researcher, 65–71
  supplements for, 226–28
Time for Kids, 105
Time magazine, 51
Tomorrow25, 51
Top Ten College Hooks, 25
transcripts, 155
Trayes, Lily, 23–24
Trinity College, 73, 77, 125, 163, 186
triumph-over-adversity essay, 218–20
Trojan Vision, 85
Tufts University, 62, 63, 145, 166

Union College, 69, 144, 163
U.S. Army Science Fair Award, 68

University of Buffalo, 227–28
University of California, 104, 140, 142, 164, 167
  at Los Angeles (UCLA), xi, 31, 39, 142
  at San Diego, 12–13
University of Central Florida
  (UCF), 55
University of Chicago, 167, 170
University of Georgia, 31, 184
University of Kansas, 17, 163
University of Massachusetts, 164
  essay to, 218–20
University of Michigan, 44, 45, 55, 151, 154
University of North Carolina, 104, 151, 167
University of Pennsylvania, 141, 142, 145, 149, 164, 190
  Wharton, 170
University of Richmond, 125
University of Rochester, 89, 163
University of Southern California (USC), xiii, 81–85, 89, 104, 105, 153, 164
  essays for, 205–206, 209–11
University of the South, 186–88
  Young Writers' Conference, 78
University of Virginia, 112, 142
  Young Writers Workshop, 78, 83
updates with new information, 180–81
U.S. News & World Report, xii, 8, 55, 89, 163, 196
USA Today, xii

Vanderbilt University, 133, 134, 145, 163, 175–77
  Early Decision, 166

essay for, 206–207

PreVU days, 179

supplemental material to, 226–28

Villanova University, 115, 175, 176

essay for, 220–21

Virginia, University of, 112, 142

Young Writers Workshop, 78, 83

Virginia Tech, 55, 115

visits to colleges, 33

volunteerism, 46, 57, 63, 70

wait list, 186–97

athletes and, 187–88

case studies, 191–94

four choices for, 186

letter written by a parent and, 196–97

quick tips for working the, 195–97

reaction to, 189–90

tip for, 189

Wake Forest University, 166

Walk for the Cure, 63

Wall Street Journal, xi, 59, 65

Washington and Lee University, 13, 128

essay for, 217–18

Washington University, 104

Wellesley College, 69, 133, 163, 164, 167, 170, 176

Wesleyan University, 59–63, 134–35, 141

wait-listed at, 191–92

Wheaton College, 151

William and Mary, College of, 151

Williams College, 32, 142, 147, 185, 187

Witherspoon, Reese, 175

women's colleges, 164

Woodward, Chas, 186–88

writer's block, 131–35

leading with an anecdote, 132–33

playing it straight from start to finish, 134

rules to overcome, 132

winning with a one-line lead, 134–35

Writer's Market, 78

writing hook, 73–78

bright ideas for, 78

essay for, 129–30

supplements for, 228–30

Yale University, 29, 52, 81, 106, 141, 145, 167

Young Epidemiology Scholars Competition, 70

Young Playwrights, Inc., 78

Young Technology Leaders Conference, 54

Youth Advisory Committee of Montgomery County, Maryland, 75

Youth for Understanding, 35, 36, 38

Zemeckis, Richard, 82